THE NEW SOCIAL WORK PRACTICE

To
Elizabeth, Emma, Richard,
Adam, Amy and Sara

The new social work practice

Exercises and activities for training and developing social workers

Mark Doel and Steven Shardlow

LONDON AND NEW YORK

First published 1998 by Ashgate Publishing

Reissued 2018 by Routledge
2 Park Square, Milton Park, Abingdon, Oxon, OX14 4RN
52 Vanderbilt Avenue, New York, NY 10017

Routledge is an imprint of the Taylor & Francis Group, an informa business

Copyright © Mark Doel and Steven Shardlow 1998

The materials that appear in this book, other than those quoted from prior sources, may be reproduced for education/training activities. There is no requirement to obtain special permission for such uses.

All rights reserved. No part of this book may be reprinted or reproduced or utilised in any form or by any electronic, mechanical, or other means, now known or hereafter invented, including photocopying and recording, or in any information storage or retrieval system, without permission in writing from the publishers.

Notice:
Product or corporate names may be trademarks or registered trademarks, and are used only for identification and explanation without intent to infringe.

Publisher's Note
The publisher has gone to great lengths to ensure the quality of this reprint but points out that some imperfections in the original copies may be apparent.

Disclaimer
The publisher has made every effort to trace copyright holders and welcomes correspondence from those they have been unable to contact.

A Library of Congress record exists under LC control number:

ISBN 13: 978-0-367-14753-2 (hbk)
ISBN 13: 978-0-367-14754-9 (pbk)
ISBN 13: 978-0-429-05327-6 (ebk)

Typeset in Palatino by Raven Typesetters, Chester

Contents

List of figures vii
Acknowledgements ix
Preface xi

Entry: Supervision and reflective practice 1
      Reflections on supervision 3

PART I   Foundations of practice 13

1 Orientation 15
    Who takes sugar? 17
2 Worldview 23
    Believe it or not 25
3 Professionalism and self-presentation 33
    Boundaries 35
4 Feelings and actions 43
    Taboo 45

PART II   Direct Practice 51

5 Introduction 53
    Playing field 55
6 Inquiry 63
    Open ends 65
7 Advocacy 69
    In my view 71

8 Beginnings, middles and endings	79
Tree	81

PART III Agency practice — 95

9 Making priorities	97
Sticky moments	99
10 Recording the work	105
Matter of fact	107
11 Managing a workload	115
Perfect timing	117
12 Running a meeting	123
Topical islands	125
13 Purchasing and providing services	131
Travel agent	133

PART IV Themes of practice — 145

14 Care and control	147
Dial 'D' for Danger	149
15 Family-centred practice	157
Whanau	159
16 Culturally competent practice	165
Ethnic realities	167
17 Empowering practice	177
Steps	179
18 Law-informed practice	189
Spirit and letter	190
19 Research-minded practice	201
Signposts	203
20 Generalist and specialist practice	217
Essence	218

Exit: Comparative social work	231
Gulliver's travels	232
Bibliography	239
Index	251

List of figures

P1	Diagrammatic contents of *The new social work practice* in the style of the London Underground map	xix
I	Foundations of practice	13
4.1	The Johari window	50
II	Direct practice	51
8.1	Mapping the work	93
III	Agency practice	95
12.1	The intrapreneur's ten commandments	130
IV	Themes of practice	145
14.1	'The social worker cannot win?'	156
15.1	A typical news story	163
18.1	Approval-disapproval continuum	196
20.1	The territorial model	223
20.2	The systems model	225

Acknowledgements

We would like to thank the many practice teachers, students and trainers who have contributed to the activities in the first incarnation of this book by using them and giving us valuable feedback. Their encouragement has been essential in completing this further book. In particular, we have appreciated teaching in a team with Catherine Sawdon, David Sawdon, Philip Proctor, Dave Henry, Yvonne Channer, Jan Horwath and other colleagues. For the many opportunities to work and develop the ideas in this book with social workers, probation officers and students in agencies in the UK and abroad, we would like to thank, in particular, Mary Citron, Lorna Bell, Lorna Felix, Maggie Heyhurst, Sheila Holland, Steve Hunt, Marina Kurchian, David McGee, Judy Moore, the National Organisation for Practice Teaching, Volodimyr Poltavets, Shulamit Ramon, Joy Rhodes, Gayla Rogers, Boris Shapiro, Mavis Sharpe, Elka Todorova, Harry Walker and Marion Whibley. In the text, we also acknowledge the specific help and creativity of colleagues in relation to particular activities. We wish to thank Kevin Kallaugher for allowing us to reprint his cartoon (p. 156). Finally, our thanks go to Jo Gooderham at Arena whose enthusiasm, encouragement and support has been invaluable.

MD
SS

By the same authors

Doel, M. and Marsh, P. (1992), *Task-Centred Social Work*, Aldershot: Ashgate.

Doel, M. and Sawdon, C. (forthcoming), *Teaching and Learning Groupwork Practice*, Aldershot: Arena.

Doel, M. and Shardlow, S.M. (1993), *Social Work Practice: exercises and activities for training and developing social workers*, Aldershot: Gower.

Doel, M. Shardlow, S.M., Sawdon, C. and Sawdon, D. (1996), *Teaching Social Work Practice*, Aldershot: Arena.

Doel, M. and Shardlow, S. (eds) (1996), *Social Work in a Changing World: an International Perspective on Practice Learning*, Aldershot: Arena.

Shardlow, S.M. (ed.) (1989), *The Values of Change in Social Work*, London: Routledge.

Shardlow, S.M. and Doel, M. (1996), *Practice Learning and Teaching*, Houndmills, Basingstoke: Macmillan.

Shardlow, S.M. and Payne, M. (eds) (1998), *Contemporary Issues in Social Work: Western Europe*, Aldershot: Arena.

Preface

The more things change...

This book is about teaching and learning social work practice. Its first appearance in 1993 was in a workbook format, as part of the Gower series of training manuals. We have updated and revised *Social Work Practice*, replacing some of the activities and materials and substituting completely new chapters in a number of areas which are central to current (and future) social work practice. The initial intention was to provide a second edition of the Gower manual, but as our work progressed, it became apparent that this was more than a second edition – it was a new look at social work practice.

In updating the book, we have responded to feedback from readers that the format of 'Activities' followed by 'Notes' for each of the topics is a stimulating way of teaching and learning, so we have maintained this style. Users of *Social Work Practice* also suggested that a section on supervision would provide a welcome overview of the rest of the book. In 'Entry' we consider the supervision process alongside the concept of the reflective practitioner (Schön, 1995), in order to place the rest of the topics in context.

Presented with this opportunity to return to *Social Work Practice*, we also wished to introduce aspects of practice which were emerging at that time, and which are now a firm feature of current practice: for example, the increasing division between the purchasing and the providing of services (Chapter 13). We have added themes which have been long-standing and recurrent in social work practice (such as care and control in Chapter 14; and general and specialist arrangements for practice in Chapter 20). The final chapter on generalist and specialist social work uses a historical approach in order to help the new generation of social work students 'take the long view'. In this way, we feel they will be better equipped to face the future, and to contribute to the profession's definition of itself.

Indeed, we have attempted to anticipate future developments in the final section – 'Exit' – by alerting students towards the globalization of social work. This section on comparative social work also reflects the welcome interest in *Social Work Practice* from practitioners, students and teachers around the globe, and our own attempts elsewhere in the book not to rely exclusively on our 'home patch' in the UK, but to present illustrations of social work practice from diverse national settings.

... the more they stay the same

As we worked on a new edition, it became evident that in looking forward we were also looking back. Choices about what to include and what to exclude are, in effect, decisions about what social work is, or should be. We might think that this question is especially pressing as we approach the new millennium, yet a trawl of the key texts over the last fifty or so years puts the present discussion in context. It seems there always has been uncertainty about the nature of social work practice, and that the profession has long felt the need to try to define and describe 'the essential social worker' (Davies, 1994).

This strong sense of revisiting long-standing themes in social work practice while exploring the new social work practice, furnished the title and subtitle for the book. Whether it be general and specialist practice, care and control, power and oppression, these are central and recurring themes in social work – even if the words to describe the concepts alter.

Aims of the book

The intention of the original workbook remains intact: to guide and stimulate learning about social work practice. The book aims to achieve this purpose by presenting various aspects of social work (topics and themes), using differing settings and contexts as illustrations, and supplying activities to promote discussion, understanding, learning and better practices. Taken together, the topics and themes in the book define the essential elements of a curriculum for social work practice.

Learning to practise is a process which continues beyond any formal period of training. The activities which 'kick-start' each chapter are as relevant to staff development as they are to practice teaching, and they have been used for these purposes as well as for the development of students' practice. The activities can be addressed at different levels, and we have found that even the most experienced practitioners have found them challenging and stimulating.

Social Work Practice was written in response to frequent requests for materials from hard-pressed practice teachers and staff supervisors without the time to create their own teaching activities. We have long advocated a magpie approach to training materials, borrowing ideas and activities from a variety of sources and adapting them to your own purposes, so that you do not have to rely on creating all your own work. (See Huczynski, 1983, for a useful encyclopedia of training methods.) *The new social work practice* is a response to the changes in social work practice which necessitate renewal and replacement of some of these materials. As we have noted, it is paradoxical that these changes have sharpened our sense of what is *not* changing, and what *always* seems to be changing about social work practice! In responding to the legislative and agency requirements of social workers 'on the job', the profession must be able to articulate what makes the job essentially 'social work'. The content of this book is what we consider to be the non-negotiable core of professional social work practice.

Our intention in *The new social work practice* continues to be to provide 'oven-ready' activities with clear guidelines so that they can be used without too much preparation. However, we have reservations about a cookbook approach, and encourage you to 'make your own toppings'. In most cases you can use an activity as it stands – and please note that you may photocopy these pages – but sometimes you will want to adapt it to your own setting. Each activity contains much condensed material, so you will need to 'add water' – in the form of time. Time for discussion, reflection and practice. The particular style of the practice teacher or staff leader and the individual response of the student or staff member will make the experience of each activity different. The 'Notes' elaborate on the topic of the activity, providing additional material, a digest of some of the relevant literature and pointers to other helpful sources. (The 'Notes' cannot provide more than an introduction and overview of the topic or theme in question.)

The following is a brief guide to the topics and themes covered in each chapter:

Entry: Supervision and reflective practice: purpose and functions of supervision; placements and learning; group supervision; accountability; the reflective student.

Part I Foundations of practice
1. Orientation: making new contacts; the skills of discovery and initiation; making links with prior learning and experience; planning and doing work tasks.
2. Worldview: the impact of personal beliefs on professional practice; engaging in dialogue; the ability to reason and to conceptualize; linking theory and practice.
3. Professionalism and self-presentation: the skills of self-disclosure; ethical beliefs and professional values; views of clients; handling dilemmas and paradoxes; developing self-awareness; understanding personal style and agency culture; expressing professional authority.

4 Feelings and actions: handling taboo areas; making connections between beliefs, values, feelings and actions; understanding power and discrimination.

Part II Direct practice

5 Introduction: tuning-in skills and anticipation; communication and writing skills; systems thinking – who is the client?; professional purpose.
6 Inquiry: understanding and using a framework for interactional skills; confronting skills; listening skills; broadening the repertoire of skills.
7 Advocacy: checking assumptions and hidden agendas; being assertive; balancing inquiry and advocacy; strategic thinking; non-verbal communication.
8 Beginnings, middles, endings: working over time with people by exploring and re-framing problems, building partnerships with clients, helping to agree priorities and negotiate goals; problem-solving techniques; working with reluctant people; planning ends as transitions, time limits; evaluating process and outcomes; getting feedback.

Part III Agency practice

9 Making priorities: questioning established patterns of work; developing explicit criteria to help decide priorities; ranking criteria; notions of accountability.
10 Recording the work: purposes of records; recording skills; facts and opinions; challenging jargon and assumptions; writing records with clients.
11 Managing a workload: developing criteria to decide how to use time, diary planning; using unplanned time; flexibility and reliability, avoiding burn-out.
12 Running a meeting: taking part in meetings successfully; chairing meetings; following procedures; negotiating skills; understanding the 'hidden' organization.
13 Purchasing and providing services: factors important in the idea of 'choice'; stages in making care in the community; a history of community care; assessment, care planning, contracts and inspection.

Part IV Themes of practice

14 Care and control: identifying levels of risks; types of risk; deciding when to intervene; balancing care and control.
15 Family-centred practice: understanding the idea and reality of *family* deficits and strengths models; decision making with families as allies.
16 Culturally competent practice: developing self-awareness of culture and community; valuing diversity; challenging cultural incompetence.
17 Empowering practice: insider and outsider groups; multi-dimensional nature of oppression; partnership; barriers to empowerment; full participation in society.

18 Law-informed practice: sensitization to a legal framework; demystifying the law and legal process; practice dilemmas; seeking advice.
19 Research-minded practice: sensitization to research; parallel processes in social work and research; purposes of research; the notion of practice wisdom.
20 Generalist and specialist practice: the common base for social work practice; historical trends; territorial and systems models of generalist and specialist practice; generalist methods.

Exit: Comparative social work: social work practice in its national and cultural context; international comparisons; forms of social work; boundaries with other professions.

We think that the four areas – 'Foundations', 'Direct practice', 'Agency practice' and 'Themes' – are essential for good practice, and that the topics in the chapters provide a sound basis for social work practice. They provide the transferable skills often associated with an initial period of practical learning – a practicum.

Although individual activities can be used on a one-off basis, it is better to get acquainted with the entire book beforehand, and to return to activities at different stages in the student's learning to see what progress is being made. The topics in Parts I, II and III are in no strict chronological order, and the themes in Part IV run through the whole of social work practice. A knowledge of the total curriculum for general practice will help when searching for the right activity for the occasion. A 'teachable moment' occurs when the learner is particularly receptive to the teaching, and a well-timed activity can help these moments to happen (see Knowles, 1983).

Inevitably, our desire to be comprehensive has been tempered by the need to be selective. We know that every reader will be able to think of other areas which could, maybe should, have been included, for example, activities on multi-disciplinary practice, or the effects of poverty. This will depend on the national and local context of your social work practice. In *Social Work Practice*, we suggested that any additions to the curriculum of activities should be compensated by removing others. This kind of pruning is essential to prevent an ever-expanding curriculum which places demands on teachers and learners that are unlikely to be fulfilled. We have followed our own advice – though you might see the amalgamation of beginnings, middles and endings into one chapter as a cheat!

Accelerated learning

The activities in this book are as uncomplicated as possible: they do not require elaborate technical assistance or hours of preparation. The focus of this book is on *learning for professional practice* and a belief that learning flourishes in a climate where it is safe to take risks, like tight-rope walking above a net.

There are different ways of learning. *Learning by doing* is one, and it has been used heavily by student supervisors in the past. The student experiences direct practice with clients and learns on the job, with some preparation beforehand and discussion afterwards with the supervisor. The student gains an authentic experience of the coalface but this method of learning to practise tends to perpetuate existing practices – good and bad – and often fails to highlight the learning which may have taken place. When learning opportunities come solely via direct practice it is difficult to pace them in a way that can match the individual student's needs and abilities.

Live teaching in the same room uses direct practice with clients as a learning opportunity (see Evans, 1987). The practice teacher can give direct feedback to the student about his or her work, and this has an immediate impact on the student's practice in a way that is not possible when the practice teacher is absent. The advantages of such immediate feedback are clear but the presence of the practice teacher has to be carefully managed.

Another way of learning, illustrated by the activities in this book, is by using materials which *simulate practice situations*. These can be very close approximations to practice, like flight simulations used to train pilots, or activities which – by their very distance from direct practice – help to cast it in a new light.

We have described the advantages of using these kinds of teaching material elsewhere (Doel and Shardlow, 1996b). Simulated practice is a relatively safe environment for learning because the pace of action can be controlled and the consequences of taking risks are not serious. In these circumstances, the learner can feel free to experiment and be open to new approaches. The learner can also take the time to reflect on the issues which underlie the practice, especially the assumptions and values which might otherwise remain hidden or unchecked. The practice teacher can regulate the degree of challenge facing the student, so that it is sufficiently stretching to break new ground, but not so demanding that it breaks the student. Activities which simulate or represent aspects of social work practice can *accelerate* learning by encouraging risk taking.

Practice placements are scarce, so there are economic as well as educational pressures to consider how opportunities for simulated learning might be constructed independent of the agency setting. However, activities such as the ones in this book are not a substitute for direct practice at some point in the student's learning. Direct practice is essential to put that learning into action, to test it out, and to experience a sense of imminence and of responsibility (Doel and Shardlow, 1996b).

Participative learning

Activity-based learning is participative in a number of ways. The teacher and the learner are undergoing a similar process, whilst recognizing their different roles. The teacher is not a repository of knowledge who fills the student's empty vessel; rather a person with considerable experience who is prepared to look at practice critically and reflectively. This applies to the teacher's own practice as well as the student's. Activity-based learning acknowledges that students bring knowledge, beliefs, values and skills which will have a vital impact on their practice and, perhaps even more crucial, on their ability to learn practice (see Sawdon, 1986).

In using these activities, therefore, practice teachers must be prepared to be open about their own practice. Learning flourishes in a creative and energetic climate, but evoking this environment in the midst of day-to-day practice is not easy. The activities can add spice to student learning and staff development, and we would be surprised if they did not have an impact on the teacher's own practice. Constant reappraisal of practice is the mark of a good practitioner.

In summary, the activities are participative in two ways: as a method of learning which is engaging and active, but also as a process in which all participants (whether they are styled teachers or learners) are learning.

'Skilled incompetence'

If risk taking is an essential ingredient of learning, so is *unlearning*. Perhaps the biggest blocks to learning are the patterns of belief and behaviour which have become so habitual that they are second nature. The opportunity to be a teacher of practice is an opportunity to question your own practice and reflect on it. This can be a difficult process because, as we become more 'experienced', we face greater demands to appear competent and to deny the need for renewed learning. We can become so good at preventing ourselves from learning that the consequence is *skilled incompetence*. Senge (1990) defines those possessing this as 'people who are incredibly proficient at keeping themselves from learning' and suggests that most organizations encourage their workers and managers to develop skilled incompetence. In an atmosphere where making mistakes is not acceptable, we spend so much time covering up our mistakes that there is no time to learn from them.

The activities which introduce each chapter in this book are designed to help participants to explore issues in practice as well as enhance technical skills. The activities develop an ability to learn, which we believe is a necessary condition to develop a competence to practise. The practice teacher will need to make links between the learning which takes place via these activities and the student's direct practice with people using the agency's services.

The activities can be used to assess students' practice learning as well as to develop it. In particular, revisiting an activity towards the end of the placement or review period with a member of staff is a good way to measure changes in understanding of practice. Participants should always be clear about the purpose of any activity and what uses may be made of it.

Devices for teaching and learning professional practice

The teacher of social work practice is constantly looking for ways to help students make the necessary connections in their learning – ways of simplifying complicated and messy processes without losing sight of their genuine complexity. There is an increasing amount of useful information available from research, both qualitative and quantitative, identifying those aspects of placements students find useful or satisfying and what helps or hinders learning; see, for example: Leung, Tam with Chu (1995); Kissman and Van Tran (1990); Nixon, Shardlow, Doel, McGrath, and Gordon (1995): Marsh and Triseliotis (1996), Secker (1993), Walker, McCarthy, Morgan and Timms (1995).

We have developed the idea of 'topography' of social work practice, using a map of 'Socialworkland' to describe the current social work scene (Doel and Shardlow, 1996a, p. 74). This simulacrum, or schematic representation, achieves a balance of generality and specificity which allows it to 'travel' successfully. Everyone understands the idea of geography, even though each identifies different distinguishing topographical features: the 'mountains of workload management' become 'volcanoes' in the American Pacific Northwest; the 'lake of social work values' transforms to 'thermal springs' – even 'boiling mud pools' – in New Zealand. Similarly, everyone can conceive the idea of the social work 'landscape', though different countries at various stages in their development will highlight diverse aspects. The British ghost town of 'Patchwork' is the thriving settlement of 'Community Development' in many parts of the world.

One of the best-known examples of a successful simulacrum is the London Underground map. This design icon has helped millions of people to navigate a large city, and its success lies in its ability to distort the places it portrays, both in terms of relative distance and position. (The powers-that-be initially complained that it was an inaccurate and misleading guide to London's complex configuration.) However, we – the travelling public – know that the diagram's success lies in its emphasis on connections and linkages, because

> [it presents] an orderly simulacrum for a disorderly, disjointed accumulation of urban villages, only barely discernible from one another on the ground, yet possessed with all the pride and exclusiveness of true communities ... what matter if Chelsea was nowhere to be seen in this orderly array, nor Mayfair, nor Bermondsey? They'd be fitted into the newcomer's mental map sooner or later, once the basic linkages had been absorbed. (Garland, 1994, p. 7)

The Underground is an excellent analogy for the difference between social work practice 'on the ground' and the ability to present that practice in an accessible manner. The task of the practice teacher and the staff development worker is to create a design, 'an orderly simulacrum', based on the confidence that an element of distortion can help learning rather than hinder it, because the missing parts and the chaotic aspects can be fitted into

Preface xix

the student's 'mental map sooner or later, once the basic linkages [have] been absorbed'.

To illustrate this point, we can choose to present the contents of this book in the conventional linear fashion (see pages xiii–xv) or as an Underground-style design (see Figure below).

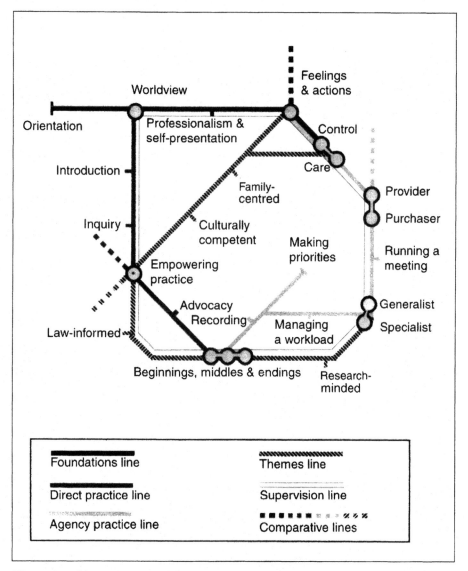

Figure P1 Diagrammatic contents of *The new social work practice* in the style of the London Underground map

Reproduced from *The new social work practice* by Mark Doel and Steven Shardlow, Arena, Aldershot

Which do you find the more illuminating – the sequential presentation or the design? Some will prefer the former, others the latter. Some might be attracted to the idea of the design, but find its execution wanting (for instance, the reliance on grey shading rather than colour is too obscure). Ask yourself why you are more attracted to one format than another.

It is important to reflect on your own response to these different approaches because – collectively – you as teachers will mirror the different responses of learners of social work practice. The search for variety is a vital ingredient of effective teaching and learning. The topics in this book, and their attendant activities, should provide a lively and diverse experience, but it is necessary to use them alongside other methods as well, such as live teaching. It also helps to think of different *arrangements* for the practice learning: one-to-one; small groups, and so on (see Payne and Scott, 1982). Although an understanding of the student's preferred approaches to learning is needed, it is also useful to broaden these preferences. Students should not cut themselves off from certain kinds of learning opportunity.

Making use of the opportunities to link simulation and live practice, learning and doing, is part of the art and science of practice teaching. The simulated activities give you and the student a common frame of reference to make sense of what happens in direct practice, and a chance to rehearse practice dilemmas. We hope this will make the live practice a more coherent experience for the student.

Anti-discriminatory practice

Moves towards modular approaches to curriculum development draw into question how fundamental aspects of practice, such as anti-discriminatory practice, are to be included. If there is a special focus on anti-discriminatory practice in a particular module, there is a danger that it can be marginalized – something that is 'done' and then forgotten. However, if we rely on a model in which anti-discriminatory practice is suffused throughout the curriculum, there is a danger of a dilution effect. What is needed is an approach where dimensions such as anti-discriminatory practice are both *weft and weave* of the curriculum (Phillipson, 1992).

In addition, we must beware the pressures to mouth the right sentiments whilst doing little to promote practical learning. Learning depends on risk taking, and this is not easy if, for example, we pounce on each other because we have failed to use correct terminology. Let us explore the meaning behind the words before we make any judgements.

As well as providing chapters and activities which focus specifically on the themes of power, oppression, anti-discrimination and empowerment (notably Chapters 4, 16 and 17), we have considered it vital to bring the anti-discriminatory dimension to all the activities, most of which already raise these issues. There are ways in which you, too, can introduce this dimension to an existing activity. For example, 'Boundaries' (Activity 3) could be discussed in the light of specific differences, such as the way in which the answer 'it depends' would be influenced in the case of a female student with a male client, an older student with a younger service user, and so on.

The power dynamic between the practice teacher and the student is also an important feature. There are many subtle and obvious differences in power between teacher and learner, assessor and assessed, and these should be openly discussed (Doel, Shardlow, Sawdon and Sawdon, 1996, p. 67). Similarly, practice teachers and students bring their own ethnic, gender and other personal attributes to the situation, so that teaching and learning occur in a specific context. There are many opportunities during these activities for practice teachers and students to explore their differences and similarities: the practice teacher has a responsibility to make sure that they are discussed not just as part of the initial learning agreement but throughout the placement.

As authors of this book, we have tried to keep aware of the impact of our own backgrounds and attributes on our view of social work practice learning, as white males from northern England. For this reason, we have been keen to continue to develop the activities with many different people. This applies both to the activities first presented in *Social Work Practice* and to those appearing fresh in this book. The feedback has been very valuable in shaping the activities as they appear in this book, and we hope their influence is evident.

Framework of each chapter

Each chapter comprises four parts:

- **Introduction**   The first page gives an overview of the chapter, which includes a brief description of the activity, an outline of its purpose, a step-by-step guide to using the activity and an indication of the likely amount of time needed.

    There are brief suggestions about 'Variations' to the activity which the practice teacher might wish to make. With each activity, we have had to make a decision about the kind of setting in which to place it. Our experience of using the activities is that, for most of them, diversity is a stimulus to fresh thinking. However, there are a few activities where we advise practice teachers to adapt the activity to their specific circumstances.
- **The activity**   The activity is designed as a focus, a trigger, a 'kick-start' to the particular topic or theme of the chapter. Each person participating in the activity will need a copy of it.
- **Notes for practice teachers**   Each chapter contains notes to guide both practice teacher and student. These are not exclusive to either practice teacher or student, but they have a different focus. The 'Notes for practice teachers' provide background to the activity and elaborate the particular topic which it addresses, describing in more detail how the

activity can be used. These 'Notes' recognize that practice teachers are not necessarily familiar with all these topics and themes, and that it is helpful to have some further explanation and teaching material. In the first four activities there are 'Examples' to illustrate the way an activity has been used in a practice tutorial (student supervision session). Ideally, practice teachers need to become familiar with the activities by doing them themselves.

We use the term 'practice teacher' throughout the book as short-hand for 'teacher of practice', whether this is in an agency or an educational base (see Doel and Shardlow, 1996, p. 184 for a discussion of different terminology as used in different countries). The activities are relevant to a broad range of professional development, not just formal training: they take practice teaching as a starting point, whilst recognizing the close links with staff development. Other authors have taken staff development as their start, but have a similar relevance to practice teaching (Douglas and Payne, 1988).

- **Notes for students** Again, these are not intended to be exclusively for students, but they provide suggestions for follow-on, usually after the practice tutorial. Some additional exercises build on the activity which the student has completed with the practice teacher, perhaps taking a slightly different angle on the same topic. The activities described in the students' notes can be done with the practice teacher or independently by the student.

Feedback

Always remember to allow time for feedback about the activity itself. Make sure that no one is left feeling 'short-circuited' and that any residual feelings after completing an activity are expressed. Some of these activities (for example, Activities 4, 16 and 'You are what you eat' in the 'Notes for students' on page 173) can evoke a powerful response which needs careful handling.

Entry and Exit

In addition to the twenty chapters on aspects of social work practice, we have included two 'bookends' – an entry into the book via the issue of supervision and reflective practice, and an exit from the book via comparative social work. These two sections provide context for the work in between: the inward-looking context of the processes and arrangements which will aid the student's understanding and practice of the topics which follow, and the outward-looking context of the development of social work elsewhere, which we hope will help students to consolidate their learning of practice in their home setting.

A note on terminology

We have decided to continue to use the word 'client' as the main (though not exclusive) term to describe the persons who use the services of a social work agency. Where possible we use 'person', but sometimes this does not differentiate from others in the same sentence (such as the student or practice teacher). The inadequacies of 'client' are well documented, but the word remains in currency and has the advantage of being short. We use it to denote people living in their own homes, people in residential care, people in custody and users of day services. We are all clients in one way or another.

In the absence of a neutral gender pronoun we have tried to address you, the reader, as 'you' (which refers to the practice teacher in 'Notes for practice teachers' and the student in 'Notes for students').

When referring to the student in the introduction to each chapter and in the 'Notes for practice teachers', we have used plural forms, even when this is not grammatically correct.

Please note that names have been changed in the newspaper items which are used in some of the chapters; in other respects, the news items remain unaltered, except for minor editing.

Finally ...

Your comments have been very helpful in our work on this revised version of *Social Work Practice*, so please keep them coming:

Mark Doel,
School of Social Work
   and RNIB Rehabilitation Studies,
University of Central England,
Perry Barr,
Birmingham, B42 2SU, UK.
e-mail:mark.doel@ucl.ac.uk

Steven Shardlow,
Department of Sociological
   Studies,
University of Sheffield,
Sheffield, S10 2TN, UK.
e-mail:s.shardlow@sheffield.ac.uk

Continue to have fun with these Activities!

M. Doel
S.M. Shardlow

Entry: Supervision and reflective practice

About Entry Activity: Reflections on supervision

'Reflections on supervision' is a trigger to encourage both practice teacher and student to examine their expectations about the content and functions of supervision. The practice tutorial (supervision session) is the linchpin of the student's learning and the assessment of their practice abilities, yet it has complex purposes and may reflect very different understandings of these purposes.

Purpose

'Entry' is concerned with the way in which supervision is put to use. There are a number of different functions and purposes which need to be untangled; otherwise it is difficult to achieve the best use of the practice tutorial.

Method

- Ask the student to read 'Reflections on supervision', explaining that each of the 25 statements is taken from a collection of articles on supervision.
- Ask the student to make a quick response to each statement, pencilling a number from 0–10 to indicate their responses (from 0 = strongly disagree to 10 = strongly agree). (Blue-coloured circles around statements

from 0–3, green from 4–6 and red from 7–10 will give an immediate, graphic summary of the student's views.) Do the exercise yourself, too.
- Where are the student's highest scores?
A grouping of high scores towards the top of the page (that is, more red circles in this area) indicates an emphasis on the managerial and administrative functions.
Highest scores in the middle region suggest a focus on the educational and developmental functions.
High scores in the bottom third of the page indicate most concern for the supportive and nurturing functions.

How do the students' clusters of scores compare with your own?

Variations

If you ask the student to complete 'Reflections on supervision' early and late in the placement, you can gauge if there has been any change in emphasis as a result of the experience of the placement. It is also an opportunity to get feedback from students about your supervision style and practice, and to explore any wide differences in your expectations.

Notes

Like driving, we all slip into poor practice. Supervision should be the central reflective tool for us to remind ourselves of personal standards as individual professionals, as well as the agency's preference for monitored service delivery. (Sawdon and Sawdon, 1995, p. 10)

The supervision session is pivotal in bringing together all the different aspects of the work with the student. Frequently, it is a one-to-one encounter, which provides a rare opportunity to focus on the individual student's learning needs and to tailor the work to their particular circumstances.

'Supervision session' is a term also used in respect of the supervision of staff by agency supervisors, and many of the activities in this book are as relevant to staff development as they are to practice teaching. However, there are also differences, and we have used the term 'practice tutorial' to describe the event which brings the practice teaching of students into focus (Doel, Shardlow, Sawdon and Sawdon, 1996, p. 127; Shardlow and Doel, 1996, p. 105).

Purposes and functions of supervision

The practice tutorial is a complex meeting with many purposes. The various functions of supervision have been described and categorized

Entry:
REFLECTIONS ON SUPERVISION

How strongly do you agree or disagree with the following statements?
Rate each one from 10 = strongly agree to 0 = strongly disagree.

1. Supervision means being able to demonstrate that what is expected from the student is actually achieved.

2. Supervision is where objectives and tasks are agreed to produce a required level of service.

3. Supervision must ensure that clients get an even service.

4. Assessment is a major area of the supervisor's role.

7. Supervision must ensure that the best use is made of the skills, time, and resources available.

8. Student and practice teacher have shared responsibility to ensure supervision sessions take place.

6. Having created a trusting relationship, the practice teacher should use supervision to present the priorities, philosophies and policies of the agency.

5. The needs of the client should be the starting-point for all the work done in supervision.

9. Supervision is intended as guided self-observation which gives shape to that which the student experiences as fragmented.

10. As supervision requires two parties with unequal power to make an effective working relationship, issues of values, rights, responsibilities and goals have to be explored.

11. It is important to draw up a contract which acknowledges the joint expectations of student and practice teacher.

12. The practice teacher should create a climate that enables and empowers the student to talk about thorny issues, especially race and racism.

13. Supervision enables students to consider different ways of handling situations.

14. Supervision acts as a powerful role model for the management of difference and the use and abuse of authority.

17. Supervision is a deep well from which to draw strength and wisdom.

16. Practice teachers must establish how the student learns and adapt according to that style.

15. Supervision provides the opportunity to look at work critically in a way that is professionally developmental.

18. Supervision is not about giving false reassurance, but providing an opportunity to replenish and motivate students, valuing their strengths, effort and commitment.

19. Good practice teaching, as well as being stimulating, can also be painful.

20. Supervision is a helicopter that lifts from danger.

22. A practice teacher who says 'just tell me about the case', invites unconscious misrepresentation as to what went on between the student and client, therefore invalidating the whole thrust of the session.

21. Supervision is the student's most essential helping relationship.

23. Supervision is a warm wall to give support in bouncing ideas off.

24. The practice teacher should be able to say 'I don't know'.

25. The practice teacher can help the student to discover how, in the implementation of the rules and policies, the victim inside the student may have colluded with the victim inside the client.

Reproduced from *The new social work practice* by Mark Doel and Steven Shardlow, Arena, Aldershot

The statements above are taken, in a modified form, from 'Staff Supervision' in *Community Care*, 30 July 1992. Contributors were: Jean Moore, 'Staff supervision: are you satisfied?'; Tony Morrison, 'A question of survival'; Chris Payne, 'A map for different models'; Elizabeth Ash, 'Piggy in the middle'; Jane Metcalf and Clive Curtis, 'Feeding on support'; Anne Hollows, 'Resources for courses'; Joy Francis, 'Results without racism'.

many times, so we know a great deal about what *should* happen in a supervision session, but much less about what actually happens.

At some point, at some time, in some practice tutorial, one or more of the following will be occurring:

- Accounting ● Advising ● Assessing ● Challenging ● Checking ● Clarifying
- Confirming ● Controlling ● Correcting ● Empowering ● Enabling ● Encouraging
- Evaluating ● Explaining ● Helping ● Learning ● Listening ● Managing ● Mediating
- Modelling ● Monitoring ● Negotiating ● Nurturing ● Planning ● Probing
- Recommending ● Reflecting ● Reframing ● Reviewing ● Rewarding ● Supervising
- Supporting ● Teaching ● Testing ● Theorizing ● Valuing

To make sense of all these activities and behaviours, a number of authors have attempted to identify the different functions of supervision. A common categorization is based on the three functions of *administration* (managerial accountability), *education* (teaching and learning) and *support* (helping, enabling, facilitating). Richards *et al.* (1991) add a fourth, *mediation*. The recent focus on competencies might also suggest that *appraisal and assessment* needs to be considered as a discrete, fifth element, separate from the administrative function.

To what extent are these functions compatible or in conflict? It is possible both to establish the accountability of the student to the organization and to promote the student's development as a professional person; indeed, properly accountable work *is* professional practice. However, the balance between these two concerns can be difficult to maintain, and practice tutorials or supervision sessions which spend much of the time on the management and administration of the student's workload will inevitably crowd out the opportunity for reflection and active learning. Whether as practice teacher or agency supervisor, you should find ways to 'audit' your sessions with students and staff, to discover the profile of your supervision and to bring the various functions into balance. This proactive approach is likely to bring the different elements of your supervision practice into better proportion.

Some authors suggest that supervision is different from practice teaching, identifying the latter solely with the educative functions. Pritchard (1995, p. 196) makes what we think is a false dichotomy, suggesting that practice teaching is 'directed towards helping the student to do the job, that is developing skills and knowledge', whereas supervision 'is about helping the student to do the job better'. In *The Anatomy of Supervision*, Gardiner (1989, p. 19) avoids the use of 'practice teaching' because he believes that an emphasis on *practice* and *teaching* is in danger of reinforcing the limitations of the classical model of supervision, which he exposes with ruthless care. He also thinks that the term 'practice teaching' may perpetuate what he refers to as 'concept-leakage', which is the transfer of psychotherapeutic approaches from the practice environment into the supervision process. In the worst cases, students find themselves subjected to enforced therapy. Concept-leakage is not in itself a bad thing, and the leakage can happen in either direction (for example, techniques and theories of learning are leaking back into practice methods, such as task-centred social work); but it rather depends on which concepts are doing the leaking!

Whilst not wishing to become tied up by terminology, we understand 'supervision' and 'practice teaching' to be descriptions of the same phenomenon, viewed from different angles. Early attempts to differentiate what goes on with students from what goes on with workers were a legitimate attempt to uncouple student supervision from the prevailing model of staff supervision. However, what we now know as the practice teaching model of supervision is increasingly seen as appropriate to the supervision of employees – certainly in those organizations which view their workforce as learners and not mere operatives.

Types of supervision

As a practice teacher, what type (or combination of types) of supervision and supervisory methods do you use? This may not be a question you have asked yourself before, but Bourne (1996, p. 11) suggests a useful typology:

- *Coaching supervision* The supervisor works alongside the supervisee, demonstrating, observing, advising, encouraging, and so on. This form of supervision is very close to training and is most often employed with new staff as part of an induction programme. It is also the forum of supervision favoured in industry and commerce.
- *Live supervision* This is similar to coaching supervision, except that the supervisor may not be directly present, although will often be observing through a one-way mirror, and may have some form of audiolink or time-out procedure. This approach is widely used in family therapy circles.
- *Reported supervision* Reported supervision takes place away from direct practice, and relies substantially on information provided by the supervisee, either directly, or indirectly through their behaviour during the session, or their relationship with the supervisor.

Apart from the three direct observations required by CCETSW, social work supervision is often almost exclusively reported supervision. There are limitations in relying on one method of supervision: it is important to question the accuracy of this particular form of supervision and the wisdom of relying on it.

For an alternative classification of types of supervision, see Hawkins and Shohet (1989, p. 44).

The placement as a learning experience

> Managing a field education learning environment is like setting the stage for a play. The stage is the agency and the community is in the wings. (Thomlison and Collins, 1995, p. 223)

It is possible to discern a number of 'tides' in the way the various aspects of the activity we call supervision has, and continues, to progress. Currently there is a pull between the educative function, with an emphasis on the student as a learner and the use of a variety of teaching methods, and the assessment function, with an increasing concentration on the student's ability to demonstrate competencies. In this latter case, there is a danger that the processes of teaching and learning become buried beneath the weight of minutely detailed competencies.

We would like to keep the spotlight on the placement as a learning experience, not a work experience. 'The primary responsibility of the [practice teacher] is to facilitate the student's ... educational plan through the service delivery system of the agency' (Thomlison and Collins, 1995, p. 225). The agency is primarily a service organization, and the education of students for professional practice is not a core concern. In these circumstances, practice teachers have a major role to help mediate between the needs of the student and the requirements of the agency.

There are indications that some organizations are beginning to view their workforce as 'learners for life'. This might be in a formal sense, such as when businesses make adult education classes available in the workplace or in informal ways, for example emphasizing staff development, which reflects a commitment to employees as whole persons with lives and interests beyond the workplace. It is ironic that these developments are appearing in organizations designed for profit, and that human service agencies are more likely to borrow management styles now being abandoned in the business sector. (This perhaps mirrors the search for credibility by the 'soft sciences, adopting the empirical, quantitative methods now found wanting by the 'hard' sciences.) Your supervision work, as practice teacher or staff supervisor, can play its part in developing your agency as a 'learning organization' (Senge, 1990).

What goes on in supervision?

> We appear to know very little about what takes place within supervision. (Brodie 1993)

In an attempt to discover more about what happens in supervision Brodie's study explored three aspects:

- the content (subjects covered within supervision);
- the techniques used by practice teachers within supervision;
- references made to theory within supervision.

In terms of content, 64 per cent of all supervision time was devoted to case or work discussion, though there was a degree of variability within the sample studied. In terms of techniques, four activities made up 86 per cent of all coded practice teaching activities. These were: offering opinion (34 per cent); questioning (22 per cent); clarifying and summarizing (17 per cent); and information giving (13 per cent).

> The regularity and consistency with which practice teachers did offer unsubstantiated opinion raised interesting ... questions: What sense did students make of these statements? Is this opinion-offering indicative of social work's alleged reliance on practice wisdom rather than theoretical propositions? (Brodie, 1993, p. 82)

Full-time practice teachers used clarifying and summarizing techniques twice as much as practice teachers who took occasional students (singleton practice teachers). 'When used together, *questioning* to encourage exploration and *clarifying and summarizing*, student participation in supervision was positively enhanced' (Brodie, 1993, p. 82). The same difference between these two groups of practice teachers was noted in relation to reference to theory in supervision: 'full-time practice teachers made significantly more frequent, more explicit and more expansive references to theory' (Brodie, 1993, p. 82). Where reference was made in theory in supervision, students reported that they found this helpful.

Brodie suggests that the transfer of practice skills (such as encouraging exploration, information giving, and clarifying and summarizing) is a necessary, but not sufficient, skills base for practice teaching. He identifies some barriers to student learning and terms these *minimalist supervision*, 'characterized by the student telling the case, with the practice teacher checking and providing practical information, occasionally providing factual information and repeatedly missing opportunities to encourage the student to make sense of practice issues and dilemmas' (Brodie, 1993, p. 84). Moreover, the minimalist supervisor displayed no interest in the academic world of the student.

Your own supervision practices will develop if you have the opportunity to scrutinize them. Some post-qualifying programmes in practice teaching require you to submit a video extract from a practice tutorial with a student, accompanied by your commentary on what you think worked well and what you would change, with the benefit of hindsight. Even without this formal requirement, you should consider how you might 'capture' a practice tutorial, in order to answer the question 'What goes on in one of my supervision sessions?'

Context

We rightly value the learning which people bring to their work from their previous life experiences. However, it is easy to assume that all experiences labelled 'learnt' are beneficial or, at least, benign. The reality is that learning can be relatively useful or relatively useless, be put to good ends or to poor ends, develop into productive patterns or into destructive ones. The difficulty of 'unlearning' should not be underestimated.

An example of unhelpful learning which becomes established as a pattern is the tendency to repeat an error. This is noticeable when we take a wrong turn on a journey: if the journey is repeated, the likelihood of taking the same wrong turn is strong, unless we make a conscious effort to unlearn the original pattern.

How can your supervision value and respect the individual's past experiences, whilst identifying patterns of learning which are not proving helpful or productive? This needs to be addressed directly in the supervision contract, which is the agreement negotiated between practice teacher and student, supervisor and supervisee, preferably before the beginning of contact.

It is not possible in this chapter to address in any detail the skills needed to perform supervision, but you will need to consider how to develop these skills. Shulman (1982) provides a thorough overview of the skills of supervision and staff management, taking an interactional approach and including a section in each chapter to report on research findings from his supervision study (conducted with Robinson and Luckyj). However, it is important to keep in mind that supervision is more than a technical skill, and that the context of supervision has a significant impact. In particular, your perspective as a man or a woman, as black or white, and the perspectives of the person you are supervising, all influence the supervisory process. It is crucial that issues of power are addressed openly in order to achieve supervision which is anti-oppressive.

Group supervision

One of the ways in which different perspectives can be incorporated is to consider arrangements for practice tutorials which include other practice teachers and students. In a study of the effects of reflective team supervision, Thomlison (1995, p. 234) found that students felt that they received more feedback in this than in one-to-one supervision; team and group supervision gave them information about how other students experienced them and how they came across to others. There were some concerns, too, about the need to adapt to different supervisors' styles and the anxiety of being observed. Used with care, group supervision can provide a more rounded experience for students and staff, and helps to bring different perspectives and a potential power shift into the supervision.

Bourne's study (1996) perhaps explains why group supervision is not prevalent in social work. The group supervision in four out of the five teams which he studied folded shortly after the spotlight of his research terminated. He points to the public nature of group supervision (it takes a confident team leader to 'perform' in front of the full team), and the difficulties arising from the different supervisory needs of the group members as key reasons for the relative absence of groupwork approaches to supervision. In addition, it is important for teams to be clear about the place of the group supervision sessions in relation to their other meetings: group supervision has to be qualitatively different from other forums, otherwise it becomes yet another time-consuming meeting.

Conversely, group practice teaching might have more success because of the relatively common purposes and standing of students on placement.

Lines of accountability

An important element of supervision is the monitoring of the quality of the work done with service users. In many ways it is the power of accountability which differentiates supervision from consultation (Brown and Bourne, 1996). As a practice teacher, you have a mediating role between the requirements of the student's learning and the standards of the service to the agency's clientele. What are the lines of accountability in this situation?

As Payne (1995, pp. 215–6) notes, lines of accountability are elaborate and unclear in any case, especially in the post-Griffiths system of community care. In the light of this uncertain backdrop, there are a number of questions which you need to answer in relation to your *own* work in the agency, before you can begin to consider the student's position:

- How much autonomy and responsibility do front-line workers have?
- Do service users feel that they are dealing with somebody who can make decisions, or are they told they will have to wait for a decision 'from somebody else'?
- How flat or deep are lines of accountability in the agency?
- How does the agency monitor the quality of its service to clients?
- What support system are there for agency staff (in terms of professional supervision, personal support, or group support for staff, such as a black workers' group)?
- If something goes wrong in the handling of a case, who carries the can?
- If something goes well in the handling of a case, who receives the recognition?

Although students have a reference point in the agency which is different from an employee's (they cannot be neatly added to the bottom of the hierarchical pyramid), their experience of learning on the placement will be underwritten by the kinds of responses you have made to the questions above.

Moreover, it is proper to question the usefulness of the practice tutorial as a tool to monitor the service people are receiving. You are a user of a number of services: what do you think would be an accurate and efficient way to monitor quality in respect of your doctor/hairdresser/bus conductor and so on? The functions of supervision go beyond the event of a particular session. The practice tutorial is a forum to facilitate a good-quality service by the student with the user, but direct observation of the student's practice is a more effective way of monitoring that service and making it accountable (Doel, Shardlow, Sawdon and Sawdon, 1996, pp. 147–9).

Liaison between college and agency

The student's placement experiences typically constitute one half of their period of learning, with the other half located in the educational establishment. It is an important task of the practice teacher to help students to integrate these different inputs, a task which is shared with the college tutor. Sheafor and Jenkins (1982, p. 121) argue that the college liaison tutor should not be seen solely as a troubleshooter, and that an active and regular involvement is necessary. Certainly, it is practice wisdom that the student's placement should be supported by consistent contact with a tutor (field liaison), which by tradition has meant a visit before the placement, another at the mid-point, and a final one towards the end. However, it is not clear that these individual linkages are as significant as the general integration of the practice and class curricula. Fortune and Abramson (1993, p. 108) concluded that tutors can offer more by helping, advising and consulting with practice teachers and less by monitoring the individual student. In a later study by Fortune, Miller *et al.* (1995), the experiences of over 300 practice teachers (field instructors) were analysed in relation to two models of liaison between college and field – the 'Intensive Model' and the 'Trouble-Shooting Model'. Surprisingly, the evidence suggested that the practice teachers involved preferred neither model over the other, suggesting that the Trouble-Shooting Model might, therefore, be a better use of scarce resources.

As a practice teacher you need to know whether the contact with the student's programme is likely to be routine or 'as needed'. Whatever model of tutoring and liaison is in operation, the most significant factor is that it should be coherent, with the mutual understanding and support of practice teachers, students and college tutors.

The reflective student

The notion of supervision and practice teaching in social work needs to be informed by ideas of professional education in general. With reference to this wider canvas (which, for instance, includes musicians and architects), Schön describes the notion of a practicum, and characterizes it as

> a setting designed for the task of learning a practice. In a context that approximates a practice world, students learn by doing, although their doing usually falls short of real-world work. They learn by undertaking projects that simulate and simplify practice; or they take on real-world projects under close supervision. (Schön, 1987, p. 37)

The view that existing professional knowledge cannot fit every case and that not every problem has a right answer leads Schön to the notion of reflection-in-action, by which 'students must develop new rules and methods of their own'. It relates to a central tenet of social work education – the concept of the transferability of knowledge; in other words, learning is not about experiencing every possible contingency (clearly an impossibility) but about making links and connections from one situation to another, and by creating a greater whole out of the sum of the parts.

Practice learning for professional education transcends both the agency work setting and the educational establishment, but must not become divorced from them. Schön goes even further, suggesting that

> in order to be credible and legitimate, a practicum must become a world with its own culture, including its own language, norms and rituals. Otherwise, it may be overwhelmed by the academic and professional cultures that surround it (Schön, 1987, p. 170)

This moves a long way from the notion of professional education as an apprenticeship, in which supervision is primarily concerned with regulating the student's behaviour to fit the requirements of work tasks. In this vision of practice learning, the student enters a distinct world created for the purpose of learning reflective practice. This is essential in order to establish professional practitioners as opposed to skilled technicians.

Crucially, supervision which nurtures the reflective student guarantees a future for the reflective practitioner. For further ideas about the development and practice of supervision/practice teaching, see for example: Bogo and Vayda (1987); Ford and Jones (1987); Shardlow and Doel (1996); Schneck, Grossman and Glassman (1991); Thompson, Osada and Anderson (1994).

I

Foundations of practice

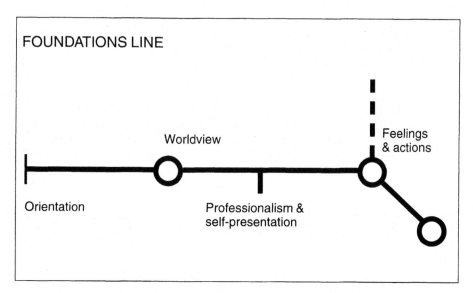

Chapters 1–4 focus on the student's beliefs, values and feelings, and how these relate to social work practice and to the student's work in agencies:

- Orientation (Chapter 1) makes the induction process explicit rather than haphazard, helping students to settle into new work settings.
- The second chapter, Worldview, focuses on the way beliefs influence how the students view the world. It also opens up opportunities to

explore a student's attitude to the relationship between theory and practice.
- Professionalism and self-presentation (Chapter 3) introduces students to the first of many paradoxes in social work practice: the need to be warm and approachable at the same time as keeping a cool, professional distance, and is concerned with questions of personal style and the verbal and non-verbal messages which students give to clients and colleagues. This chapter examines differences between friendships and *workships* (working relationships) and how different settings may have different codes of professional practice.
- Finally, Feelings and actions (Chapter 4) explores how students deal with strong emotions or feelings which they find unacceptable or disturbing; and how students' feelings and actions are mediated by their values.

'Foundations of practice' is intended to introduce the social work learner to a number of practice dilemmas. The purpose of these chapters is to help students learn how to think critically about their own practice in the light of these dilemmas, and to develop self-aware practice. Put simply, this means *knowing why you're doing what you're doing when you're doing it*.

The development of an understanding of the significance of factors such as race, gender and class for the student's personal outlook is paramount in all the chapters. These factors influence what we do in a profound way and are an essential component of self-aware practice.

It is important to establish a good climate for learning, so that students feel able to take risks safely. By working jointly with students on the activities contained in the chapters, practice teachers are showing commitment to improving their own practice. The activities do not rely on 'right answers', because these are usually elusive, but they do depend on a willingness to be explicit about the knowledge, the values and the beliefs which are the foundations for the practice. This is more demanding than learning 'facts'.

Students who successfully complete 'Foundations of practice' will have a better understanding of their own beliefs and values and how these influence their practice. They will broaden their repertoire of styles, consolidating the strengths they bring from their previous experience and developing a commitment to work on areas which need improvement. They will have a good foundation in basic skills which are often taken for granted, but which need careful learning.

1 Orientation

About Activity 1: Who takes sugar?

The orientation exercise consists of a number of questions which students are asked to complete during the first few days on placement, as part of the induction to work in the agency. This chapter contains two sample exercises designed to serve as models on which you can base an activity of your own invention and design. In developing an activity specific to your area of practice, it is essential to frame the questions in such a way that they help the student to get to know key people and find out about significant places and information.

Purpose

Finding your way around a new place is seldom easy. Remind yourself of when you started a new job and you will have an idea of how the students feel when they start a placement. The purpose of this activity is to help students to orientate themselves to the placement as quickly as possible in a way that reflects the active approach they will be learning to practise throughout the placement.

Method

- This is an activity best completed by students acting on their own, and it can be introduced on the first day. The purpose of the activity needs to be carefully explained as:

- an example of the kind of activity the student will be doing;
- a means to see how the student completes a task;
- an entertaining way to feel at home and find out about the placement.

Tell students what your expectations are: you expect them to complete most of the questions, but there may be a few they have not been able to answer. (This introduction should take about 15 minutes.)

- Arrange a time later the next day to find out how the student is getting on. You are not expecting everything to be completed by then, but it will give you both an opportunity to see if there are any major difficulties. (This will take 5–10 minutes, but more time may be needed if the student is experiencing difficulties.)
- Arrange a time three or four days into the placement to review the student's work on the Orientation exercise. (Allow about 30 minutes.)

Variations

This activity can be used in any setting, though the questions need to be tailored to the specific placement. When devising a similar exercise, ask yourself which people and places are likely to be significant for the student during the placement, so you can construct appropriate questions. Are you going to have 'true–false' questions or open ones? How far are the questions going to focus on the 'inside' or lead the student into the community?

Two examples of the activity are provided, one based on the example of a home for older people, 'Who takes sugar in Oakbrook Home?'; the other 'Who wears the sandals in the office?', based on community practice. One uses true–false questions; the other requires students to provide more detailed information. In producing your own version you will need to decide which format to use, whether to mix and match, and how testing or controversial to make your questions. In the examples provided students will be forced to confront some significant issues – you may decide that these should be introduced later in the placement.

You will need to consider whether to consult people in advance: you want this to be a positive experience for the student and not everybody takes kindly to questioning.

Activity 1   WHO TAKES SUGAR?

Who takes sugar in Oakbrook Home?			Who wears the sandals in the office?
	True	False	

Who takes sugar in Oakbrook Home?

	True	False
The oldest resident is Ivy Pinner		
The friends of Oakbrook raised £1500 last year		
The hairdressers visit on Fridays		
The Red Lion pub has a ramp to the side door		
The senior staff group decide how to spend the annual budget		
Residents can eat a meal at any time they want		
Relatives can visit residents at any time		
There are no black residents		
The deputy principal is the only fully qualified first-aider		
There are no vegetarian residents		
John and James are an 'out' gay resident couple who share a room		
Residents can furnish their own rooms as they choose		
Ann is the only staff member who takes sugar in her tea		
The average stay for residents is seven years		
Oakbrook home was last redecorated six years ago		
All residents must be in bed for 11.00		

Who wears the sandals in the office?

Where is the nearest post office?

How long is the waiting list for a place at the local day nursery?

How does the user committee at the day centre for people with physical disabilities work?

How much does it cost to hire a room at the community centre?

Why did the support group for lesbian single mothers have to close?

How many Asian home helps work in the area?

What different kinds of care does Oakbrook Elderly Persons' Home offer?

Where are the foster homes in the area?

What is the availability of interpreters for the principal minority language group?

When is the rights and advice centre open and how does it get its funding?

What are the average waiting times for council tenancies in our area?

Who wears the sandals in the office?

Reproduced from *The new social work practice* by Mark Doel and Steven Shardlow, Arena, Aldershot

Notes for practice teachers

Students are likely to feel strange during the first few days of the placement. Reactions to new learning experiences are many and varied (Shardlow and Doel, 1996, pp. 164–7). They may not know many people nor where things are, and they have to fathom the often complex relationships among their new colleagues. They do this with very little knowledge of the history of existing relationships and the culture of the agency. Above all, the student is aware that, though this is the beginning of the placement, the end is already in sight and that the contact with the agency is limited.

Anticipating students' feelings means giving care and attention to the details of their introduction and taking account of their needs, ensuring they are included on any rosters, or that their name is on the signing-out board, that they have a desk or workspace complete with information packs and stationery, and that they are introduced to immediate members of the team. You need to welcome the student personally (you can suggest a student starts the first day an hour after you, to give you time to deal with anything that needs your immediate attention). A warm welcome is a considerable improvement on the pile of unallocated work which has been known to greet a student on their first day.

Preparation for the placement is a process which predated the placement, with informal contact and a meeting to work in more detail on the learning objectives. Once the student has begun the placement, a guided introduction is important if the student is to make quick progress in the agency. However, as the practice teacher, you have your own work demands which mean you cannot be responsible for all of the student's time. Moreover, the student does not want to feel like an extra limb, incapable of any independent action. How can students be guided through the workplace, getting a broad-brush feel of its work and make the acquaintance of various people, without feeling led by the hand?

Orientation exercise

A simple fact-finding exercise can help to achieve these aims. The practice teacher can point the student in specific directions by the nature of the questions in the exercise, and the students can work at their own pace to answer them. The exercise can be revised before each placement so that the information which the student collects is relevant and beneficial to you and your team (the student's enquiries may help you to document some changes).

'Who takes sugar?' orients a student to a residential home for elderly people, and 'Who wears the sandals?' to work in the local community. You should design the orientation exercise around the working community which the student needs to get to know. The physical layout of the work place affects the contact, or lack of it, between colleagues. In a tower block for example, contact with people on different floors does not happen by chance, so an effort is necessary to establish a pattern of meeting colleagues whose advice or support may be important, but whose habitat may feel unfamiliar. The 'shape' of a small unit or local team may become quickly familiar, but links with people outside may be hard to establish, reinforcing inward-looking patterns of work. How can 'Who takes sugar?' be supplemented to point the student outside the immediate setting of the home?

In addition to focusing on people and places, the exercise should also point to issues which you will be addressing during the placement, for example client and user power, decision-making processes and ethnicity. It is hoped, too, that the student will build on these contacts in order to find out more about the jobs of other workers and the perceptions of people who use the agency.

Students can be encouraged to think about their experiences as newcomers to the agency in comparison with those of clients, who are also new to the agency. The experiences of clients have been graphically summed up in the title of a chapter in Davies's (1994) *The Essential Social Worker*: 'First encounter: the client enters an alien world'. Thinking about the similarities and differences between the experiences of students and clients can help to develop students' empathy with their clients.

Let the student know how an activity may be used. For example, if the exercise is part of the examination of the student's competence, this must be made explicit before the work begins. An activity such as 'Who takes sugar?' would not normally be part of the examination of the student's practice, though the creation of such an exercise by the current student for use by future students could be part of the formal assessment. The emphasis of the orientation exercise is on *learning* rather than *performance*.

Students who return to the practice teaching session with most of the information, who enjoyed the encounters with other people, who connect with the issues and with the people they meet are likely to be a joy to have around. But what if a student returns with muddled or terse responses and little information? You will want to find out how the student set about the task and make links between this and the ways such a student might approach the work with clients.

Examples

Mary had been hesitant about doing the orientation activity and gave bare answers in the practice tutorial.* She gave the impression that she thought it all a waste of time, and her terse replies led the practice teacher to wonder how much face-to-face contact she had managed in preparing her answers. Mary's initial hostility to the activity gave

---

* The term 'practice tutorial' is used to refer to the face-to-face teaching session between student and practice teacher. 'Practice' emphasizes the nature of the content, and 'tutorial' expresses the educational form and context of the learning. Other terms used for the same activity are the rather long and inelegant: 'practice teaching session', or 'supervision session', with its managerial overtones.

way to an acknowledgement that she found it difficult to approach new people. The activity had been difficult, because she found new situations awkward. The practice teacher made links between the activity and the situations which Mary would encounter in the work with residents. She emphasized her commitment as Mary's practice teacher to help her to develop the interpersonal skills to give her more confidence. Together they began by listing the situations in the orientation activity in their order of difficulty for Mary, and rehearsed some of the first contacts.

Brian came to the practice tutorial with only a few of the answers to the exercise. When the practice teacher asked him to explain in detail how he had approached the task, it emerged that he had taken a very literal approach. In serial fashion he had started at the top and worked down. Unfortunately, he had difficulty catching the home care organizer, so he became stuck at that question and ran out of time. He seemed genuinely disappointed to miss out on making all the contacts and confessed that although he had been to the advice centre, he didn't think to ask them about the question on the orientation sheet, because he 'hadn't come to that one yet'. The practice teacher acknowledged her responsibility to recap the purpose of the orientation work, and to plan with Brian ways in which he could approach the task, such as getting an overview of the task and reviewing his diary for likely opportunities to find out the information.

Howa came to the practice tutorial with a complete set of answers to the orientation activity. The responses were concise and clear, but she said she couldn't really see the point of the exercise because she had no difficulty making contact with people and that this was rather a time-consuming way of proving it. The practice teacher felt confused by this response – a successful outcome with such an apparently unsuccessful process. She wondered if Howa's obvious satisfaction with her own competence might prevent her from taking risks, or indicated a lack of imagination. Nevertheless, she was also alive to the possibility that Howa does indeed make contacts very easily, has a low boredom threshold and that the activity fell below it. (Although the activities in this book have been well received by students, it is important to adapt the activities to individuals – and you won't always be successful.)

Notes for students

There are many different ways of getting to know new places and new people. The orientation activity is designed as a guided introduction to the placement – a way of finding out about the setting for your placement.

First impressions

It is always difficult to know how reliable our first impressions are, and usually we forget them as we acclimatize to a new setting. Nevertheless, it is interesting to compare first impressions with later ones and to think about the ways the early impressions have been changed or confirmed.

Make a note of some of the impressions you have gained from the experience of the orientation activity. These are your private impressions, though you may want to discuss some of them with your practice teacher as you go through your responses to the activity. Or you may just want to log them. These are some suggested headings:

- The 'climate' in the unit or team
- The way clients are received at the front door or front desk
- The feelings workers express about the organization
- The attitudes of workers towards the clients
- The physical appearance of the unit or office
- The opportunity for privacy or quiet space
- The 'pace' of work compared to what I'm used to.

Towards the end of the placement, it will be interesting to reflect on these first impressions. How do they look now that you have got to know the setting and your colleagues better? In particular, which impressions have deepened with experience and which ones have changed?

An afterthought

You may want to consider compiling your own orientation activity for the next student; after all, you are in as good a position as anybody to know what this should contain. In addition to the orientation activities you undertook, and with the benefit of hindsight, what information and contacts would have been useful in those first few days? Discuss this with your practice teacher and see if you can revise the orientation exercise in preparation for the next student.

Reproduced from *The new social work practice* by Mark Doel and Steven Shardlow, Arena, Aldershot

Some further reading

In respect of learning generally see Knowles (1972) and Schön (1987), and for learning on placements in particular see Doel, Shardlow, Sawdon and Sawdon (1996) and Shardlow and Doel (1996). See Danbury (1994) for an account of the necessary practical preparations.

Reproduced from *The new social work practice* by Mark Doel and Steven Shardlow, Arena, Aldershot

2 Worldview

About Activity 2: Believe it or not

'Believe it or not' takes a look at social work from several different points of view. Brief quotations present examples of different views about social work. Students are invited to consider with which statements they agree.

Purpose

The reasons why people come into social work are numerous. Some have clear, well-rehearsed positions and others have difficulty identifying their motives and beliefs. Some subscribe to an '-ism' or two, and others have muddled views with no obvious guiding principles. We all have some kind of personal philosophy – ways of looking at the world and explaining it – but are we aware of what these are? The purpose of this activity is to help students reach a better understanding of how the way they view the world influences their work; in other words, how beliefs interact with actions.

Method

- This activity is best undertaken by a student and practice teacher jointly, or by a group of three or four students. Give a clear explanation of the purpose of the exercise, emphasizing the exploratory aspects and making sure the student knows that there is no pressure to take up any particular position.

- The student reads the various statements in the 'Believe it or not' activity and writes down responses to each of the statements. (If a group of students is working together you can also then ask them to discuss their responses to these statements.) Arrange a time when you can exchange comments (probably the next practice tutorial) and suggest that the student makes a few notes ready for this discussion.
- Encourage the student to enter a dialogue about the statements and your mutual preferences. It is important to avoid preaching or trying to enforce a consensus: the discussion is an opportunity to share the ways you each view the world or, if these are not clear, an attempt to articulate previously unspoken worldviews.
- Help the student to relate worldviews to social work practice. What are the implications of each of these statements for practice? How do different beliefs affect the choices social workers make about what they do? (About 1 hour in total.)

Variations

You can substitute different statements about social work from a wide variety of perspectives. The views expressed in this activity can easily be substituted for different ones (for example Moslem, behaviourist). Alternatively, you can use different viewpoints about particular aspects of practice (for example child care, work with older people). In many respects, it is irrelevant which views are discussed with the student: the purpose of the activity is for students to become aware of their own views by looking at the world as others see it.

You can use this activity at an early stage in a student's placement. It is also the type of activity that can be revisited using either the same or different extracts later in the placement to help students identify how their worldview has or has not changed.

Note

A commentary on the extracts and their sources is to be found in the appendix to this chapter. It is strongly suggested that you do *not* consult this appendix until you have completed the activity and had the opportunity for discussion.

Activity 2   BELIEVE IT OR NOT

Consider the following FIVE brief extracts about social work, and ask yourself:

- Which if any of these statements do I agree with, and why?
- What are the ideological beliefs that underpin each of these statements?

The ruling class uses social work primarily to support and protect the expansion and legitimation of its power. The social services are provided for the subject class and its casualties, in order to improve the health and social functioning of the labour force, and to mitigate the worst effects of the structural inequalities. Social work is especially important in legitimating the values of the ruling class by its emphasis upon the socialization process. Paradoxically, social work reinforces the underclass clientele's identity as irresponsible and immature.

Although feminist theory offers an alternative theory of service delivery and method, it operates itself on a system of received ideas about women – a system without commonly agreed theoretical explanations or practical operational outcomes. Bluntly, feminism is ambiguous; it means very different things to different people. To this end, we would suggest that, like Marxism and the traditional approaches to social work, feminism offers a flawed approach. In particular it assumes a unanimity on the subject – women's oppression – which does not exist.

In so far as there are common elements in social work, they are best described by the notion of *maintenance*. Society maintains itself in a relatively stable state by managing and making provision for people in positions of weakness, stress or vulnerability; society maintains its own members by virtue of social work's commitment to humanist endeavour, and its emphasis on the idea of respect for the client, optimism for the future, and faith in the essential, or at least potential, unity of society.

There is a tendency in the social work profession to disengage social work practice from political debate and political advocacy. Yet, social work in itself is 'undeniably political'. This anomaly is usually couched in a liberal approach to social work, which may embrace the ideology of 'individual freedom' but need not concern itself with societal flaws that are fundamental barriers to individual freedom – barriers like sexism, racism, and other oppressions. A liberal social worker gets so involved in the so-called 'individual freedom'; that s/he tends to accommodate *all* individuals, irrespective of their socio-economic, educational or cultural backgrounds, in his/her pluralistic view of society. So the result is trying to please *everybody*.'

Our present model of so-called client-centred social work is basically sound, but in need of a better defined and less ambitious mandate. Social work should be explicitly selective rather than universalist in focus, reactive rather than preventative in approach and modest in its objectives. Social work ought to be preventive with respect to the needs which come to its attention; it has neither the capacity, the resources nor the mandate to go looking for needs in the community at large.

Reproduced from *The new social work practice* by Mark Doel and Steven Shardlow, Arena, Aldershot

Notes for practice teachers

There are as many worldviews as there are people to hold them. What we know as '-isms' (socialism, feminism, and so on.) are such cogent worldviews that we often refer to them as theories. A theory is a coherent explanation of why the world is as it is. It often provides both an analysis of some aspect of the world and prescriptions about how the world might be changed to rectify wrongs that are evident in the analysis. For example, Marxism proposes changes in the ownership of the 'means of production', that is, that factories and the like should be communally owned. Feminist theory proposes changes in the social roles ascribed to women to bring about changes in social structures, such as the family or workplace.

If you were to ask students 'cold' about their personal philosophy, you would probably get an equally cold response. It is a very personal matter to be asked about the way in which we view the world and the beliefs we hold, and there may be many reasons why we have learned to be careful about revealing them. It is important to find a way of starting from an objective position and move at the student's pace to a more subjective point. The notion of *accelerated learning* can be used to speed up the process of mutual discovery (see page xv).

An example of this objective technique, which approaches potentially difficult issues obliquely, is described by Heap (1979) in a groupwork context. A group for people with socially disabling stutters was finding the going tough, with long periods of silence and no eye contact. On one occasion, a group member arrived with her dog, which made itself at home in the middle of the circle. Gradually, the group members found that they could communicate with each other by addressing comments through the dog. In time they were able to lift their heads and speak to one another directly. Perhaps this is an extreme form of a universal process called beating about the bush. Opening up about professional values and the beliefs we hold to explain the world is helped by an activity such as 'Believe it or not'.

Nevertheless, it is difficult to remain disengaged, and the activity triggers sympathies, antipathies and discussion of general issues. For example, how does the use of language differ from one statement to the next, and is this significant? What do we make of the similarities and differences between aspects of the extracts?

It is important to be open about your own beliefs. It may be difficult to avoid dispute with an opinionated student and 'giving answers' for a diffident student, but your aim is to open up a genuine dialogue. At this stage you are not making a judgement about the student's worldview; you are exploring how it is likely to influence the student's work.

Examples

Molly was eager to discuss 'Believe it or not'. She had read it carefully beforehand, as the practice teacher had requested, and had made notes on the extracts. However, she was quickly critical of the crude representation of the viewpoint in extract three and claimed that the others were an irrelevance in the face of a feminist critique. Molly gave a forthright and articulate account of her views and referred the practice teacher to Langan and Day (1992) for a good perspective on different feminist positions. The practice teacher's suggestion that it might be a good idea for Molly to write a feminist position and commentary to use as part of the exercise met with short shrift on the grounds that a caricature would debase feminism and that there wasn't a feminist worldview, just interpretations of it. The practice teacher's views were, in fact, similar to the student's, but she was unhappy that Molly's manner prevented her (the practice teacher) from sharing her own beliefs.

'How do I feel?' the practice teacher asked herself fifteen minutes into the activity. The answer came, 'like a hurricane is blowing me away'. She decided that it was time to turn the session into a more reflective mode and gently shared her impressions with Molly, who was initially surprised. When Molly began to reflect on her approach to the session, she realized that she had assumed that she would be expected to give a good account of her own views. Although she had denied it to herself, she had been nervous but she was determined 'to get it right – to my own satisfaction'. This explained her earnest single-mindedness. 'I suppose I've played the good little girl to your schoolteacher and I resented it, but I realize now that wasn't what you were looking for.'

Molly's approach could easily have been interpreted as rigid and, in part, it did point to a tendency to get hold of the wrong end of the stick. However, Molly's honesty and intelligence proved an asset to her work. She had no doubts about the rightness of her philosophy, but she increasingly understood that what motivated her did not necessarily motivate other people.

James was very quiet during the discussion of 'Believe it or not', tending to follow the practice teacher's lead. When he was asked more directly for his views he suddenly became dismissive of issues which he had earlier been nodding at. He felt that people were trying to make social work out to be more than it was and that he 'just gets on with the job, finding people as they are'. He didn't think it mattered which statements he agreed or disagreed with. In his opinion it was much more important to learn about social work skills and to get on with the business of just doing your best for people.

The practice teacher should not make assumptions about James's practice from this one reaction, rather discover what these views indicate. For reasons which are not yet clear to the practice teacher, abstract discussion with James has not been successful. Perhaps it would be helpful to introduce a concrete example from practice familiar to James. If this is constructed in order to illustrate a practical dilemma, the practice teacher can help James to find the principles which lie behind his practice, by teasing out the reasons for the choices he makes in the face of the dilemma. James will need reassuring that he is not being asked to adopt an '-ism', but to look at the approaches which he uses, perhaps instinctively, in his own practice and how these pull together. Revisiting 'Believe it or not' later in the placement would show how much James had developed; if he is still unable to conceptualize, this would lead to serious questions over his competence in this area.

Notes for students

Everybody has a worldview, even if it is not very clear or consistent. A worldview is just a word meaning how we make sense of the world, including personal theories we use to explain what goes on around us. Problems can arise if we have views which exclude other interpretations to such an extent that we are unaware of other people's worldviews; problems can also occur if we are not aware of the personal beliefs which lead us to act as we do.

Take an example from your previous work experience (this could be social work or it could be some other area). Think of a *case path* (a way of describing the person's contact with the organization from start to finish) for a particular user, customer or client of the organization where you worked. Look at the case path from the perspective of the writers of the extracts in the 'Believe it or not' activity. How does each viewpoint affect your explanation of the person's situation? How does this influence what you do? What effect might this have on the case path?

You have been looking at different worldviews, but how about the view which you carry all the time – what does that look like? We get so used to looking at the world through our own particular spectacles that we often forget that we have a particular and distinctive point of view, not necessarily shared by others. The statements below should help to trigger your thoughts about this; what statements do you feel attracted or repelled by?

- Blood is thicker than water.
- People have a lot of control over their own lives.
- Women experience oppression in Western societies.
- Under the skin we're all essentially the same.
- People don't usually like being reminded of their responsibilities.
- In general, people respond to reason.
- British culture doesn't encourage people to be assertive.
- There's a lot of untapped goodwill in the community.
- Never judge a person until you've walked in their moccasins.

Compare your responses to these statements with those of fellow students in order to develop explicit ideas about your own worldview. You might also like to:

- Make a note of how some specific beliefs you hold have been influenced by your experiences on the placement.
- Relate your own beliefs to a particular piece of work (with an individual, family or group) during the placement. How were your actions influenced by your worldview?

Reproduced from *The new social work practice* by Mark Doel and Steven Shardlow, Arena, Aldershot

Using these various approaches you can develop an awareness of your own worldview, whether it is a well-articulated or 'fuzzy' one, and understand how this influences your practice.

Clients' worldviews

The clients of the agency where you are on placement have their own worldviews, too. For instance, their belief in the possibility or impossibility of change is a strong factor in the success or failure of your efforts with them.

Do you think it is important to find out what the client's worldview is? If so, how can you do this? One approach is to review the range of research about clients' views of the world, such as Mayer and Timms's (1970) seminal text, or the more recent synthesis of research studies by Lindow and Morris (1995). You may discover that the client's worldview is in sharp contrast to yours, perhaps even in strong disagreement, and you need to consider whether you would disclose this. How might it affect your work with them (see Chapter 13). Can you think of occasions when it would be appropriate to challenge the client's worldview?

Some further reading

For a discussion of the nature of theory and social work, see Howe (1993) and Payne (1997). Coulshed (1991), Davies (1997), Hanvey and Philpot (1994), and Lishman (1991) give overviews of different theories and approaches in social work.

Reproduced from *The new social work practice* by Mark Doel and Steven Shardlow, Arena, Aldershot

Appendix

The extracts in Activity 2, 'Believe it or not', are taken from the following sources:

Extract one

Leonard, P. (1976), 'The function of social work in society', in N. Timms and D. Watson (eds), *Talking about Welfare*, London: Routledge & Kegan Paul, p. 261.

This extract is an expression of a Marxist analysis of society and social work. The writer sees social work as a mechanism for maintaining the existing order of society – an order that he regards as exploitative of the working class and therefore to be opposed. For a discussion of the practice implications of this view see Simpkin (1983), who advocates trade union activity for social workers.

Extract two

Davies, M. (1981), *The Essential Social Worker* (first edn), Aldershot: Gower, p. 3.
In this extract, social work has a particular function to perform to maintain a stable society. This is a humanistic approach, and – in sociological terms – a functionalist approach. Social work is described as a benign influence, a force that will contribute something positive to the future. Contrast this with the previous extract.

Extract three

Rojeck, C., Peacock, G. and Collins, S. (eds) (1988), *Social Work and Received Ideas*, London: Routledge, p. 113.

This extract does not make a positive statement about any aspect of social work, but criticizes feminist thinking directly and Marxism indirectly. It suggests that feminist social work is grounded in an inaccurate sociological analysis.

Extract four

Ahmad, B. (1990), *Black Perspectives in Social Work*, Birmingham: Venture Press, p. 44.

This extract is written from a Black perspective and calls for social workers to become more involved with problems at a societal level, rather than focusing exclusively upon the individual. It states that the overconcentration on the individual has resulted in a social work that is failing.

Extract five

Pinker, R. A. (1982), 'An Alternative View' Appendix B in P. M. Barclay (1982), *Social Workers: Their Role and Tasks* (The Barclay Report), London: Bedford Square Press, p. 237.

This extract represents a political view to the right of centre. In the opinion of the writer, social work should have a limited role in society, and should not be overly ambitious in what it seeks to achieve. Hence social work should be 'targeted' on those who are most in need.

3 Professionalism and self-presentation

About Activity 3: Boundaries

'Boundaries' consists of a number of questions designed to expose practice dilemmas. These dilemmas focus on the 'distance' social workers place between themselves and the people who use their services. The activity also encourages students to explore the impressions that they might make on others and how these are, or are not, consistent with being a professional social worker.

Purpose

Students often find it difficult to know what a professional relationship means in practice and how it differs from a personal relationship. This activity is designed to highlight the differences between *friendships* and what we might call *workships* (professional working relationships between practitioners and other people). It helps students become more skilled at deciding where the boundaries between the personal and professional should be drawn. It also encourages students to reflect on how they might be perceived by others, according to how these boundaries are defined.

Method

- This activity achieves best results with four to eight participants, but it can be undertaken by a single practice teacher and student. Arrange a

time to meet and outline the purposes of the activity, but not the details – you want spontaneous responses.
- Give each person a copy of 'Boundaries' and take each of the seven sections in turn to trigger discussion (about 5 to 10 minutes for each section). Start the first item yourself with a 'Never', 'Always' or 'It depends' and invite others to join in with their responses.
- Relate the discussion to actual experiences in order to avoid idealized replies. Encourage dissent and try to tease out any general principles which have emerged from the discussion.
- Sum up the main areas of consent and dissent and write down any general principles which have come out of the discussion. Ask for feedback from everyone about the usefulness of the exercise. (About 1 hour total.)

Variations

This activity has been used successfully in many different settings, usually in the early stages of the placement (and even as part of a pre-placement meeting). Alternatively you may wish to divide the exercise and use parts of the activity at different points in the placement.

A particularly useful variation is to ask students to complete the activity and then present the activity to a group of clients and ask them how they think social workers ought to behave. Some agencies provide excellent opportunities for this, for example those already working with groups of clients (in residential centres for children and older people, in day care centres, and group projects for adolescents). The comparison between the views of students and clients may prove very interesting and highly informative in helping students to define the boundaries of professional behaviour.

You may wish to tailor the details of 'Boundaries' to your particular work base. For example, if you are a social worker based in a hospital, it may be the boundaries between the health care staff and the social work staff that you wish to highlight. There are dilemmas, too, in the patient–doctor relationship which you could compare with client–worker activities.

You can use 'Boundaries' to highlight a particular dimension of practice for example an anti-oppressive framework. Students can be asked to consider how issues of race or gender affect or alter their responses.

Activity 3 BOUNDARIES

- Where do we draw the boundary between personal and professional relationships?
- How should social workers present themselves to their clients?
- Can you answer 'Always' or 'Never' to any of the questions below?
- If your answer to a question is 'It depends', what does it depend on?

Reciprocation

1. Do your clients call you by your first (given) name?
2. Do you call them by their first (given) name?
3. Would you accept a service from a client:
   - Let them knit you a jumper?
   - Advise you what is wrong with your car?
   - Mend an electrical fault in your home?

Self-presentation

4. Do you wear:
   - Jeans and trainers when you meet with clients?
   - Body piercing; visible tattoos on placement?
   - Formal dress for a case presentation?
5. Would you wear a badge, when meeting clients, that stated:
   - 'Campaign for Nuclear Disarmament'?
   - 'I've run a marathon'?
   - 'Jesus lives'?
   - 'Proud to be gay'?
   - 'A woman's place is in her union'?
   - 'Have a nice day'?

Interview culture

6. On a home visit would you accept
   - A cup of tea or coffee?
   - An alcoholic drink?
   - A meal?
7. In the unit, ward or group room would you:
   - Talk about personal matters with other people present?
   - Make a cup of tea or coffee for the client?

Social contact

8. Would you accept from a client:
   - A wedding invitation?
   - An invitation to a party?
9. Would you avoid frequenting a place where a client worked?
10. Do you lend money to your clients?

With acknowledgements to Kate Langford

Self-disclosure

11. Do you compare life experiences with clients:
    - Let them know how you feel about their circumstances?
    - Let them know what sort of day you've had?
    - Talk about your work with other clients?
12. Do you share personal information with your clients:
    - Good news, such as your partner has been promoted?
    - Bad news, like your father suffers from Alzheimer's?
13. Would you give your home address or phone number?

Touch

14. When you meet a client would you"
    - Shake hands?
    - Kiss socially on the cheek?
    - Embrace?
    - Make a physical gesture?
15. Would you touch a client who is upset:
    - On the arm?
    - Round the shoulders?
    - On the knee?
16. Would you cuddle or romp with the children of clients?

Looking the other way

17. Do you ignore your client's illegal activities:
    - Claiming benefit when they are working?
    - The presence of a cannabis plant in their home?
    - Electricity that has been reconnected by the client?
    - An absconder who is being harboured?
    - Unlawful sexual activity?

Sexuality

18. Would you:
    - 'Flirt' with a client?
    - Discuss your HIV status with a client?
    - Consider having a sexual relationship with an ex-client?
    - Help a severely disabled person find a prostitute?

Reproduced from *The new social work practice* by Mark Doel and Steven Shardlow, Arena, Aldershot

Notes for practice teachers

Guidance about how to behave with clients often seems to be paradoxical. Take the following statements about practice that might be given to students:

- You must be engaging, personable and able to step into people's shoes.
- Act natural.
- Be warm.

- You must be purposeful, objective and able to stay outside the situation.
- Be professional.
- Keep your cool.

It is not surprising if students feel that making a successful professional relationship is like squaring the circle. Asking somebody to be personal and impersonal at the same time is confusing. Students need to consider how the way they present themselves to clients can influence the nature of the professional relationship.

Discuss this paradox early on: it gives you and the student a reference point later, when things happen in the student's work which illustrate these dilemmas.

Different expectations

Students behave now as they have learned to behave in previous settings, which may have been very different from yours. A student who has been working in a residential setting with disabled people may be used to a lot of physical contact and informal relationships: this student may not understand the different expectations of a formal office setting, and vice versa. Richards (1988) describes three spheres of practice which illustrate these differences very well.

Students are at an early stage in their careers and may have a strong desire to help people, perhaps resulting in close identification with the client and an emphasis on personal friendship. In practice, this could mean an interview in a pub, intimate talk by a resident's bedside, or activities like motor biking with groups of adolescents in the evenings. All of this may be fine, but that is not always the case: professionals exercise considerable power in their work and students need an early appreciation of the dimensions of their power (Hugman, 1991).

On questions of professional standards, the difference of opinion about what is acceptable is striking. For example, Jayaratne, Croxton and Mattison (1997) point out that 'virtually no empirical studies of professional standards exist ... in effect, practitioners and those who judge practitioner behaviour are making decisions with relatively little guidance from the profession'. Their own exploratory study in Michigan examined professional social work behaviour and beliefs in the following areas: intimate relationships; dual relationships (that is, a social relationship); mixed

Professionalism and self-presentation 37

modalities (by which they mean using other methods such as prayer, yoga, and so on alongside social work); giving advice; financial transactions (of particular relevance in the United States where, increasingly, social work service is dependent on appropriate insurance cover); and boundary behaviours. They found that hugging or embracing a client was commonplace; the acceptance of expensive gifts and lending or borrowing money rare. Bartering for goods or services from clients instead of services was considered appropriate by over a third of the 826 practitioners in the sample. There were no clear majorities either way for: commenting on clients' physical attractiveness; cursing or swearing during sessions; discussing one's religious belief; and providing a home telephone number. In other words, social workers said these were acceptable and not acceptable in roughly equal numbers.

The following example shows how students who have been used to keeping clients at arm's length might respond to the prospect of a placement where the users of the agency are not kept at such distance. We also see how 'Boundaries' can be used to judge the suitability of a placement before it is planned.

Example

Yusef, an Asian student, and **Jim**, a black American student on the same programme, were interested in a placement in a Neighbourhood Family Resource Centre used mainly by the local black community. So far, they had experienced field social work, which was their intended career, and they wanted the chance to have a placement together to run groups for young people. The tutor thought that the style of the Centre would be a contrast with previous experience and arranged a meeting for Yusef, James and the two black practice teachers from the Centre.

The practice teachers, Carmen and Nalini, began by saying that the people who came to the Centre were called users, not clients. They had chosen five specific dilemmas from 'Boundaries' which they felt highlighted the work at the Centre and they invited Yusef and James to add any others. The subsequent discussion revealed that the boundaries which the practice teachers drew around their relationships with the users were more permeable than Yusef or Jim had known.

Yusef queried some of the boundaries drawn by the practice teachers, but he said that the Centre's relationship with its users would be a new experience and he was interested in the contrast. He had reservations about the effects on his family life, especially the policy of letting users have his home phone number.

Jim answered all the questions with 'It depends', complaining that the circumstances in each case needed elaborating before he could give an opinion on the basis of the information available. When the practice teachers asked him to explain what he thought it depended on, Jim said that he would have to meet each situation as it came: 'It would depend on what felt right at the time.'

After the meeting, the practice teachers and the students reflected separately on what had been said. Rejoining the meeting, Carmen and Nalini said they thought Yusef would have an interesting placement and his past experience would be a nice challenge to their own work. They understood the strain this work places on domestic lives and they would respect whatever decision he and his family came to.

They had concerns about Jim's inability to state his position on any of the dilemmas. They had no problem with 'It depends' as an answer, but they would expect James to be able to say what it depended on. More to the point, the users of the Centre would expect that, too: an answer which relied on whatever 'felt right at the time' would not be acceptable to them.

The activity gave everybody a chance to find out about the expectations at the agency and whether they would be acceptable. It was also a useful assessment for the practice teachers to find out how willing the students were to question their own judgements. For example, giving your home phone number is neither professional nor unprofessional; but failure to question the principles behind the decision *is* unprofessional.

Developing a style

Your task as practice teacher is to create a climate which enables the student to make conscious choices in terms of style (the unique way that each student defines and expresses the boundaries between themselves and clients) and personal presentation.

Perhaps an analogy will illustrate this: the Norwegians have a saying that there is no such thing as bad weather, just bad clothing. In other words, what is appropriate in one circumstance is inappropriate in another. It is the same with style and personal presentation. It is not that a particular style is right or wrong in itself, but that certain styles might suit particular occasions (though there are some styles, it is true, which suit no occasion). Students need opportunities to 'try' different clothing and to experiment to find the style that suits them and is consistent with agency expectations.

During the placement you will be evaluating the student's ability to define professional boundaries and use of style. If most interviews seem to take place in pubs or if every client is told to attend the office for appointments, you may have concerns about the student's ability to respond flexibly to the different needs of people. A preferred style may have become one which is fixed.

Students need to become aware of any unintended messages due to their presentation. For example, warmth and friendliness can be interpreted in the wrong way, perhaps as a willingness to give more than the student can or should offer. Sexual attraction does not respect client–worker boundaries. A dress code often carries different messages from one situation to another: a male student wearing an earring may be 'right on' in some places and suspect in others. This does not necessarily mean that the student should spend his time taking his earring on and off – just that he should be aware of the possible impact of his appearance. Style is one of those personal issues which affects the student's ability to work as an effective professional. Don't be surprised if the student challenges you on your style, or where *you* draw the boundary in your professional relationships.

Notes for students

'Boundaries' places you in the position of a professional person. It reflects some of the dilemmas you will face when making working relationships with people coming to your agency.

Let's turn this situation on its head, and think about times when it is you who receive a service. This helps you learn about what you think shows professional behaviour.

- As a patient with toothache,
  what would you describe as professional behaviour by the dentist?
- As a borrower with debts to pay,
  what would you describe as professional behaviour by the bank manager?
- As a householder with three inches of water in your cellar,
  what would you describe as professional behaviour by the plumber?
- As a parent of a child finding school-work a struggle,
  what would you describe as professional behaviour by the teacher?

Think of your positive and negative experiences as a user of services. You can do this on your own, but it is more fun with a small group of students. Use the examples above, or choose different ones. Use flip-chart paper to make two lists: one for the positive experiences and the other for the negative ones.

From the lists, draw up a number of guidelines for professional practice and prioritize them into four or five main principles. How do these principles relate to professional social work practice, do you think?

By the way, do you know where you might find guidelines for professional practice specifically for the social work profession? (See Some further reading, page 41)

Process and outcome

Does your view of professional behaviour depend on the outcome? In other words, does the relief of pain by the dentist indicate professional behaviour or is it possible to think of situations when the pain was relieved but the behaviour was unprofessional; or when the pain was not relieved, but the behaviour was professional?

How important is outcome when evaluating the professionalism of a social worker?

Reproduced from *The new social work practice* by Mark Doel and Steven Shardlow, Arena, Aldershot

Agency culture

Organizations develop their own patterns of behaviour and expectations which become so much a part of the furniture that people are often unaware of their influence. We can refer to this general style as agency culture. It affects the atmosphere in the organization, which in turn influences factors such as how decisions are made and how staff are expected to present a professional face in their work with people. The organizational culture is mediated, to a greater or lesser extent, by professional culture, and by local culture (the particular team or unit, and so on). Finally, it is shaped by your own individual style. In some work settings there is little opportunity for individual expression: for example, cabin crew on airlines all wear identical clothing and they are trained to provide a uniform response to passengers. The similarity of clothing between crew members symbolizes the uniformity of service. Should social workers, perhaps all working for the same agency, wear a uniform, and if not, why not?

Working in some agencies may feel woolly, like 'knitting fog', because of the lack of clear pathways for decisions, whilst other agencies may have very centralized, policy-driven cultures with very clear expectations about professional behaviour. Where there is no clear agency expectation, practitioners have little option but to rely on personal values and beliefs about how to present themselves to people. This is made more difficult because agency practice is fluid and constantly changing – interacting with our professional and personal values (Shardlow, 1989).

Your practice teacher will have opinions about 'appropriate' styles and boundaries, and these may be in harmony with the agency's views or they may be critical of them. We have been focusing on your self-expression as a student, but would you draw the limits differently for your practice teacher?

It is vital to consider how you might collect feedback from your clients about your personal style and definition of professional boundaries. A study by Baird (1991) showed that several clients commended things like punctuality, a sense of humour and style of dress, and that 'clients generally seemed pleased to be able to discuss their opinions of the help given by the student'. Chapter 8 provides more detail about how you can receive feedback from clients.

When you are half-way through your placement, make a note of how you feel these different layers (organization/team/unit) have influenced your personal style. Do you think the influence of agency culture where you are placed is strong or weak?

Reproduced from *The new social work practice* by Mark Doel and Steven Shardlow, Arena, Aldershot

Some further reading

You can find out more by looking at the various codes of practice for social workers, for example:

- British Association of Social Workers (BASW) UK (1996)
- National Association of Social Workers (NASW) US (1996)
- International Federation of Social Workers (1994)

For a comparison of codes of practice see Banks (1995, chapter 4), and for a discussion of their value see Watson (1985); Coady and Bloch (1996). Jayaratne, Croxton and Mattison (1997, p. 188) comment on the limitations of the standards in NASW's *Code of Ethics* which 'contains no historical or case references, interpretative guides, or formal or informal opinions'.

4 Feelings and actions

About Activity 4: Taboo

In this chapter, the activity 'Taboo' takes a specific situation which aroused feelings which are uncomfortable and difficult to admit to. The student and practice teacher reflect first on the example, and then consider the ways they handle their own feelings which make them feel uncomfortable.

Purpose

Most people are aware of a gap or dissonance that sometimes exists between what they are feeling 'inside' and what they are saying 'outside'. 'Taboo' explores this gap and the student's response to it. It examines how the student handles taboo subjects.

The activity also concerns the student's view of learning. How do beliefs, feelings and actions influence openness to learning?

Method

- The practice teacher and the student work individually, spending about 10 minutes reading 'Taboo' and thinking about each discussion point in turn (direct the student to the additional notes on page 49).
- Discuss each point together and make brief notes.
- Consider actual situations which have aroused difficult feelings.
- Ask the student for feedback about the usefulness of the activity and discuss any residual feelings that it has aroused.

Variations

'Taboo' can easily be adapted, for example, by reversing the races (black patient/white doctor) or introducing gender or age factors as the significant differences. The activity has the greatest impact when the account is given so that the student can identify closely with the patient. The example in 'Taboo' is from the point of view of a white woman.

The case scenario can easily be replaced with an alternative of your choice: perhaps there is an example from a student's direct experience that can be used. Think carefully about the implications of using an alternative scenario. The 'Taboo' example has been designed to give students something of a sense of being a client, by way of the patient's experience. By locating the example in the health care sector and using the example of a doctor the sense of vulnerability is heightened.

This activity deals with difficult material, so we recommend that it is used with particular care and by a practice teacher/student pair. However, two or more pairs can get together later to compare their discussions.

Activity 4 TABOO

> A white woman is admitted to hospital after a climbing accident on holiday. She is conscious, but unable to move without racking pain, and feels extremely vulnerable and dependent. These feelings of pain and vulnerability are new and somewhat shocking to her, because she is usually healthy, strong and independent.
>
> When the doctor comes in for the examination, the woman looks up and see that the doctor is black. For a split second, her reaction is negative – feelings of vulnerability and dependency increase.
>
> The next split second, she feels ashamed, guilty and horrified by these feelings and is determined to try to overcome them, and not to show any trace of them to the black doctor.

Discussion points

- Was the patient's reaction racist?
- Was the patient's reaction 'normal'?
- How could you explain the patient's initial feelings?
- The patient has previously expressed anti-racist views. In the light of this, how do you view the patient's first reaction to the doctor?
- How do you view the patient's attempts to hide the initial feelings by covering them up?
- If you were the doctor, what would be important to you?
- If you were the doctor, what would you DO in this situation?

Reproduced from *The new social work practice* by Mark Doel and Steven Shardlow, Arena, Aldershot

Notes for practice teachers

The 'Taboo' activity uses race as an example, but it is not just about race. It is designed to help the student to question whether it is insincere for people to act differently from the way they feel and how they handle these feelings when they are considered to be 'taboo' – unacceptable.

As a response based on the colour of a person's skin, the patient's feelings were racist. Is this, then, a racist response or a racist person? Ask the student to explain the patient's feelings, both from the patient's point of view and the doctor's (see Fanon, 1970, for a classic exploration of 'being black'). They occurred under great duress, when pain overcomes the usual inhibitions: the patient perhaps fears language difficulties or cultural misunderstandings that would delay the relief of pain, which is felt so urgently. Or is the white patient thinking that the black doctor is not going to be as competent as a white doctor? Might a black patient have the same fears about a white doctor? A woman patient about a male doctor, and vice versa?

Does the student think that these are reasons or rationalizations? Feelings may be unfair and unjustified, but they have causes, and an understanding of these causes is needed.

Ask the student what they think about the contrast between the patient's public beliefs and her private feelings. Is this a lack of integrity or a sign of sensitivity to others?

Having thought about it from the patient's viewpoint, ask the student to think about the doctor's position. What would the student want to happen if they were the doctor?

'Taboo' is an example of the way values come to mediate between feelings and actions. Let us assume that the patient's values were 'truly' held but they failed to overcome a 'gut reaction'. The patient's behaviour was changed to hide the gut reaction, which was rejected as unacceptable, so as not to make the reaction public through non-verbal communication (Pease 1984). What lessons does the student think this carries for professional development?

'Taboo' raises fundamental issues about the relationship between values and actions, and attitudes and behaviours in the workplace. Other examples of such dilemmas are explored in Rhodes (1986) and Reamer (1993), but very little is known about how students learn about ethics on placement (Findlay, 1995). Intuitively, we know that students are learning how to put these pieces (values and actions) together, and how to question the habitual patterns they have developed in fitting them together. Accepting and learning from feelings which we do not like – because they are considered taboo – is an essential aspect of professional development. It is only possible to manage these feelings when we can accept them, for good or bad.

Example

Peter had just completed his first week on a placement in a voluntary agency, working with substance abusers. During the first session with his long-arm practice teacher, Peter spoke positively about the contacts he had made during the week: he had found the 'Orientation' activity really helpful and interesting, and he and the practice teacher had a lively discussion about 'Believe it or not' (Activity 2), relating it to different theories to explain why people might abuse substances. Just as the session was ending, Peter mentioned that he had also looked at the 'Taboo' activity and, although it wasn't scheduled for discussion now, it related to incidents during the week which he wanted to raise.

Peter told the practice teacher that Mike, one of the volunteers at the project, was being 'unaccountably hostile' towards him and he recounted a number of incidents to support this feeling. When asked why he thought the volunteer was behaving this way, Peter hesitated, and then said 'I think he's homophobic.' Peter explained that he was gay and, though he didn't shout it from the roof-tops, he was open about it. He thinks one of the other volunteers at the project had told Mike and that this made him act quite differently now.

The practice teacher expressed her concern, but suggested that they look at 'Taboo' first, and then relate it to Peter's own experience. Peter agreed with this approach. Discussing 'Taboo', he referred to the notes he had made 'as a gut response' where he felt that the patient's response was very wrong. When he considered it in more detail, he felt that if 'Taboo' were expressed as a gender issue, he could see how a woman might react adversely to a male doctor, particularly if she had a genito-urinary disorder. What interested Peter was the question of when it was right to express these feelings and when it was right to cover them up. In the case of the black doctor, he thought that the patient was right to put her values between the initial feelings and 'what showed on the patient's face'. However, he thought that a woman would have every right to show her feelings and request a female doctor. Peter and the practice teacher discussed the differences in these points of view.

The practice teacher returned the discussion to Peter's own situation. It seemed that homophobia was the most likely explanation for Mike's hostility, though Peter felt that it was difficult to challenge him because he felt it was a taboo subject with Mike, who had such an indirect way of expressing his hostility.

What did Peter think should happen now? In an ideal world Mike would not feel the way he did, but Peter would be satisfied if Mike could just keep his feelings to himself. 'If Mike could become more aware of his own feelings and be honest with himself, it would help ... I don't expect to cure his homophobia, but I do want him to behave differently towards me. One of the workers at the Centre said that we're paid to manage our feelings; well, I can swallow my feelings when it's necessary, and I think it's right to expect Mike to swallow his.'

After discussing different options, Peter decided that if Mike couldn't keep his feelings to himself, he would prefer him to express them directly and openly, and he would like to give him an opportunity to do this. Peter and the practice teacher rehearsed one of the incidents which Peter had already described, with Peter practising different ways of revealing what seemed likely to be a taboo area for Mike. He felt sufficiently prepared by this session with the practice teacher to look out for a chance to face the issue directly with Mike.

The student's own experiences of discrimination (on this occasion in relation to homophobia) were important in making links with the experiences of substance users at the project. This was an able student who, on his own initiative, had made connections between one of the activities in the curriculum, 'Taboo', and his own experiences, thinking carefully about the complex links between feelings, values and behaviours.

We all need safe situations to discuss those areas where we feel or have experienced discrimination (see Goffman, 1968). In creating a climate for learning, the practice teacher is also creating this safe environment.

Notes for students

Your practice teacher has asked you to read 'Taboo' in preparation for discussion later. Read the three paragraphs which make up the 'Taboo' example (page 45) and jot down your gut responses. Do this now before reading any more from these notes.

When you have finished discussing 'Taboo' with your practice teacher, go back to the brief notes you made at the very beginning. That was your gut reaction to the incident in the hospital. Have you had any second thoughts about what you wrote, in the light of the discussion?

At some point later during your placement re-read 'Taboo' carefully and consider each of the discussion points in turn, making brief notes.

'Taboo' is about how we handle unacceptable feelings, with race used to illustrate this. How do we manage the differences between what we feel, what we think and what we do?

Can you think of occasions like this in your personal life? For example, what do you say when you get a birthday present that you don't really like? How do you share feelings of anger or sorrow with family and friends? (For a discussion of similar responses to common situations see Berne, 1966.)

Think back to your previous work experiences. Make a note of an occasion when your first feelings were disguised quickly so that you didn't let them show (for example, working in a home for older people and feeling disgust at the smell from a colostomy bag).

Make a note of the experience of meeting or getting to know a person of a race or culture different from your own. The example you select may have occurred during your adolescence: if so, you may like to compare your experiences with Hewitt's (1986) ethnographic study of relationships between black and white adolescents in South London.

Confronting a taboo area often means revealing something about yourself, and the art and skill of self-disclosure is not easy. Named after its creators, Joseph Luft and Harry Ingram, the Johari window (Figure 4.1) is a well-known way of looking at the differences between what you make public and what you keep private, and also about the things you know and do not know about yourself (from Douglas, 1976, p. 118).

Extending the public area (window pane 1) and reducing the other panes can open up new areas of insight and prevent the need to divert energy into maintaining secrets about ourselves. Soon after the start of your placement use the Johari window to think about what you make public and what you keep to yourself. Towards the end of the placement, return to your 'window' to look at any changes which have occurred. Have you gained any new insights into yourself (pane 3)? Is there anything which was known only to you, but which others now know (pane 2)?

Reproduced from *The new social work practice* by Mark Doel and Steven Shardlow, Arena, Aldershot

4 UNKNOWN AREA What I DON'T know about myself and What others DON'T know about me	3 BLIND AREA What I DON'T know about myself and What others DO know about me
2 HIDDEN AREA What I DO know about myself and What others DON'T know about me	1 PUBLIC AREA What I DO know about myself and What others DO know about me

Figure 4.1 The Johari window

Reproduced from *The new social work practice* by Mark Doel and Steven Shardlow, Arena, Aldershot

II

Direct practice

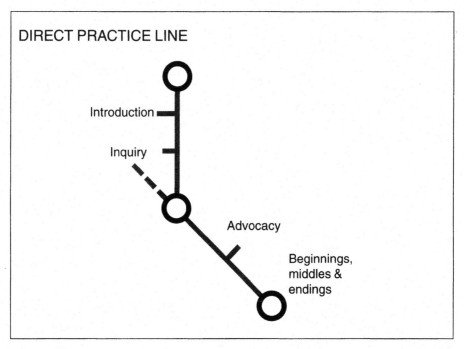

Chapters 5–8 help students (or agency staff) to learn skills in direct contact with the people who use the agency's services. The activities concentrate on planning and communication skills necessary to make these encounters

successful. These skills are important both for single encounters and also for working with people over a longer period of time, and for learning about the importance of evaluating the work together with clients.

Chapter 5, Introduction, considers the impact of the first contact with a person and the 'career path' towards becoming a user of the agency's services. The tone of the early contact, and the method and means of introduction are each considered.

Inquiry (Chapter 6) and Advocacy (Chapter 7) each focus on interpersonal skills. Students are taught to recognize their current patterns of communication and to extend this repertoire by choosing different approaches. Advocacy skills are closely associated with assertiveness and are necessary if students are to express their views and judgements persuasively. The two chapters should be seen together, since one of the aims of skilled practice is to balance inquiry with advocacy.

Chapter 8 (Beginnings, middles and endings) takes the student through a practice method. The term *practice method* sometimes alarms practitioners, who often profess themselves eclectic: of course, the true eclectic is the practitioner who has got to grips with a number of *different* practice methods. The method used to illustrate the process of working over time is based on task-centred practice, though the notion of beginnings, middles and endings is presented in order to transcend any particular practice method.

Students who successfully complete 'Direct practice' will be able to consider what sanctions their work with potential clients, to identify different kinds of communication skill and to practise using them. They will learn how to prepare, structure and end contacts with people, and how to work systematically over time.

5 Introduction

About Activity 5: Playing field

'Playing field' focuses on the student's understanding of what is 'in touch' and what is 'out of touch', in terms of the initial contacts with a potential client of the agency. It helps the student consider the areas of uncertainty (the 'grey' areas), and also how the person's concerns, problems and requests must be set in a broader framework.

Purpose

Students need to develop a good sense of the scope of work of the agency where they are placed. 'Playing field' uses a games metaphor to help the student consider when work is 'in' or 'out' of play. It is not especially difficult when the ball is in the centre of the agency's concerns or well outside this area; it is more problematic when it is on the margins, and in those circumstances when there is a clash of professional conduct and agency procedure.

Method

- The student should consider their work with a particular person, family or group. It helps if this can be a relatively complex situation, where each of the four sectors of the playing field are relevant.
- How does, or did, the student work with the different concerns? In

particular, how do they identify what is in the agency's remit, and what happened to those concerns which were outside the remit?
- Discuss with the student whether there were any disagreements or conflicts about which part of the field a particular concern lay in. (About 1 hour total.)

Variations

In the first instance, students should do this activity retrospectively, taking a situation with which they are now more familiar. They should then return to 'Playing field' at the initial stage in their work with a new service user.

It helps to develop your own case example for the student to work with. In this way, you can ensure that there are concerns, problems or requests in each of the four sectors. You can introduce situations which are controversial, with plenty of activity in the grey areas.

Contact with practice teachers and students in other settings gives students an opportunity to consider how different agencies define their own playing fields, and how strongly or faintly they paint the lines of demarcation.

Activity 5 PLAYING FIELD

Based on your work with one particular person, write one example of a concern, problem or request in each quadrant.

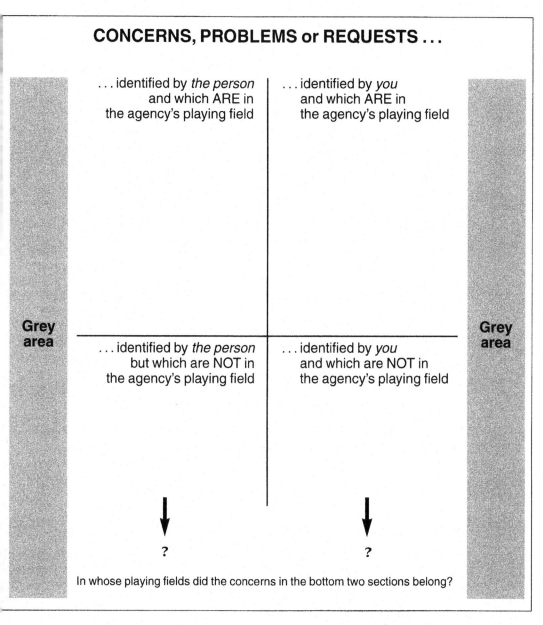

Reproduced from *The new social work practice* by Mark Doel and Steven Shardlow, Arena, Aldershot

Notes for practice teachers

> Prior to making contact with a social service agency, the majority of people have usually considered other options such as seeking advice from friends and relatives.
> (Coulshed, 1991, p. 15)

Expectations

If we extend the metaphor of the playing field, we can see how the first encounter with a client or a potential service user is like wandering on to a football pitch with few rules or 'painted lines' for guidance. The first encounter between social worker and potential client should include a negotiation about where those lines are to be drawn.

There is a whole host of expectations which each player brings on to the field. Students need to become acquainted both with the general kinds of expectation which people have of the agency, and also the particular ones which each new contact brings. Do most people become clients of the agency willingly or because there is an element of compulsion? Students must begin to discover what the agency's field of operation is, so that they have an understanding of whether the client's concerns are in line with what the agency has to offer.

The negotiations do not take place in a vacuum. Some agencies have painted very determined lines which leave little room for manoeuvre: potential service users may think they are entering an uncharted arena, only to be met with a non-negotiable response from agency staff. Students might discover themselves more restricted than they had anticipated; alternatively, they may be surprised by the size of the grey area in which they can exercise discretion.

The student must learn about the way boundary disputes between this and other agencies are resolved. Do people find themselves bouncing between agencies? And, finally, the agency has to live with societal expectations, which may be near or far from the reality of the work.

In short, the student is learning to question whether there is 'a mandate' for work and, if so, where the boundaries of this mandate lie (Doel and Marsh, 1992, pp. 10–22).

Existing networks

If you have a problem, it is unlikely that your first thought is to share it with a social worker. Unless they already have a history of contact, most people have been referred on to the social work agency, formally or informally, by friends, relatives, neighbours or other professionals. It is rare, therefore, that the student will be the first person with whom the person has discussed their concerns.

Part of the process of introduction involves tracing the path which has led the person to knock at the agency's door. This may have entailed many 'rehearsals' (for example, how many others have they been obliged to tell their story to?). These rehearsals may have reframed the person's view of their situation. All this information is germane to the student's knowledge of how this person or these people have come into contact with the agency.

The networks for some clients are provided by the agency itself. Long-standing clients, those who are very vulnerable and dependent, residents in the care of the agency – all these groups of people are likely to know much more about the agency than the student. Even so, it is important that expectations and 'rules' are checked out, just as they would be if the person were completely new to the agency. The fact that the student brings a new outlook can sometimes help long-standing clients to reappraise the service they are receiving from the agency.

Students need to consider the path which has brought the client into contact with the agency. This may extend backwards for some time (especially for long-standing residents and families with a string of social workers under their belt). Whatever the timescale, an understanding of the person's entry into the agency's orbit will develop the student's ability to focus the subsequent work. This ensures that the client's 'career' with the agency is not aimless and neglected. (See Chapter 8 for more details.)

Just following procedures?

According to the rhetoric of social work practice, agencies are moving from resources-led assessments to needs-led assessments. In the former the user is matched up against a list of agency 'goodies' and, if none of these suit, no service is available. The practitioner starts with the list in mind, and does not consider concerns or requests from the service user which fall outside it.

In contrast, needs-led assessments are those where the practitioner starts with the concerns as expressed by the client, and together they explore what might be available to meet these needs. This approach is considered to be more responsive and participative, and requires greater creativity and networking on the part of the practitioner.

Smale (1993) describes three models to explain different approaches to making assessments in community care:

The procedural model

The agency prescribes what information the practitioner needs to gather to see if certain criteria are met. This determines whether the person is eligible to receive services. The criteria are usually designed by others at a senior level who have control of the allocation of resources. It is a quick approach, because staff can be trained to follow the relevant procedures and use the documentation, and they are not expected to make judgements. The workers act as gate-keepers to limited resources, which the criteria are designed to distribute fairly.

The questioning model

The professional is seen as the 'expert', gathering information from the client and other significant people (carers, etc.) in order to arrive at a reasoned judgement of the situation. The expert advises on possible solutions and uses experience, skill and judgement to diagnose what is needed and to help the clients decide on a course of action (such as a package of care). The questions reflect what the professional needs to know to arrive at their assessment of the situation.

The exchange model

The client is their own best 'expert', and the practitioner's role is to help clients to articulate their concerns and opportunities. Two or more people come together to exchange their perspectives on the situation and to achieve a mutual understanding. The worker negotiates agreement between all those concerned, about what the problems are, how they might be addressed, and who will do what. This is a time-consuming process with no 'typical' solution, so it requires the professional to be very open minded to alternative solutions.

The procedural model has its primary focus on the agency and how it will distribute its services and resources; the questioning model centres on the practitioner's skill and expertise and how this can be used to best advantage; and the exchange model focuses on the negotiation between the various parties who have an interest in the clients' welfare, starting with the clients themselves.

It is important to be open with yourself and with the student about which model best describes your own practice and the agency's in general. You might aspire to the exchange model, but it is very intensive and is not always the most appropriate (for example, when the agency's resources are stretched to breaking point). Reviewing these models with the student gives you the opportunity to raise questions at the heart of social work practice:

- What is the purpose of agency procedures?
- How large is the gap between the formal and the informal organization (that is, between the procedures which are written down and to which the agency subscribes, and what actually happens, in terms of following, bending or ignoring these procedures)?
- Where is the line between bureaucrat and professional?
- How can the idea of professional discretion be reconciled with notions of fairness and non-discriminatory practices?

Appeals and complaints: a level playing field?

Students can feel relatively powerless when they start their placement in an agency, despite your efforts to ease their own entry (see Part I). They are likely to be new to the work, to have no working knowledge of the agency's services, and very conscious that their performance is being assessed. This can make it difficult for students to understand how powerfully they can be perceived by their clientele. The potential service user may not see the process of negotiation about services and concerns and problems as being played on a level playing field.

Return to Activity 5, and consider with the student who makes the final decision about what happens to the concerns which fall in the grey area. What recourse to appeal does a person have if their concerns are not considered to be 'in play'? How do people learn of their right (or not) to appeal? What is the agency's track record in terms of appeals and the exercise of complaints procedures?

Addressing these issues at such an early stage may seem premature, and you certainly want to avoid frightening the student unnecessarily. Nonetheless, students should know what 'tilt' there is on the playing field, and be able to advise people accurately about their rights in relation to the agency's responsibilities. There is a parallel with the preparations for the student's own placement: is everybody clear about the procedures if there is disagreement or things go wrong? – for example, if you have concerns about the student's competence, or your student is dissatisfied with your availability to give supervision.

Notes for students

The first contact with a potential client sets the tone for the rest of the work. The initial contact may be a personal encounter or it may be a written introduction, such as a letter. Whatever the means, it is important to make careful preparations for the contact.

At some time during your training and education for social work, it is important to have experience of writing letters of appointment and introduction, especially if these have not been a central part of your present placement.

Introduction by letter

In *Social Work Practice* (Doel and Shardlow, 1993, pp. 51–2), we took four examples of a letter written to the same clients but in very different styles. Letters convey a particular style reflected in your choice of words. A familiarity–formality continuum is one way of looking at style. This links with the discussion in Activity 3 concerning the differences between friendships and 'workships'. It takes practice to establish a style which conveys a sense of purpose in a friendly manner. You need to strike a balance between over-familiarity on the one hand and starchy professionalism on the other. It is helpful to discuss with your practice teacher how the purpose of your contact should influence the tilt of that balance.

Another quality which is important to consider is optimism. A positive view about the possibility and desirability of change is an important factor in the success of any work. There is a balance here, too. A Pollyanna optimism in the face of unremitting grief is not appropriate, and an over-ambitious agenda for change in the client's life can lead to disappointment and loss of confidence. However, cynicism about the prospects for change and a belief that changes are imposed from outside are unhelpful, even when they reflect the client's own feelings. At some point in the initial or early contacts, a sense of realistic optimism should be conveyed. Do you feel this can, or should, be conveyed in an introductory letter?

A clear, open message about the reason for your contact will tend to reduce rather than increase any anxieties the client might have. However, there are some issues which it is difficult to be open about. Shulman (1983) refers to them as taboo topics: for example a letter of appointment is not usually an appropriate place in which to introduce the question of physical abuse when the status of that information is not clear. The first contact should start with the topics which the client is likely to want to focus on these may or may not be the most pressing ones, but they are likely to be the ones which are most acceptable in terms of remoteness from any taboos.

The ability to convey professional purpose in a friendly manner and to

Reproduced from *The new social work practice* by Mark Doel and Steven Shardlow, Arena, Aldershot

write clearly in a way which invites participation is one worth practising, even if most of your first contacts on your placement have not been made by letter.

Introduction by telephone

Let us assume that you have the telephone number of a person who has been referred to the agency where you are on placement. In what circumstances would you consider making a first contact by telephone rather than by correspondence? What do you feel would be the advantages and disadvantages of making a phone call to introduce yourself?

Introduction in person

There are many placement settings in which introductions are informal and unplanned. You are unlikely to write a letter to a resident for whom you are key worker! However, you should think carefully about the means of the first contact, and use whatever seems the most appropriate in terms of allowing you both to be adequately prepared. If your first contact is in a group (for example, in the residents' lounge), how might you plan a person-to-person session?

Introducing your practice teacher

One of the best ways you can develop your practice is by getting direct feedback. There are three main sources of feedback:

1. *You* You are giving feedback to yourself all the time and it is important for you to learn how to recognize this and respond to it. How do you feel you are doing, and what do you do with these feelings?
2. *The person or persons you are working with* Much of the time this feedback is not explicit: it comes from reading the verbal and non-verbal behaviour of the client and from making assumptions on the basis of these readings. However, it is important to learn how to seek explicit feedback, so that you can question these assumptions. See Activity 8 in respect of encouraging direct feedback from clients.
3. *An observer* The third source of feedback is from an observer, preferably one who knows what to look for and how to give feedback helpfully. Practice teachers are in a good position to be observers, giving you feedback from their observations of your work with users of the service (and in Britain they are required by CCETSW to observe your work as a

Reproduced from *The new social work practice* by Mark Doel and Steven Shardlow, Arena, Aldershot

student). In some settings, such as group care and day care, practice teachers are likely to be able to see you in direct work with the clients as a part of their own daily work. These settings are open, with the work taking place in full view of other people. In other settings, such as field social work and probation, opportunities for direct observation with clients of the service must be created. (Of course, the 'observer' can also be an audio or video recorder.)

A first step in creating these opportunities for feedback is the introduction of your practice teacher to your direct practice with clients:

- *By letter* Take a letter you have already written by way of introduction, and include a passage to introduce your practice teacher, requesting that they accompany you on the visit. How do you explain their job and the purpose of their presence? What are the pitfalls you wish to avoid in the letter?
- *By telephone* Rehearse a phone contact to a person you are working with (this can be a client or a professional from another agency). How might you frame your request for the practice teacher to accompany you when you next meet? What factors would make the request relatively easy or difficult?
- *In person* In most circumstances you would prepare clients for your practice teacher's visit in order to give them the opportunity to decline. However, as we have noted, direct observation by your practice teacher might be a daily occurrence, and not something you have to arrange specially. What are the advantages and disadvantages of this kind of spontaneity? Are the residents and centre users aware that your practice teacher is 'observing' you?

Name your learning

Keep a record of one of your first contacts from early in the placement. This might be a letter of introduction or it may be a brief description of a personal encounter in the unit or establishment. It will act as a base-line for your practice.

Towards the end of the placement, review this record. If it is a letter, how might you rewrite it now you have the experience of writing several letters of appointment? If it is a personal encounter, how would your preparation for the encounter differ, now that you are more experienced with these contacts? This review, taken together with the base-line from the beginning of your placement, will demonstrate the way your practice has developed.

Have you identified any factors which have had a consistent influence on the way you go about your introductions? For instance, does the age of the client affect the way in which you introduce yourself and the kind of language which you use?

Reproduced from *The new social work practice* by Mark Doel and Steven Shardlow, Arena, Aldershot

6 Inquiry

About Activity 6: Open ends

'Open ends' presents a brief transcript of a client speaking. The student is invited to consider a number of options for a response to the client and to discuss the implications of choosing different lines of inquiry.

Purpose

The act of *finding out* is a great pleasure. It springs from a basic human impulse – curiosity. In Chapter 3 we described the paradox of expectations that a social worker should be warmly human and coolly professional at the same time. In this chapter, we introduce another tension: the need to be both curious and disinterested at the same time.

This chapter helps students to develop the professional skills of inquiry out of the social skills associated with curiosity. Integrity and authenticity are evident when students are able to channel their natural curiosity into skilled inquiry.

Method

- Separately, you and the student read 'Open ends' and make a note of the two questions which most closely fit the line of inquiry you would each wish to take, and the two questions which you feel would be most inappropriate. Each make your own brief notes to explain your choice. (About 10 minutes.)

- Compare these notes at the practice tutorial, opening up a discussion about different strands of inquiry and the likely consequences of taking different routes. (About 30 minutes.)
- Subsequently, the student should use the 'Open ends' approach with an audiotape of an interview with a client. The student should choose one of the client's statements and make a note of three or four possible questions which could have been asked at that point. Then the student describes why they took that particular line of inquiry, with any suggestions for changes, having had time to reflect.

Variations

You might want to match the 'Open ends' example to your own setting, using case material that is specific to the student's placement. On the other hand, we have found that the issues and the learning points transcend any particular example of 'Open ends'. Students do not have to be familiar with alcohol dependency, depression or any of the other specific aspects of John's situation in Activity 6 in order to use the learning points, though they may need extra encouragement if they are not very confident or imaginative. Indeed, if the territory is too familiar, case material can sometimes be a block to new learning, because of a natural tendency to rely on established patterns of thinking when the circumstances feel cosy.

Activity 6   OPEN ENDS

A man calling himself John comes into the neighbourhood drop-in centre. He looks in his late twenties, but he doesn't want to give any details about himself: 'I just want to talk to a social worker.' After a bit of preamble this is what John says:

> *I had my first drink when I was about fourteen. My dad died, I think in an accident, and my mother wasn't taking it too well ... (pause) ... I was sickly as a boy ... no brothers or sisters, and it was all too much. Dad was depressed before he died and I don't think they were happy with each other – Dad and my mother. And then I got into trouble with the law, but I didn't get sent away, thank God. Me, I think it's ... what do they call it? ... social drinking. I went to that group, but it was more so's I could meet some new people – I was lonely – not to stop drinking. I mean, I can hold my job down – it doesn't interfere, not really ... (pause) ... Moira, she thinks different, like, and now we're going steady and she's told me ... (pause) ... she told me straight that it's her or the bottle. She got really frit when I missed a red light – I mean, anybody can do that can't they? I bet you've done that sometime or other. But she says I've got to choose – her or the bottle. No drinking, social nor nowt. I don't know what to do ...*

What leads could the social worker follow? The number of possible lines of inquiry are infinite, but you are going to limit yourself to ones which begin with *How, What, When, Where, Who* and *Why* (see Priestley, et al., 1978). These are interrogatives which introduce open-ended questions and which can't be adequately answered with a *Yes* or *No*.

Out of the twenty questions below, choose two which most closely fit the line of inquiry you would wish to follow with John after he has spoken, and choose two which you would most wish to avoid. Explain your choices.

1   How old are you, John?
2   How do you connect your first drink at fourteen with your drinking now?
3   How did your father die?
4   How were you sickly as a child?
5   What do you think your father was depressed about?
6   How do you feel about your parents' unhappy marriage?
7   How did you get into trouble with the law?
8   Why did you get into trouble with the law?
9   When did you go to that group you mentioned?
10 What did you do at the group sessions?
11 Where did you do most of your drinking?
12 How often and how much do you drink?
13 When do you drink?
14 Who do you drink with?
15 What do you think is the difference between social drinking and a drink problem?
16 Why do you think Moira has given you this ultimatum?
17 How do you feel about shooting the red light?
18 What feelings do you have for Moira?
19 What do you think the future holds if you carry on drinking?
20 What is your job, John?

Reproduced from *The new social work practice* by Mark Doel and Steven Shardlow, Arena, Aldershot

Notes for practice teachers

Social skills

There are many ways of looking at interactional skills. John Heron (1975) uses six categories (informative, prescriptive, confrontive, cathartic, catalytic, supportive). Reid and Epstein (1972) use two categories (systematic and responsive). We are using two from Senge (1990): inquiry and advocacy.

We use the term *inquiry skills* to mean the ability to initiate and sustain a dialogue with the client – a dialogue which moves with careful purpose to a clearer picture of the client's concerns and wishes.

'Open ends' is designed to help students become aware of the pattern of responses which they use when talking to clients. The aim is to broaden the repertoire of these responses, so that students are making clear choices rather than relying on habit.

People who are helping or interviewing tend to pick up on leads which confirm their own theories of human behaviour (Ivey and Authier, 1978). Not surprisingly, clients follow the helper along this line of inquiry: they consider helpers to be experts who know what they are doing, so they are inclined to answer the questions accordingly.

The following three steps will help students to consider their present repertoire of responses and how they might expand it.

Step one: the student as navigator

The student's first step comes with an understanding that each intervention (verbal and non-verbal) moves the work in a certain direction. The student needs to be aware of this process. It is not wrong to be directive, in terms of taking responsibility for the direction of a session: abdicating this responsibility is a little like sitting in a car with the handbrake off and wondering why and where the car is moving. The student's aim is not to take over in the driving seat (after all, it is the client's car), but to help with the navigation.

Ask the student to reflect how lines of inquiry beginning with questions 3–6 in the 'Open ends' activity might come to different conclusions from inquiries beginning with questions 11–15. The first set of questions points down the road to 'current problems as a consequence of past traumas' whilst the second set of questions points down another route to 'current problems as a basis for here-and-now problem management'.

Step two: a repertoire of responses

Students need an understanding of any established patterns of inquiry which they bring to their work. Continuing with the metaphor of riding in a car, it may be that one student has a preference for navigating down main roads, whilst another has a preference for back routes. If this 'works' and helps clients to get where they want to go, that's fine. If, however, a student seems always to take right-hand forks, or drives straight forward even when the road bends, the journey is likely to be unsatisfactory!

Self-aware practice means the student can develop a broader repertoire of inquiry skills, and understand how the shape of questions now influences the outcome of work later. Students should be able to inspect their own practice in order to get this particular perspective. Audio- or videotapes are extremely useful ways for students to hear and see themselves.

Step three: choosing a response which meets the occasion

The third step is to gain a greater feel for when different kinds of response are appropriate. 'Appropriate' always seems unsatisfactory because it is so ill-defined, but there is no neat answer. The student's ability to reflect on successful and unsuccessful responses will help them get nearer and nearer to the elusive definition of 'appropriate'.

When John finishes his story in the 'Open ends' activity, inquiry is only one of a number of different responses which the student could make. Below are some examples of other kinds, adapted from Heron's categories (1975):

- A supportive response: *'I want to do all I can to help you because I can see how difficult it is to make this kind of decision alone.'*
- A reflective response: *'It seems to me that you're not sure what you want to do at present, but perhaps just talk about these things without feeling you have to make any decisions yet. Is that right?'*
- An empathic response: *'I can see how very difficult this situation is for you and what a large load you're carrying; I'd find it really hard to know what to do in your situation.'*
- A prescriptive response: *'In one sense it doesn't matter whether you call it social drinking or not; it's a problem because of the choice Moira has given you. Perhaps you ought to join an alcohol management group, to show Moira you were doing something, responding to her worries.'*
- An informative response: *'A lot of people at some time in their life cross the boundary back and forth between social drinking and problem drinking. We can work out how many units you are drinking on average every week and see how this compares with what is considered a reasonable maximum.'*
- A confrontive response: *'John, you say that you don't have a drink problem and yet I don't think you'd be sitting here telling me this if you weren't worried yourself.'*

The answer to the question, 'Which kind of response would you choose?' is, of course, 'it depends'. The characteristic of good practice is the ability to say what it depends on. Discuss with the student the factors which would lead you each to choose a particular kind of response.

Notes for students

Blocks to using inquiry skills

It is difficult to continue in a spirit of inquiry when you disagree strongly with the views of the person. Are there are times when it is right not to continue the inquiry? For example, when would you inquire further into a client's racism?

Jack is a 79-year-old white member of the Day Centre at Oakbrook Elderly Persons Home, where you are a student on placement. A year ago, Jack had an accident when he stepped in front of a young motorcyclist. The cyclist was driving carefully, but Jack had failed to look properly. The motorcyclist was a black youth and this feeds Jack's strong racist feelings. Jack is in poor health and, over a cup of tea, he says:

> It was all very different before the coloureds started coming into the area. It was a nice area. People looked after it. Now, they've taken all the jobs so our kind gets thrown on the heap. I wouldn't be here now if a coloured hadn't run me over; I could look after myself in my own home, I'd be able to get about more. But what's the point of going to the shops now? They're all owned by them.

Your first response to Jack might be to formulate a confrontive response ('I can't accept what you're saying, Jack, and I think you're denying your own responsibility for that accident') or a prescriptive response ('You shouldn't make racist comments like that, Jack; you'd be better looking at your own responsibility for the accident').

However, for the purpose of practising inquiry skills, think what lines of *inquiry* you might follow with him. Make a note of the different kinds of lead you could take. Try taking 'Jack' into a role play, in order to get practice in sticking with inquiry skills even when you have strong feelings of disagreement.

Don't jump to solutions

Another block to inquiry can occur if you formulate a solution for somebody's problems. Why bother continuing to find out more when you already know what will solve the problem? However, it is important not to jump to solutions before you have a full picture; it is always preferable if your inquiry can bring clients to a point of solution for themselves. In that way you guarantee it is the client's solution, not yours. You avoid the danger of suggesting clients do something which they might already have tried unsuccessfully, which can feel demoralizing.

For a comprehensive account of interpersonal skills, see Lishman's (1994) *Communication in Social Work*.

Reproduced from *The new social work practice* by Mark Doel and Steven Shardlow, Arena, Aldershot

7 Advocacy

About Activity 7: In my view

'In my view' presents seven possible 'hidden agendas' at a hospital ward round. The student wants to advocate for the client's return home, but each hidden agenda might explain the ward round's reluctance to accept the student's view. The activity helps students to practise whether and how they might open up hidden agendas.

Purpose

This chapter helps students to learn how to express their views clearly and how to work with other people's agendas, when these are in conflict with their own.

The term *advocacy skills* is often used to refer to the practitioner's work on behalf of the client. In this activity we use the word advocacy to mean the skills of expressing your own view, even when it comes into conflict with other people's. The expressed views may, indeed, be on behalf of a client. This activity helps students to learn how to advocate both for their clients and for their own purposes.

Method

- Both you and the student read 'In my view' in preparation for the practice tutorial. You each agree to prepare a short, verbal summary of the

hidden agenda items, taking three or four each (ward round politics, and so on). (About 20 minutes.)
- In the practice tutorial, you and the student present the prepared verbal summary of each hidden agenda item, as though you are speaking to the ward round. You discuss the merits and problems of each item after it has been presented, and consider in what circumstances you would actually open that particular agenda item. (About 1 hour.)
- Finally, the student makes a priority list of the hidden agenda items, based on those items the student considers are most likely to help them advocate for their view that the client should return home. Which items, if any, does the student feel should remain hidden? (About 20 minutes.)

Variations

You might want to adapt 'In my view' to your own setting. However, as with 'Inquiry' (Activity 6), the case material is used as a hanger for the learning points, so it is not important for the student to be familiar with the case material itself.

Situations may have occurred in the student's own practice which relate to 'In my view'. The activities in this book serve as simulations of direct practice, so they can be followed at a pace which promotes the student's learning. Although the pace may be slower than live practice (because you can stop and start and re-run simulated situations), paradoxically this can *accelerate* the student's learning. It is important, however, that the learning which takes place in simulated conditions is tested in live conditions. You need to look for examples in students' direct practice which illustrate the learning they have experienced in simulated practice (Doel and Shardlow, 1996b).

Activity 7 IN MY VIEW

Mr Sahid is 72 and he is a patient at St Francis' General Hospital. He was admitted to Ward 14 two weeks ago after he was found on the floor at home: he had fallen and injured his thigh, and when admitted to the hospital it seemed that he had been neglecting himself. He was widowed last year and his only son lives in a distant town, with the care of a disabled daughter. Mr Sahid speaks faltering English and it is necessary to take time when conversing with him. At the previous ward round, it was clear that most people were advocating that Mr Sahid should remain in hospital and that a place in residential care should be sought. You are of the opinion that Mr Sahid could return home, with domiciliary services, and that this is what he wants.

Hidden agendas

These are some hypotheses that you have made concerning the many agendas which you suspect are influencing the decision about Mr Sahid's future.

- **Misunderstanding Mr Sahid's wishes**
  You have taken time to help Mr Sahid talk about what he would like to happen and you think he is aware of the risks. You suspect that others have not been as conscientious.

- **Ward-round politics**
  You have noticed a pattern in which Dr Jenkins, who seems to have a genuine concern for his patients, always swings behind the views of the physiotherapist, but you don't know why.

- **Double standards**
  You are fairly confident that if there were immediate pressure on beds on Ward 14, Mr Sahid would be going home right away.

- **Race and gender**
  You wonder if Dr Jenkins, a white, male doctor, might view Mr Sahid's position differently if Mr Sahid were a woman. Are men thought to be less able to care for themselves in the community? It is also possible that the fact that Mr Sahid is Asian could have some bearing, but you have no hypothesis at present.

- **Generalizing from a previous case**
  The death at home of a patient who was discharged too early has made the hospital very cautious in these circumstances. You surmise that it is this previous patient's 'needs' which are being (belatedly) met and not the present needs of Mr Sahid.

- **Care in the community undervalued**
  You have a feeling that your medical colleagues underestimate the extent of domiciliary services and that they feel more comfortable if they know patients are going to receive institutional care rather than care in the community.

- **Your own feelings**
  You are aware that when you become old you think that you would prefer to return to your own home, even if you were alone, with no family support. The risks would have to be greater than you think they are with Mr Sahid before you would go into residential care. You are trying to be careful that this does not influence your view of what Mr Sahid wants.

At the next ward round, you will be sharing the reasoning which has led you to your view of Mr Sahid's position and your recommendation that he return home with domiciliary care.

Which of the seven hypotheses above do you think you should address and how?

Reproduced from *The new social work practice* by Mark Doel and Steven Shardlow, Arena, Aldershot

Notes for practice teachers

Advocacy and assertiveness

There are many links between advocacy skills and assertiveness. Successful advocacy, like successful assertiveness, does not start with the premise, 'There is an argument to be won,' but with an ability to express a viewpoint and to inquire about other people's viewpoints, too.

The ability to state a view and how you arrived at that view is essential to good practice. The first stage in this aspect of students' learning is to be able to formulate their own view and to articulate it for themselves, explaining the reasoning which informs that view. This provides the student with a rehearsal for the next stage, which is the ability to explain these reasons to other people. If the student's view differs from other people's, they need also to be able to think about the reasons for these differences and incorporate them into their reasoning.

Sometimes it is particularly difficult or intimidating to express a view. This is especially true where other people have more power than we do. In the ward round example, lines of power and authority are not stacked in the student's favour. This does not mean that students should abandon their view to the powerful majority, but it does mean that they will have to be especially clear about their reasoning and strategic in the way they express their views. Students may, for example, seek out individual members before the ward round to run through their reasoning on a person-to-person basis; they may seek your help and support to present their ideas.

These are some tips for successful advocacy taken from Senge (1990):

- Make your own reasoning explicit: say how you arrived at your view and what it is based on.
- Encourage others to explore your view: 'Do you see gaps in my reasoning?'
- Encourage others to provide different views: 'Do you have different information or different conclusions, or both?'
- Actively inquire into others' views that differ from your own: 'What are your views?' 'How did you arrive at your view?' 'Are you taking into account information that is different from what I have considered?'
- If you are making assumptions about others' views, state your assumptions clearly and acknowledge that they are assumptions.
- State the information upon which your assumptions are based.
- When you or others are hesitant to express your views or to experiment with alternative ideas, encourage them (or yourself) to think out loud what might be making it difficult.

Balancing inquiry and advocacy skills

Encourage students to think how they can combine the inquiry skills in Chapter 6 with the advocacy skills in this chapter.

> When two advocates meet for an open, candid exchange of views, there is usually little learning ... Advocacy without inquiry begets advocacy [because] the goal of pure advocacy is to win the argument. When inquiry and advocacy are combined the goal is no longer to win the argument, but to find the *best* argument. (Senge, 1990, p. 198)

Also, pure inquiry is limited because we usually do have an opinion and we can use incessant questioning as a screen. The client is often interested in our perspective and may actively seek our advice or views.

Non-verbal communication

Only part of our communication is verbal and explicit. The way in which the words are spoken also reflects our meaning: the same phrase can sound sincere or sarcastic depending on the tone, gestures, facial expressions and body posture which accompany the spoken words. Sometimes the content of the verbal communication and the message conveyed in other ways can be quite different (Pease, 1984).

Encourage the student to observe non-verbal communication and to recognize occasions when this differs from the verbal communication. This ability is particularly helpful when the student is helping others to reveal their inner thoughts (see 'The left-hand column', page 76).

Direct observation: 'You can talk the game, but can you walk it?'

As expressions of late twentieth-century pop philosophy, American T-shirts are illuminating. 'You can talk the game, but can you walk it?' nicely sums up the chasm between chat and action.

A considerable leap is needed to move from talking about the skills of inquiry and advocacy to practising these skills. It is possible to think that we have learned something because we have got to grips with the concepts and the terminology (and this understanding is an important first step), but our behaviour may be unaltered.

How do you find out whether the student is learning to 'walk the game'? It is important that observation of the student's practice is a regular feature of your teaching (and it is a requirement by CCETSW). Direct observation becomes much more relevant if it is focused on a particular topic, rather than a casual look at how students get on with their clients. An agreement before the observation takes place about the scope and focus of your feedback makes the occasion less stressful because you and the student are clear about the purpose of the observation. In this case, the focus of your feedback will be the way in which the student has balanced inquiry skills and advocacy skills.

You will find that direct observation of the student's practice becomes a more acceptable part of the student's learning if the student has also had the opportunity to observe you directly. Your ability and willingness to talk about the balance of inquiry and advocacy in your own work will encourage students to be open about their work, too. (See Doel, Shardlow, Sawdon and Sawdon, 1996, p. 147, for a model of introducing direct observation into your practice teaching.)

Notes for students

Negotiating styles

Work with an individual client often requires negotiating skills: negotiating on behalf of the client with other members of the family, community or other agencies; negotiating between the client and other people; or negotiating between the client and your own agency.

Fisher and Ury (1983) describe the shortcomings of traditional ways of negotiating, where the people who are trying to reach an agreement chip away at each others' respective positions. They show how 'positional bargaining' fails to live up to three criteria for an acceptable method of negotiation:

- It should produce a wise agreement, if agreement is possible.
- It should be efficient.
- It should improve, or at least not damage, the relationship between the parties.

Fisher and Ury set out to change the rules of negotiating, by moving to 'principled negotiation', or negotiation on merits. There are four main points to this way of negotiating:

- *Separate the people from the problem* Try to understand the situation from the different angles of the persons involved, and acknowledge their feelings; be 'hard' on the problem and 'soft' on the people.
- *Focus on interests, not positions* Interests are the concerns and desires which are 'the silent movers behind the hubbub of positions'; in other words, it is important to find out about the wishes and fears which lie behind a person's position, because these might lead to solutions that have not yet been considered.
- *Invent options for mutual gain* Conventionally, negotiators see their task as narrowing the gap between positions rather than broadening the options available, yet 'skill at inventing options is one of the most useful assets a negotiator can have'. In other words, rather than trying to halve the distance between straight line A————B consider other positions – C D E – which do not lie along the line at all.
- *Insist on using objective criteria* This means developing fair standards and fair procedures which 'concentrate on the merits of the problem, not the mettle of the parties'.

These are useful skills for you to develop in your work with, or on behalf of, clients.

Reproduced from *The new social work practice* by Mark Doel and Steven Shardlow, Arena, Aldershot

The left-hand column

Some cultures are more open than others when it comes to expressing inner thoughts and feelings. Most situations have a 'subtext' of unspoken thoughts – the kind of conversation we are accustomed to keep inside our heads. This was illustrated in the film *Annie Hall*, when Woody Allen and Diane Keaton meet at a party and the verbalized conversation between them is subtitled with their private, internal thoughts. Needless to say, the open conversation and the private one are quite different, but it is interesting how the characters' non-verbal behaviour reveals some of their inner thoughts.

Of course, there are inner thoughts which it is better not to reveal, but often it is the inner conversation which directs our actions, and for that reason we need to find ways of expressing the subtext openly, and encouraging others to reveal theirs. Senge (1990, p. 196) describes a technique called 'The left-hand column' in which you select a specific situation where your interaction with a client or colleague does not seem to be working. You write out a sample of the exchange in the form of a script on the right-hand side of the page. On the left-hand side you write what you are thinking but not saying at each point in the exchange. For example:

What I'm thinking	**What is said**
I don't think that's his opinion – I bet he's got it from the physiotherapist.	Dr J: in my view I think Mr Sahid would be better off in residential care.
I've spent a long time with Mr Sahid and I know he wants to go home.	Me: I'm not sure Mr Sahid sees it that way.
You feel guilty because you sent Mr Greaves home too early and he died.	Dr J: He'd be at considerable risk left in his own home.
You don't think much of domiciliary services, do you?	Me: Well, we've got good domiciliary services and they've told me ...
And I wish you wouldn't interrupt me like that.	Dr J: Unfortunately, they can't be around all the time, and he'd get company in Oakbrook Home.
I don't suppose you've wondered what he might feel like as the only Asian man in the home ...	Me: Well, they do give a comprehensive service. And I'm not sure how 'at home' Mr Sahid would feel at Oakbrook.
Where would you like to spend your last days?	Dr J: I think we should give it a try – it's better than him neglecting himself at home.
This is a terrible decision, but you're more powerful than me so I'll keep quiet.	Me: Mmmmm.

Reproduced from *The new social work practice* by Mark Doel and Steven Shardlow, Arena, Aldershot

The reason it is important to bring the left-hand column to the surface is that it is often these hidden assumptions which influence our actions. My assumptions about Dr Jenkins lead me to tread too softly, and I lose an opportunity to tell him I think there is a problem.

How might I have shared my own views from the left-hand column?

Reproduced from *The new social work practice* by Mark Doel and Steven Shardlow, Arena, Aldershot

8 Beginnings, middles and endings

About Activity 8: Tree

'Tree' is a metaphor for the primary processes in direct practice. The ground level is the 'here and now', with the trunk representing the concerns which have brought the person into contact with the social work agency. The roots are the various causes which have been feeding the concern and which often lie hidden. The branches are the opportunities for change and growth, the options available to help address the concerns.

Purpose

This chapter looks at processes and outcomes in social work practice. The concept of a practice method is demystified by linking it to the generic processes of beginnings, middles and endings in work with clients. The chapter illustrates how students can learn to work in a systematic and methodical fashion.

Method

- 'Tree' should be used when practice teacher and student have had an opportunity to work together with a client (perhaps after an initial assessment or meeting).
- Each person (practice teacher and student) should consider the three elements of the 'tree':

- *The trunk* This represents the concerns as seen by the practice teacher, student, client(s) and any other significant persons.
- *The roots* These represent the causes of the concerns.
- *The branches* These represent the aspirations and wants of the client, and the various options for achieving them.

● Practice teacher and student compare their 'Trees'. How similar or different are their perceptions of the concerns, problems and difficulties which make up the trunk? How much attention would each pay to the root causes? What range of options was identified? Draw fruit on those branches which you think are likely to lead to a successful outcome. (About 1 hour total.)

Variations

Although the concerns are represented by the one tree trunk, these are often perceived differently by the people involved (just as the trunk's colour, shape and texture vary from different angles).

It is important to think as widely as possible about the options available to help work with the concerns which have been identified, and ways of alleviating them. Do the client's aspirations differ from those of their carer, family or the agency?

When the student has gained more familiarity with the work, it helps to return to the 'Tree' and discuss how far it is useful to dig for the causes of present problems and concerns.

Activity 8   TREE

What are the options?
(Which are most likely to bear fruit?)

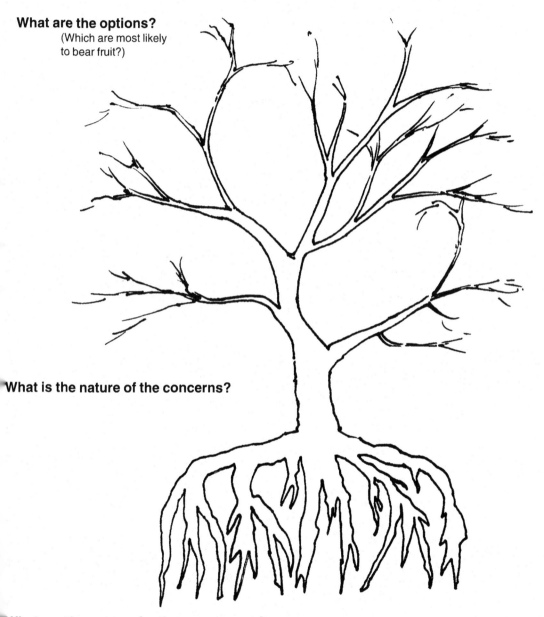

What is the nature of the concerns?

What are the causes for these concerns?

Reproduced from *The new social work practice* by Mark Doel and Steven Shardlow, Arena, Aldershot

Notes for practice teachers

Processes and outcomes

In Chapters 6 and 7 we explored the building blocks of interpersonal communication. These blocks are available to build larger constructions: an encounter; an interview; a session; an assessment; a group. In constructing a piece of work, the student needs to become familiar both with the processes involved and with the outcomes desired.

Experienced social work practitioners are often unaware of the way they are using processes to organize their encounters with clients. It has become second nature, and it saves time if it is not subject to constant scrutiny and review. However, students need to 'deconstruct' the processes so that they understand them before reconstructing them in their own practice. In addition, deconstructing your own practice in this way can be a refreshing and challenging experience.

Whether the piece of work in question is as brief as a one-off assessment, or as protracted as daily sessions over three months with a resident in care, the processes associated with beginnings, middles and endings are in play. In other words, the scale of the 'Tree' in Activity 8 could be anything from the smallest bonsai to the tallest redwood!

Practice methods

What is it, then, that connects the quick, individual assessment and the lengthy, intense involvement? These have the appearance of very dissimilar events, yet it is possible to discern common factors. One such factor is the need to organize the process into a beginning, a middle and an ending, even if the time-scale is relatively collapsed or extended. After all, a ninety second telephone call and a ninety-year lifetime both have recognizable processes of beginning, middle and ending.

The way in which these processes are organized depends on the practice method which the practitioner uses. Many practitioners put 'practice method' second only to 'theory' in their lexicon of scary words. (Practice teachers completing an information sheet for prospective students regularly answered the question 'What practice methods do you use?' with one word – eclectic.) Yet practitioners cannot avoid using methods of practice; what is significant is the extent to which they are *explicit* and *systematic*.

A practice method is:

- a way of working which is *systematic* – there is a coherent pattern of action sequences;
- explicit about its *ethical principles* – the values of the method are open to scrutiny;

- based on a particular *body of knowledge* – perhaps organized into a theory;
- refined in the light of *research findings* – regular evaluation modifies the method;
- practical and has a recognizable *technology* – there are techniques which guide practitioners who use it.

Some practice methods are more systematic than others, more explicit about their value base and the body of knowledge on which they rest, have been better researched and provide more accessible guidance on how they can be put into practice. They conform to our notion of a practice method more than other, less organized, less explicit ways of working (Doel and Marsh, 1992).

Practice methods bring purpose to the processes of the work and help the student to consider how the beginnings, middles and endings of work will relate to each other.

Beginnings

In Chapter 5 we discovered the importance of establishing a proper basis for the work with a prospective client. This is a period which prepares for the beginning of the work itself, and which Doel and Marsh (1992, pp. 10–22) have referred to as 'the mandate'.

The beginning stage of work is a period of exploration and information gathering. Wherever possible, this should be done with the client, so that the student develops a partnership with the client in their work together. However, in addition to the client's own view, there are usually a great many different opinions – including the student's – about the situation. All of these need to be included, and bringing these other perspectives into the client's perception is part of the work itself.

The student should learn ways of gathering information which are responsive to the client's concerns, and which are also systematic. In other words, the 'Beginning' stage should have a sense of purpose, but not so strong that there is no room for clients to express themselves. The following four-stage framework is one way in which students can learn to be both responsive and systematic when finding out about the client's situation (adapted from Doel and Marsh, 1992).

Scanning the range of difficulties

It is important to give people an opportunity to look at the full range of difficulties they are experiencing. Sometimes there is one obvious and definite problem which the person is seeking help with, but other times there may be quite a range of difficulties, and the student should make sure the client has the opportunity to set these out. This first stage is like gathering an agenda at the beginning of a meeting: it gives the student and the client a better idea of how much or how little ground there is to cover. In addition to the client's topics, students should make sure that they present their own, so the agenda is one they have built together.

The student should be alert to the effects of different moods: for example, people who feel very confused or emotional may be looking for space to express their feelings and not be ready to look at different problems. The student should respond to this, taking time before moving into an exploration of other problems.

Colouring in the details of each concern

Once the client and the student have a broad idea of the areas of difficulty, they can begin to find out some of the details. What is the concern, specifically? How is it a concern? Who sees it as a concern? Where does the concern occur and when? Why is it a concern? Answers to these questions give the student and the client a much clearer picture; sometimes this process helps to reframe the concern in a way which is new to the client.

Stating each concern in a nutshell

After the details of a concern have been carefully discussed, it is helpful to state it in a nutshell, a 'headline' which sums it up, with a quote from the client if possible. This checks that everybody is working on the same lines. There may be concerns which others (including the student) want to add – views of the situation which they want to be included, even if the client does not agree with them at this point. This brings any different views out into the open at an early stage.

Choosing a concern to work on

Change is not an easy process, so there is great value in focusing any efforts towards change on one or two specific areas. It may be clear by this stage where the client wishes the main efforts for change to be focused; the process of looking in very clear detail at each area of difficulty should also have given the client and the student a better idea of where change is most likely to be successful, and what exactly it is that needs to be changed.

In deciding priorities, it is important to give the client a chance to review how the concerns relate to each other. Thinking about the relationship between the different areas of concern helps clients to make informed choices: it is a balance between the concern where success is most likely and where success is likely to have the greatest impact on other areas of difficulty.

This approach is adapted from a practice method which is founded on the importance of the 'here and now'. Practice methods based, for example on psychodynamic theories of human experience would approach the client's concerns in a different manner. With reference to 'Tree', the student would learn how to dig below the surface to trace the roots back to their tips, in the belief that this is necessary to understand the 'here and now' fully.

Middles

Moving from what is wrong to what is wanted

Clients need to know that the student has been exploring their concerns as a basis to move to the next stage – a discussion of what the client *wants*. 'OK, we've been looking at what is wrong, and we've selected a particular concern to work on in detail, but now we need to think about what you want.' We use *goal* as shorthand for 'what is wanted', which in turn is shorthand for 'what is wanted and what can also be realistically achieved'.

The goal might be the concern turned on its head. For example, if the concern is 'the other kids in this home keep picking on me', the goal might be 'I want the other kids in this home to stop picking on me'. However, this may be a flawed goal (it might be unrealistic or based on faulty premises). If the concern has been reframed as 'I can't handle it when the other kids make fun of me', the goal might be something like 'I want to make more friendships outside the home'. The student helps the client to choose a goal which they can work towards together. The goal should remain true to the client's concern but, in the judgement of the student and the client, it should be framed so that it has the best chance of success.

Backward mapping

Small actions or tasks can build towards the goal, like the rungs on a stepladder. It can also be useful to think about this process in reverse.

Sometimes when we are 'Here' and we are trying to work out how to get 'There', it helps to consider this journey in reverse. As with a maze, it can be easier to track from the exit to the entrance rather than the other way round. If students consider a 'There' which has already been achieved and traces how they got there, they are 'backward mapping'. When they have a clearer idea of how they achieved previous successes in getting from 'Here' to 'There', they can use this knowledge to improve their chances of arriving successfully next time. This process of backward mapping can be used in the work with clients.

Backward mapping is not a linear process. It will include plenty of loops and diversions as new information or circumstances arise. Often there are paradoxes, like the one that strikes new seafarers when they learn that to turn to the right they must move the rudder to the left, and to turn to the left they must move the rudder to the right! The idea of a ladder (from 'Here' to 'There') is a useful device to use with the client, but in practice the progress will not be so linear. There will be twists, turns and loops in the process.

Working with people who are reluctant

It is not uncommon to hear complaints from students and practitioners about the client's lack of motivation. If this seems to be a problem, the practice teacher should ask whether the student feels the client is working towards a goal which is genuinely their own. Too often, we expect people to work towards other people's goals (usually ours) and show surprise when they do not seem fully committed.

There are times when clients are working towards a goal which they want to achieve, but events conspire against success and this affects their motivation. In these circumstances, if the student and the client were genuinely unable to foresee the extent of the obstacles, your help may be needed to renegotiate the goal with the client, or to abandon it altogether.

There are other circumstances when the agency's goal *has* to come first. For example, where the care of children is concerned it is not possible to work towards the parents' goals if these do not recognize the child's basic needs. The student needs to spell out that the agency's goals might be different from the client's. It is essential for both the student and the client to be aware of the *consequences* of failure to reach a goal. They need to be spelt out, not as a threat to clients, but as an honest statement of possible events. Understanding the consequences of not reaching a goal can help to increase the client's motivation in a positive way.

If agreement is not possible, work should stop, unless there is a legal mandate for the work to continue (see Doel and Marsh, 1992, pp. 33–4).

Power

Any partnership between a client and a student is based on differences in power. Students usually have greater power than clients in terms of their formal role, knowledge and access to the resources of the placement agency and other agencies. However, clients know their own situation better than the student (even if they are sometimes confused and upset by it). Clients may feel relatively powerless to make an impact, but they usually have much more vested interest in the work and spend far more time 'living their own life' than the student does!

The relationship is unequal, but it is not one-sided. There are different kinds of power and it is patronizing to assume that clients are automatically powerless or feel powerless. They may or may not lack power; similarly, they may or may not feel powerless.

Explicit practice methods, such as task-centred social work, are intrinsically anti-oppressive because they bring power issues to the surface: 'the principles of task-centred [practice] have much potential for empowering clients', writes Ahmad (1990, p. 51). These ways of working do not make issues of power disappear, but they do make them part of the work. Nevertheless, practice methods which are intrinsically empowering can be misused so that their effect is oppressive rather than anti-oppressive. For example, though the task-centred method is considered to be widely used

(Payne, 1995, p. 119), we cannot be certain *how* it is being used. If hooked up to the procedural model of working described in Chapter 5 (page 57), it could have quite oppressive results. Perhaps the greatest potential for oppression lies in the use of implicit practice methods, hidden from scrutiny so there are no means to review whether they are the most effective and empowering ways of working.

Another power issue to consider is the one between student and practice teacher. In particular, differences in race and gender should be discussed openly, in terms of their impact on the processes of teaching, learning and assessment (Doel, Shardlow, Sawdon and Sawdon, 1996, p. 56).

Endings

When children go on a long car journey they tend to ask the same question several times: 'Are we there yet?' Partly, this is wishful thinking and partly it is because they don't have enough information to let them know how to judge what the end of the journey looks like or how to pace their progress towards it.

The first step to knowing whether we are 'there yet' is knowing where we want to go and being able to recognize progress towards that destination. This suggests a linear approach, but such an approach is mistaken: although the general progress may be linear (from 'Here' to 'There'), the process is likely to be a series of loops.

In each of the ten destinations below, how might a person know if they were 'There' yet?

1 I want to give up smoking.
2 I want to lead a more fulfilling life.
3 I want to be rich.
4 We want to have a happy family.
5 She wants me to get a better job.
6 We want to move nearer to her parents.
7 I want to have my children back.
8 I want to stay in my own home.
9 I don't want to feel hurt in this relationship.
10 I don't want him to tell any more lies.

Endings as transitions

A piece of work without a proper ending is like a novel with the last chapter missing. Endings allow us to feel a sense of completion, and this is crucial to our morale and well-being. A properly conducted ending prevents a sense of unfinished business, which can mar the work that has already been done. A planned ending gives the student and the client a chance to review the ground they have covered and to see how far they have come. It is an opportunity to say some positive things about the work that has been done and, especially where close relationships have developed, to express any fears and sorrows that the end brings with it.

Each exit is also a new entrance. What marks the end of one stage marks the beginning of another, so that most endings can be viewed as transitions – from dependence on help from the agency to independence from the agency, from living independently to moving into care, or vice versa, or from working with the student to working with a new social worker after the placement has ended. Preparation for each transition makes the chances of success greater, so the student should never be tempted to hide the fact from the client that the placement has a definite end. It is better to embrace this built-in time limit as a help rather than a hindrance.

Difficulties with endings

It is not uncommon to experience difficulties with endings: common examples are meetings which drift on beyond 'closing time' with people leaving in dribs and drabs, and clients who introduce the crunch problem just as you put your hand on the door handle to leave.

Endings start with beginnings. Being clear from the outset how much time is available will influence the pace of the work, especially if there are reminders from time to time ('Well, we're about halfway through the time we agreed ... we've only got ten minutes left' and so on). Making short summaries, now and then, helps to rehearse the ending itself, when it is important for everybody (student, client, family, group, team) to have a shared understanding of what has been agreed and what you have all undertaken to do. The student should think of the ending as a process which starts at the beginning and speeds up to the conclusion.

Endings refer not only to single contacts, each of which comes to closure, but also to a longer period of work. Research by Sainsbury, Nixon and Phillips (1982) found examples of clients in a social services department who did not know whether their case was open or closed. Indeed, there were clients who thought their case was closed when it was not, and clients who thought that they were 'still on the books' when the agency had closed their case. They conclude that 'closing a case can be an administrative event of little emotional significance, or it can be an endorsement of the client's social competence'.

If students are working in an explicit way, they and their clients should have a common understanding of whether the work is open or closed. Indeed, using the methods we have described in this chapter, the client and the student should also have a shared understanding of how much progress they have made towards the end. If the work is not going smoothly and there have been emergencies, they should at least have an idea of how much this has disrupted their plans. The frustration of knowing the train has been diverted and delayed is nothing compared to the anger of not knowing where it has been diverted to or how late it is going to be.

Different kinds of ending

The student is aiming for planned endings in their work, but some endings can be sudden, unexpected or premature. As the practice teacher, use your own practice experience to look at the various reasons why endings differ. Even in settings where the work tends to be more open-ended, such as a drop-in centre, the fact that a student is on a finite placement creates a forced ending. The time limit of the placement can be an advantage rather than a problem, because deadlines often increase motivation by providing a reason why something should be done today rather than be put off until tomorrow.

Endings in residential settings are related more to the rhythm of the day and to patterns in residents' life cycles. The main ending for a young person in residential care is related to a transition, usually from residential care to family care or independent living, and the student's placement may or may not coincide with this time track. In residential care for the elderly, beginnings and endings come and go with each day's rhythm, with the biggest ending of all – death – often a taboo subject. Dealing with the impact of other residents' deaths and preparing for their own is a valuable focus for the student's work, if the culture of the home permits it.

'Created' endings are possible in residential settings. Meal times, sessions with key workers, meetings of staff and residents, groups such as oral history groups with elderly residents – all of these introduce patterns and routines with beginnings and endings into residential life.

Ends and means

If 'ends' describe the destination, 'means' describe how we are going to arrive there. We often make the mistake of assuming that ends and means have to be of a similar kind. For example, consider a skinny person who wants to build some muscle. This person's end is physical (more muscle) and no doubt some of the means will be physical, too (weight training). However, it may be an understanding of the importance of diet, or how to plan a training programme, or the technical skill of using the equipment properly, which is critical to success – or it could be the psychological will and motivation to achieve the end. In this case, an end which is expressed in *physical* terms is achieved by using *affective* and *cognitive* means as well as physical ones.

Journeys and destinations are sometimes seen as opposites in social work practice: 'Are you a journey person or a destination person?' Clashes in these kinds of orientation are often visible in meetings, when destination people (brisk procession through the agenda items with one eye on the clock) and journey people (meandering from one topic to another and back again) seem to inhabit different time zones. How does the student feel they can get the best from both of these camps?

Catching the moment

The student is learning how to plan their work effectively, but it is also important that they are able to make good use of spontaneous and unexpected events in their work with clients. If plans are too fixed, these events can feel disruptive and the student might lose an opportunity for a new departure in the work. The student is learning the difference between responsive and reactive practice.

Notes for students

Beginnings

Statements of concern

Arriving at a clear statement of a concern is not simple. We often express our problems and concerns in fuzzy, unclear ways; they often need unravelling, especially if clients have accepted other people's definitions of their concerns. It can be a new, empowering experience to start to question these definitions. Of course, there are further complications if the main concern as you see it is not accepted by the client as a concern at all; or if the main problem for the client is you!

Below are twelve statements which people might make in response to the question, 'What's the problem?' Can you match them to the four categories (A-D) which follow?

My concern is ...

1. He won't do as he is told.
2. I can't pay the rent.
3. You won't let us have our children back.
4. We don't know whether to let her leave home.
5. I'm overweight and it's affecting my health.
6. No-one understands me.
7. He needs to stop drinking.
8. We're not happy.
9. I want to have breakfast in this home at whatever time I want it.
10. I feel depressed and I can't get down to anything.
11. The other kids in this home keep picking on me.
12. I keep getting caught.

A: Concerns which are really goals
Sometimes we express something we want to do (a goal) as a concern. What we mean is that what we want to do is a problem to somebody else. For example, as a resident of Oakbrook Home, I want to have breakfast at whatever time I want it (no. 9), but the problem is: 'The cook won't let me', or 'There's not enough staff on and I can't get it myself'. Also, the client's goal for somebody else can look like a problem statement: 'He needs to stop drinking' means 'I want him to stop drinking'.

B: Concerns about other people
Most problems involve other people to an extent, but some statements focus only on the behaviour of somebody else (nos 1 and 11). If the other person does not recognize this as a concern, the statement has to be reframed, for example no. 1: 'I get angry when he comes home late' and no. 11: 'I can't handle it when the other kids make fun of me'. These reframed

Reproduced from *The new social work practice* by Mark Doel and Steven Shardlow, Arena, Aldershot

statements bring the concern closer to the client's control. In no. 3, you, the agency worker, are the problem. This is best expressed openly, and often it can be a focus for the work: what has to happen to get rid of the agency?

C: Concerns which are not specific
Some statements of concern need much more careful spelling out. They give you a sense of how the client is feeling, for example nos 6 and 8, but you would not be clear about what needed to change in order to alleviate the difficulty. Broad, general statements need detailing so that you and the client know whether you can take steps to help. More details help you both to decide which direction those steps should follow.

D: Concerns which are specific
Some statements are relatively clear expressions of a concern, for example nos 2 and 5. A successful outcome is more likely if the concern is relatively specific and the client is able to do something about it. However, many concerns are not like that: in these circumstances, your skill is to help the client to reframe the problem as much as possible towards a statement which is more specific and more within the client's influence. However, the reframing should not go so far that clients feel their original statement has been lost.

Middles

Goals

We all use problem-solving techniques to achieve our own goals, even if we do not think about it in these terms. Your work with clients will benefit from making links between the way you use problem-solving techniques in your own life and the methods you will be using with clients.

On a blank piece of paper, draw yourself a ladder with ten or so rungs from top to bottom. The lowest rung represents 'Now' and the top-most represents a future 'Goal'. Consider a personal goal (for example, 'I want to go on holiday') and, using the rungs on your ladder, write down the steps necessary to achieve your goal. Use 'snakes' to identify potential obstacles along the way, and consider how you might find a way round each of your 'snakes'.

Endings

Mapping the work: getting the client's views

There are two litmus tests of your work with a client: one is an evaluation of the *outcome* of the work for the client; and the other is an evaluation of your

Reproduced from *The new social work practice* by Mark Doel and Steven Shardlow, Arena, Aldershot

own *practice*. The first test measures how far you and the client felt the goal has been achieved – how near is the client to their destination? The second test measures what part you had in helping or hindering that process. For example, you can think of situations where the client felt that your involvement was very helpful, even when the goal was not achieved. Similarly, the client could achieve the goal but not think that your intervention had much bearing on this.

If we take a vertical axis to indicate the client's views about the outcome of the work (the further 'north', the more positive, and the further 'south', the more negative), and a horizontal axis for the client's views about your work (the further 'west', the more positive, and the further 'east', the more negative), we have four sectors, as shown in Figure 8.1.

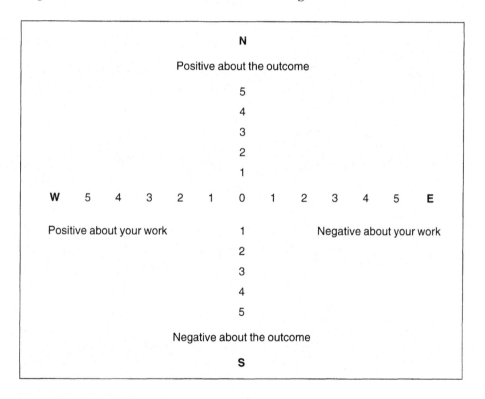

Figure 8.1 Mapping the work

In the NW sector, clients' views of the outcome of the work are positive and they also feel good about your work. In the NE sector, their view of the outcome remains positive, but they have negative feelings about your involvement. In the SE sector, the clients do not think they have achieved their goal

Reproduced from *The new social work practice* by Mark Doel and Steven Shardlow, Arena, Aldershot

and they do not think your work has been helpful, either. In the SW sector, the clients still do not think they have reached their goal, but they nevertheless see your intervention as helpful.

You will find Baird (1991), Evans *et al.* (1988) and Furniss (1988) helpful in identifying the benefits and pitfalls of finding out your clients' views, and suggesting some ways forward. The starting-point is your genuine desire to map your work.

Reproduced from *The new social work practice* by Mark Doel and Steven Shardlow, Arena, Aldershot

III

Agency practice

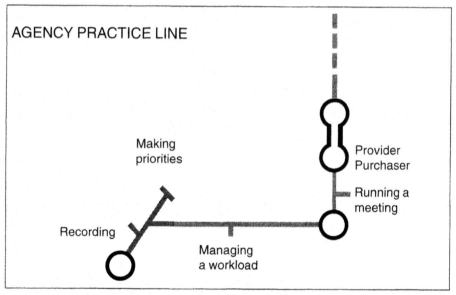

Students of social work practice must learn their art in the context of the social work agency. The idea of good social work practice is not dependent upon the agency, but neither is it unconnected with the agency. Social workers need to know how to do the job expected by the agency, while not compromising the professional task. Indeed, part of that task is to ensure that agency policies promote good working practices.

Chapters 9–13 look at how students manage their work. Central to this process is an understanding of the criteria which students use to plan their work and justify priorities. There are many different interests to be taken into account, and it is important that criteria are negotiated and open to scrutiny. The six chapters and activities in Part III also help the student to learn how to become a good team player rather than an isolated performer.

Making priorities (Chapter 9), uses a deliberately 'unreal' situation to help students find out how they make decisions. They learn to develop and evaluate criteria, and to assess their usefulness in setting priorities.

Recording the work – often considered one of the least exciting tasks in social work practice – is an excellent opportunity to develop a partnership with the client. Activity 10 helps students to learn how to differentiate fact from opinion and to question the use of language in social work recording. The student learns about open records and shared records.

In Chapter 11, Managing a workload, students learn the skills of managing their time by organizing their diary. Students also consider how they 'capture' unstructured time and get the best out of unplanned contacts and opportunities.

Social workers spend much of their time in meetings, where decisions are made which can have far-reaching consequences. Learning how to observe, how to take part in and how to chair a meeting are essential skills. Running a meeting, Chapter 12, introduces the student to a framework for meetings: first, to analyse processes as an observer; then to participate actively; and finally to use the framework as a practical procedure, as chair of a meeting.

Chapter 13 addresses an aspect of current practice which is increasingly significant in agency practice, Purchasing and providing services. This chapter explores the development of the concept and practice of care management and the stages in helping care in the community to work.

Students who have successfully completed 'Agency practice' will be developing an ability to work within agency settings, to agency guidelines. They will have learned how to develop criteria to help think critically about agency practice and to make suggestions about possible improvements to services.

9 Making priorities

About Activity 9: Sticky moments

'Sticky moments' takes a number of incidents or situations similar to ones which students will experience during the placement. Students are asked to make priorities in relation to these incidents and to think about the criteria which they have used to make these priorities.

Purpose

The purpose of this activity is to encourage students to think about how they make decisions when there are conflicting priorities. Too often, these decisions are made without an awareness of the knowledge, values and beliefs which underpin them. This activity makes these factors explicit and teaches students a framework which will help them to continue to review the way they make decisions.

Method

- The activity can be done by two people (you and the student) or by a small group of practice teachers and students. A group of students in different settings (group care and field work, for example) can address both parts of the activity, which provides interesting contrasts.
- Students should study 'Sticky moments' before the practice tutorial. Ask them to prepare whichever of the two situations relates best to

their own setting. The three questions at the end of the activity apply to both settings. Students should write down their responses to these questions.
- In the practice tutorial, ask students to describe their responses to the three questions, using their prepared written notes. Subsequent discussion should focus on the *criteria* which the student developed. (Allow 45–60 minutes.)

    – Write the criteria up on a piece of flipchart paper, adding your own and any further criteria which come out of the discussion.
    – Decide on priorities for these criteria: rewrite them in this new order on a fresh piece of flipchart paper.
    – Finally, use these newly ordered criteria to look at the six situations again. How do they change or confirm the student's original priorities?

Variations

You can use the 'Sticky moments' format to prepare six situations which reflect the specific kind of work which the student does in your setting. If you create your own 'Sticky moments', remember that your aim is to provide an opportunity for students to think carefully about the criteria they might use when confronted with choices: you are not seeking to simulate a realistic moment in the life of the unit or the kind of in-tray the student is likely to have to deal with. Each separate situation or referral is realistic, but it is unlikely they would all happen together.

Activity 9   STICKY MOMENTS

... in Oakbrook Home

- Mary (aged 91) has wet herself.
- Harry (76) is having an argument with Kathleen (79) who is very frail and deaf. Harry has a stick and is hitting the wall with it.
- A member of staff puts the tea and biscuits out on the trolley and tells you she is going out 'for a few minutes'.
- The telephone rings in the office.
- The emergency buzzer from the bathroom is sounding.
- Avis (88) keeps crying 'Out!, Out!' and is heading for the front door.

... in the team's in-tray

A
Referred by parents
Mr and Mrs Appleyard are concerned about their eldest daughter (15), who is truanting persistently and 'mixing with bad company'. They want a social worker to visit to 'give her a good talking to'.

B
Referred by a local councillor
Councillor requesting help for Mr and Mrs Brzynski who have increasing problems coping with a mentally handicapped daughter (41). 'All their requests for help have been ignored.' Mrs B. is in reception.

C
Referred by general practitioner
Doctor Chaduri is concerned about Mrs Clark (63), whose mother (84) lives with her and is confused, incontinent and increasingly demanding. Mrs Clark is 'getting to the end of her tether'.

D
Referred by anonymous neighbour
The caller claims that her neighbour, Trisha Davies, a single parent, has left her children alone in the house for over an hour several times recently. The children are four and seven years old.

E
Referred by himself, via a probation officer
Tony Ezeshi, a single parent with four children between nine and sixteen, has rent arrears and is on the verge of an electricity disconnection. He referred himself to Probation who say they can't help; can we?

F
Referred by consultant psychiatrist
Mr Francis, a divorcee living alone, was discharged from psychiatric hospital two months ago. The consultant wants a social worker to do a full needs assessment because Mr Francis is becoming depressed and drinking again.

Questions

1. What priority would you give to these six situations/referrals?
2. What further information would you like to gather before taking action?
3. What criteria have you used to help you decide your position?

With acknowledgements to Penny Forshaw, Mary Gardiner and Matt Bukowski

Reproduced from *The new social work practice* by Mark Doel and Steven Shardlow, Arena, Aldershot

Notes for practice teachers

Accountable practice

'Sticky moments' is an example of how a simulated exercise can promote learning, precisely because it is not 'realistic'. A student in Oakbrook would be unlucky to have all six of those incidents occurring at the same time; similarly, six referrals of that nature in one in-tray is not something the student expects to meet.

The value of 'Sticky moments' is that it gives students permission to reflect carefully on the reasons behind the decisions they make. In the safe environment of simulated practice, students can begin to question the reasons for their choices, because there is time to reflect on them. This helps students to make better decisions at times of great pressure, and gives a framework to evaluate the way they have made their priorities.

Good social work practice is self-aware and accountable. Students learn how to *give an account* of what they are doing and why they are doing it. Those students who can answer the question 'What am I doing and why am I doing it?' make their practice accessible, with every prospect of becoming accountable, too. Students often learn to describe what they did and why they did it *after* the event, which only improves their skills in *post hoc* rationalization. As practice teacher, you hope to improve the students' abilities to give an honest account of the choices which are available to them and to become aware of the criteria used to make these choices. This kind of activity can accelerate students' understanding (see Doel, 1988).

Ranking criteria

The criteria which help the student to make choices about the dilemmas in Oakbrook Home focus largely, but not exclusively, on physical factors such as degree of risk. The factors influencing the student with the in-tray dilemmas are broader, especially when a wide range of client groups is included: they relate to other factors such as the source of the referral or the immediacy of the problem.

Below are a dozen criteria to tease out during the discussion with the student. Ask the following questions:

- How does the student think these criteria are ranked in practice?
- How does the student think these criteria *should* be ranked?

1 *Urgency, consequences of delay and risk* How are each of the six incidents or situations likely to deteriorate if action is delayed? Is there a deadline which has to be met, such as the disconnection of fuel? Is somebody's health or safety at risk?

2 Legal obligations   What is the legal framework for the powers and responsibilities which govern the student's actions? For example, what financial powers has the local authority to help with rent arrears?
3 Agency expectations   Does the agency have any policies which determine the priorities, and are these clear and accessible? Is there a procedure manual to help the student make decisions? Are there any local practices which are specific to this unit or office?
4 Social pressures   What are the broad influences on the worker's decisions? Is there such a thing as society's priorities and expectations? How do we determine what these are and who defines them?
5 Available resources   To what extent do we make priorities in order to fit the available resources, so that resources define needs?
6 Others' responsibilities and skills   The student is not alone in the unit or office. What other people could and should be helping? When would you expect other people, in your agency or other agencies, to be involved?
7 Source of the referral   Do different referrers carry different weight and credibility? Is a self-referral likely to be more accurate and motivated? How does the referrer's authority and power influence the decision about priorities?
8 Previous knowledge   To what extent do previous assessments influence present attitudes? In Oakbrook Home, for example, knowledge of the individual residents would be an important factor in deciding what to do.
9 Degree of need and disadvantage   Can one person be said to be more needy than another and how can this need be measured? Are specific client groups particularly disadvantaged and how should this influence the way we treat particular individuals?
10 Likelihood of success   Is it important to put energies into effective work, providing help to those who can use it? How is the chance of a successful outcome to be judged and what do we do about those situations where failure is almost inevitable?
11 Personal preferences   How far does the acknowledgement of personal preferences for particular kinds of work clear or cloud the judgement? For example, there may be a preference for working with women. Is this an honest self-assessment of personal skills and limitations, or a rationalization of prejudice?
12 Problem Sensitization   Are we more likely to respond quickly and favourably to problems which we can relate to, in connection with our own personal lives?

If there are clear agency policies which define priorities, it is important to let the student know that you will be discussing these. However, agency priorities are not necessarily synonymous with professional ones and, to begin with, you want students to express their own priorities. Make sure students do not try to avoid the issues by claiming they would never have to deal with all these things alone. Of course they wouldn't, but the point of the activity is to look at reasons for making choices, not ways of avoiding them.

Alter some of the situations slightly to see how this influences the student's response (for example, Mr Francis, rather than his psychiatrist, requests help). Students can 'weigh' each criterion (in this example, the source of the referrer) by considering how a small change in the circumstances alters their priorities. If Mr Francis's case is given a higher priority because he has referred himself, the students can see how they are putting weight behind this criterion. It also sheds new light to ask students to reconsider their priorities from somebody else's point of view, such as the director of the agency, the local newspaper, or 'the man or woman in the street'.

You are not looking for a rapid response, a quick deployment of residents or referrals. A student who wants to get everything neatly wrapped up at great speed is unlikely to be open to the self-questioning which leads to a better understanding of how decisions are reached. Students should be encouraged to think about how they manage to deal with competing demands, both in the sense of making effective decisions and in terms of managing any stress they may experience (Bristol Polytechnic, 1982).

Notes for students

Triage

During the First World War the medical services were faced with the kinds of priorities we hope we will never have to make. With scant resources, they had to make decisions which were, literally, life and death.

They divided the casualties into three categories:

- Those whose injuries were such that they were likely to recover, even without treatment.
- Those whose injuries were such that without treatment they were likely to die, but with treatment they were likely to survive.
- Those whose injuries were such that they were likely to die, even with treatment.

The medical services put all their energies into the middle category, leaving the first group to recover unaided and leaving the last group to die. This method of making priorities was called triage.

Fortunately, the choices in social work are not so stark, but they are difficult nonetheless. The principle of putting your efforts where they are most likely to be effective is one you need to consider.

> Effectiveness is an important ethical consideration not only for individual workers but for the agencies in which they work. There is a disproportionate unconcern within agencies with self-evaluation. (Hudson and Macdonald, 1986, p. 11)

The latter part of this assertion, concerning agencies, may or may not remain the case, but if you used the criterion 'likelihood of success' (no. 10) as the main guideline for your work on the placement, what differences would this have make to the kinds of priorities you have made?

What do you think are the benefits and the limitations of using the success criterion in social work?

Reproduced from *The new social work practice* by Mark Doel and Steven Shardlow, Arena, Aldershot

10 Recording the work

About Activity 10: Matter of fact

'Matter of fact' is a collection of twenty entries taken from social work files in different settings. There are also twenty alternative statements made from the client's point of view rather than the worker's. The student is asked to match each file entry with the client's likely response.

Purpose

There are many different purposes in recording in social work practice. This activity helps the student to think critically about the language used in social work recording, to improve the meaning of their records, and to consider writing records as part of the work with clients.

Method

- This activity can be done by a practice teacher and student together, or by a group of practice teachers and students. A group of students who are placed in different kinds of settings produces a variety of perspectives.
- No preparation needs to be done before the practice tutorial. Each person needs a copy of 'Matter of fact'.
- Each written statement, taken from actual files and records, should be addressed in turn, with suggestions about which of the client responses

might fit best. Students and practice teachers should discuss what meaning is conveyed by the statement and what they think it says about the writer. Relate this discussion to the recording practices in your agency and the student's record writing so far. (Allow about 30 minutes.)

A suggested match of worker and client statements will be found in the Appendix on page 112.

Variations

'Matter of fact' presents a 'Top 20' of clichés common to most social work settings; indeed, they have been taken from various case files and day books. You may wish to collect your agency's own 'Top 20' (for example, a medical or psychiatric social work placement will have its own brand of jargon to add to the set in 'Matter of fact'). A list of acronyms would also be a useful way of demonstrating how professional language can exclude clients and obscure meanings.

Activity 10   MATTER OF FACT

The comments in the left column have come from case files, reports or day books. They illustrate some of social work's favourite phrases – perhaps you can add to this Top 20. The comments in the right column are responses as they might appear in the clients' case books, if they were to keep them. Apart from the first four examples, the case records and the clients' responses are scrambled.

Which clients' comments might you match to which social work records?

Social work record	Client's view
Shirley is very *manipulative*	I know how to play the system
Yusef is *easily led*	I don't know how to play the system
Julie indulges in *promiscuous behaviour*	I have a lot of sexual partners
Karl is *testing the boundaries*	I have a lot of sexual partners
Trisha is *aggressive and self-centred*	I don't know how to ask for what I want
Mrs Khan presents in a *hostile manner*	I don't know how to show my son, either
There is an ongoing *conflict situation*	We don't know what to do with him
He is *an inadequate*	I don't like your rules and I want out
He is *an inadequate role model* for his son	There is a lot of racism
The family has a lot of *inner resources*	I don't like what you want me to do
They have *rejected* him	We fight like cat and dog
He is a difficult *problem case*	I don't trust you
Mr Davy is a *needy, dependent eneuretic*	You don't know what to do with him
Samantha is an *acting-out attention seeker*	I wish I could do more for myself
Sean must prove he *responds to structure*	You don't have my taste in jokes or clothes
Winston is *oversensitive* about colour	English is not my first language
George *represses his emotions*	I know how to ask for what I want
Mr Pradish is *uncommunicative*	We get through despite everything
Polly is very *demanding*	I know very well how to ask for what I want
Claire laughs and dresses *inappropriately*	Nobody takes any notice of me

- What meaning does each statement convey to you?
  What kinds of knowledge, values and beliefs does it suggest the writer holds?

Reproduced from *The new social work practice* by Mark Doel and Steven Shardlow, Arena, Aldershot

Notes for practice teachers

Purposes of recording

Since the earliest days of the profession, recording has been considered important. Paré and Allen have summarized the early work of Mary Richmond in 1925, who gave nine reasons for recording:

1. to help workers be more effective by providing the full complications of a case
2. records allow someone else to continue treatment (sic) when workers get sick, go on holiday, or move to new points of service
3. records can be used as a starting point when people return for service years after the case has been closed
4. records help in the supervision of staff
5. records help to train new workers
6. records offer data for the study and improvement of treatment
7. records can be grouped around presenting problems to provide the opportunity to assess effective treatment
8. records contain the full and detailed descriptions that allow for problem-solving in difficult cases
9. records provide public evidence of the activities of social work
(Paré and Allen, 1995, pp. 166–7)

More recently, a BASW (1983) report cites the following as the core purposes served by social work records:

management control; continuity; self-justification; legal record; work support; supervision and teaching; information storage; personal evaluation; planning, research, financial control, agency evaluation; personal identity.

When these various purposes conflict, the student faces a dilemma. In a nutshell, this is often expressed in the question 'How much recording should I do?' Some purposes seem to suggest that the record should be full and detailed; others point to a brief, pithy approach.

With each piece of recording, students need to ask themselves what the specific purposes are. Is the recording in this case largely *procedural* (application forms for day care), or *investigative and speculative* (suspected child abuse), or *personal* (life story books with children in care), or *providing continuity* (day books in group care settings)? The student learns that being clear about the purpose of making a written record helps to decide what needs to go in it.

Students need opportunities to learn actively about recording, since it is an essential part of practice. 'When students arrive in the field [placement] they should be fully exposed to the procedures, politics, and power of the written record in social work practice' (Paré and Allen, 1995, p. 173).

Records should be high on the agenda and students should be encouraged to experiment with different recording formats. If your agency has a specific recording framework, such as the Probation Service, the student will need to become familiar with those requirements, too. Report writing is especially important in some settings, and there is a number of publications available to help you to teach the student good report writing skills (see, for example, Øvretveit, 1986 and Shemmings, 1991).

Jargon and labels

Frameworks for recording vary from agency to agency, but students will be used to their own professional language to colour these frameworks. It is important that students question the meaning and the impact of phrases which have become routine and commonplace, and begin to identify new phrases which might be in danger of becoming over-used, no matter how worthy their intentions ('empowerment', perhaps?).

Every profession has its shorthand. One difficulty which is peculiar to social work is a tendency to take relatively commonplace words such as 'relationship' and 'boundaries' and to endow them with mystique. The jargon of science and medicine is easily recognizable as such, and even psychodynamic-speak does us the favour of looking peculiar (*id, ego* and *superego* not being conversation on the Clapham bus). By comparison, social work's pet phrases can look deceptively user-friendly. Dearling (1993) has made a recent attempt to demystify some of the basic concepts of social work and a dictionary of social work is now available (Thomas and Pierson, 1995).

Social work is becoming increasingly aware of the power of language, but there are still many practices which the student should question (Payne, 1993; Billington and Paley, 1993). Particularly insidious is the shorthand which uses an adjective as a noun: for example, 'Philip is an inadequate' as an abbreviation, perhaps for 'Phillip's ability to hold a conversation with a stranger is inadequate'. The latter statement is an improvement on the former, but it still begs the question, what constitutes 'inadequate'?

What does the student think is the difference between the description 'a mentally handicapped person' and 'a person with learning difficulties'? Asking students to consider this and similar questions about the use of language in social work practice helps them to think not only about how and what to record, but also to be critical of the use of labels for people.

Fact or opinion

'Matter of fact' highlights the matter-of-fact way the social work profession can describe its clients, even though these descriptions are often not matters of fact. During the 1980s the profession became increasingly aware of the importance of distinguishing in the written record whether a statement was one of fact or opinion.

The boundary between fact and opinion is often not clear. Is the statement 'Phillip's ability to hold a conversation with a stranger is inadequate' fact or opinion? We can see how it could be made more factual. For example, 'Phillip looked down at the ground and didn't reply to Mr Smith's questions' is factual. If Phillip's behaviour is part of a pattern, it may be possible to generalize that Phillip has difficulties holding conversations with strangers; but has the observer seen Phillip with people his own age or race, for example, and is his behaviour any different then? Every statement is selective, no matter how factual it is, so that what we look for in the record are statements which are a fair reflection of patterns of behaviour which the student has observed.

It is important to emphasize how language shapes the way students see the world. Recording in a clear fashion is likely to help students to think and act clearly as well.

Open and shared records

The best way for students to check whether they are making fair, accurate and concise records of their work is to share these with the clients. Except in a few of the most sensitive cases, usually concerning child protection or mental health, writing records with clients is an excellent way of achieving good recording practice. The student receives immediate feedback from the client, both about the recording (use of language, and so on) and the work itself (the student and the client can check whether they are working along the same lines, because it is hard to fudge the record). Doel and Lawson (1986) reported on a small-scale study which identified the bonuses of shared recording as an active practice, contrasted with open records as a passive agency policy.

Process recording

No chapter on recording would be complete without a word about process records. Once a major tool in the student supervisor's* kit, process recording has been put in the shade by the use of direct observation and audiovisual feedback. Moreover, the value of reflecting at great length about the feelings evoked during an event which is now passed is doubtful. It is even possible that process recording encouraged poor practice, by emphasizing the habit of committing clinical opinions to paper as a recording method Better to use recording exercises which help students improve their ability to record practice, rather than to commit the student to lengthy *post hoc* reflections.

---

* 'Student supervisor' is an increasingly redundant term used to refer to the person in a social work agency who had a similar function to the practice teacher. It is used here to emphasize the historic nature of past practice.

Notes for students

Me as the subject of other people's records

Your clients are the subjects of the records which you write about your work with them. You are the subject of many records, too. Make a note of all the different agencies which you know will have some form of written record about you (your doctor, your bank, and so on). Are there any agencies which you suspect will have some record but which you are not sure about? How could you find out what is written about you in these files?

Open records

How would you respond in the following three situations?

Patty Johnson returns to her children's home two years after leaving it and asks to see her records. During the placement, you have read some past files which confirm your view that they contain very subjective, often destructive, opinions. Some of the workers involved are still employed in the home, but others have left. You are not sure about the Department's policy on past files. At the staff meeting, Patty's request is discussed. What's your view?

Frank Lomas is a regular visitor to the mental health day centre where you are on placement. One morning he arrives very angry because he has caught sight of his notes at the local general hospital (he opened the blue envelope carrying information about him from one department to another). He is being treated for a viral infection and the notes from the consultant to the laboratory describe him as 'a homosexual and a drug addict'. Frank is openly gay, but does not see this is relevant, and although he took an overdose in the past, he has not been dependent on drugs. Frank wants to know what he can do about this and what you can do to help.

Dr Thomas, a psychiatrist at the local hospital, writes a report to you about Mrs Bird, who is about to be discharged following her admission four weeks ago, suffering from paranoid delusions. Dr Thomas states at the bottom of her letter that she does not wish Mrs Bird to see the report because it might provoke a recurrence of her paranoia. What do you do?

Reproduced from *The new social work practice* by Mark Doel and Steven Shardlow, Arena, Aldershot

Appendix

Matter of fact

The following is a suggested match of client responses with social work recordings:

Social work record	Client's view
Shirley is very *manipulative*	I know how to play the system
Yusef is *easily led*	I don't know how to play the system
Julie indulges in *promiscuous behaviour*	I have a lot of sexual partners
Karl is *testing the boundaries*	I have a lot of sexual partners
Trisha is *aggressive and self-centred*	I know how to ask for what I want.
Mrs Khan presents in a *hostile manner*	I don't like what you want me to do
There is an ongoing *conflict situation*	We fight like cat and dog
He is *an inadequate*	I don't know how to ask for what I want
He is an *inadequate role model* for his son	I don't know how to show my son what to ask for, either
The family has a lot of *inner resources*	We get through despite everything
They have *rejected* him	We don't know what to do with him
He is a difficult *problem case*	You don't know what to do with him
Mr Davy is a *needy, dependent* eneuretic	I wish I could do more for myself

Reproduced from *The new social work practice* by Mark Doel and Steven Shardlow, Arena, Aldershot

Samantha is an *acting-out attention seeker*	Nobody takes any notice of me
Sean must prove he *responds to structure*	I don't like your rules and I want out
Winston is *oversensitive* about colour	There is a lot of racism
George *represses his emotions* Mr Pradish is *uncommunicative*	I don't trust you English is not my first language
Polly is very *demanding*	I know very well how to ask for what I want
Claire laughs and dresses *inappropriately*	You don't have my taste in jokes or clothes

Reproduced from *The new social work practice* by Mark Doel and Steven Shardlow, Arena, Aldershot

11 Managing a workload

About Activity 11: Perfect timing

'Perfect timing' consists of a set of twenty-four different activities which a student might have to fit into a working week. The student and practice teacher each construct a diary for the week ahead, incorporating the twenty-four activities. They discuss the criteria they used to manage the time.

Purpose

The purpose of this exercise is to look at the ways in which students organize their work within the working week. A set of demands and constraints which mirror the student's work on the placement is used to discover the principles which can be used to manage a workload.

Method

- This activity can be completed by a practice teacher and student together or by a small group of practice teachers and students. It achieves particularly good results with one practice teacher and two or three students. Give the students a set of 'Perfect timing' cards (either photocopy page 117 and cut out the cards, or create your own tailor-made set – see 'Variations' below).
- Before the practice tutorial, you and the student separately should organize the same set of demands (the twenty-four activity cards) into a manageable working week. (Allow 20 minutes.)

- At the practice tutorial, or in the small group, compare your 'diaries' for the forthcoming week, discussing the reasons for your decisions. The exercise can be made more or less difficult by the number of activities you put into the pack. You can upset careful planning by producing rogue cards (unexpected activities) *after* the diary has been organized. (About 30–60 minutes.)

Variations

'Perfect timing' is an activity best tailored to your particular setting, so use the generic one in this book as an exemplar. You can prepare for this before the student's placement begins by making a note on separate cards of different demands made on your time. Note what the demand was (for example, a visit to a single parent to discuss financial problems) and the length of time set aside for each demand. If the demand had to be met at a specific day or time (such as a team meeting on Wednesday from 9.30–10.30) make a note of the details on the card. Small, repeated demands, like telephone calls and re-dials, can be totalled (for example five outgoing telephone calls, with estimated time taken). If the student's work takes them outside the home base, find a map of the area with bus routes if needed.

The pace of time in informal settings, such as group care and drop-in centres, is different from the pace in more formal settings, such as field social work and probation practice. Making use of unstructured time may be a key skill in informal settings, and a similar diary exercise can be used to log the use of time.

The amount of time taken to complete visits to locations outside the office can vary considerably according to the means of transport available to your student – car, cycle, bus, train – or even walking! Take account of these differences according to local circumstances and the student's access to differing forms of transport. Other factors to be taken into account might include the distance from the office to the car park, if this is notable, and the time needed to park a car in a busy area.

Towards the end of the placement, you might wish to make a new set of 'Perfect timing' cards (or encourage the student to do so) and repeat the exercise as completed earlier in the placement. Students can be asked to consider how their organization of time on the placement has been influenced by their experiences of the agency. Are there any changes they would like to make in the way they manage time and workload? In addition, students can be asked to consider if there are any other criteria they would add to the seven which Cathy and Henry identify on pages 118–120.

Activity 11   PERFECT TIMING

Below are 24 activity cards. Arrange the activities into a diary for a working week.

ONE HOUR LUNCH EACH DAY Mon.–Fri. 1 hour *Anywhere*	VISIT TO ASSESS ELDERLY PERSON FOR RESPITE CARE est: 45 mins *Brick Street*	COURT REPORT ON JUVENILE OFFENDER written by Tuesday est: 2 hours *Office*	COURT APPEARANCE some time during Friday morning est: not known *Court*
TEAM MEETING Wednesday weekly 9.30–10.30 *Office*	5 OUTGOING TELEPHONE CALLS est: 30 mins *Office*	WORKING PARTY ON COMMUNITY CARE Wednesday fortnight 2.00–3.30 *Central Office*	VISIT SINGLE PARENT – FINANCIAL PROBLEMS est: 1 hour *Slinn Street*
10 INCOMING TELEPHONE CALLS est: 1 hour *Office*	VISIT ELDERLY MAN WANTING COUNCIL ACCOMMODATION est: 45 mins *Conduit Rd*	DISCUSS TEENAGE MOTHERS' GROUP WITH HEALTH VISITOR est. 1 hour *Clinic*	5 OUTGOING TELEPHONE CALLS (including re-dials) est: 30 mins *Office*
REVIEW ON CHILD IN FOSTER CARE Tuesday 2.00–3.00 *Hill Lane*	PRACTICE MEETING WITH LOCAL HEALTH CARE STAFF Friday, weekly 1.30–2.30 *Clinic*	VISIT CONFUSED ELDERLY WOMAN, SEE DAUGHTER est: 1 hour *Hands Road*	MEET WITH MOTHER, CHILD, STAFF AT DAY NURSERY est: 1 hour *Beet Street*
2 RECORD SUMMARIES, 3 LETTERS, 2 MEMOS est: 1 hour *Office*	5 INCOMING TELEPHONE CALLS est: 30 mins *Office*	2 RECORD SUMMARIES, 3 LETTERS, 2 MEMOS est: 1 hour *Office*	PRACTICE TUTORIAL SESSION Thursday, weekly 9.30–11.00 *Office*
VISIT TO FAMILY EXPERIENCING PROBLEMS est: 1 hour – evening *Elkmore Road*	CASE DISCUSSION WITH PART-TIME O.T. Tue., Wed. or Thu. est: 30 mins *Clinic*	STUDENT SUPPORT GROUP Friday, 1.00–2.30 (usually Thursdays, fortnightly) *Central Office*	DAY DUTY Wednesday 9.00–12.30 *Office*

The office is about a mile from the clinic and street addresses are within 10 minutes' walk of a bus route. Central office and the court are four miles away, 20–30 minutes by bus.

- What criteria do you use to decide how you will plan your week ahead?

Reproduced from *The new social work practice* by Mark Doel and Steven Shardlow, Arena, Aldershot

Notes for practice teachers

Studies of clients' opinions of social work are giving us a clearer view of what clients value (see Barnes and Wistow, 1994; Department of Health, 1995; Lindow and Morris, 1995: Mayer and Timms, 1970). Reliability seems obvious, and the ability to be where you said you would be and to do what you have said you will do is first base for good practice. Is it common?

A placement can start to go wrong when practice teachers make incorrect assumptions about students' basic abilities to organize their own time. This is the first step to managing the workload. It can seem pedantic to investigate how students remember the tasks they have set themselves, or how they collect and store information for regular use. Perhaps this is one reason why these core abilities are often assumed to be present: they are the day-to-day backdrop to the 'real work'.

However, if we begin to look at how people do sort, store and retrieve the information needed to manage their time, we discover a myriad ways of doing this. The only right way is the one which works for that particular person. For some, this means careful colour coding, filofax style; for others, it means lists of jobs to be ticked off on the diary page. Are there any general considerations behind these idiosyncratic systems?

Tasks or information?

The student needs to think about the distinction between data which are prescriptive and data which are informative. Prescriptions, such as 'Telephone Mrs Jones' and 'Arrange the residents' outing', might be described as tasks. They often refer to the short term, but not always: for example, the student may have a task to help an offender to find accommodation before release from prison in four months' time.

Other data are informative, such as the telephone number of the local social security office or the fact that a supervised access visit is due to take place later in the month. The distinction between these two kinds of data influences the way they are stored and retrieved. Useful telephone numbers will need retrieval in a different way from identifying data about a particular person, or information about a specific event.

Social workers are estimated to spend about a quarter of their time engaged in administrative work (Parsloe, 1981), yet students get a small fraction of that in terms of their training for the job. The 'Perfect Timing' activity redresses a little of that balance.

Example

Cathy and Henry were on placement in a small locally based social work team. They completed their 'Perfect timing' diaries independently, then met to discuss how they had arrived at their decisions. These principles came out of their discussion with the practice teacher:

1 *Be clear about the status of each diary entry – is it tentative or definite?* 'Can you tell at a glance what you're doing on Thursday at 2.30?' Henry confessed to making frequent scribbles and deletions; Cathy suggested using pencil until it was confirmed. 'Some feasts are movable and some aren't.'

2 *Prioritize diary entries according to urgency and others' expectations* 'Are you aware of the criteria you used to plan your diary time?' Cathy and Henry had both used urgency as their main priority. Whose circumstances warranted contact early in the week and what promises, if any, had been made about contacting people? They had made very similar decisions about this and expressed pleasure at their like minds.

3 *Pace appointments economically* 'What about the space you've allowed between diary entries?' Cathy and Henry were conscious of working in a neighbourhood and were committed to the localization of services. They were careful to group their destinations to avoid either zipping back and forth across the map or twiddling their thumbs between appointments. They had taken account of their method of transport – car in Cathy's case, foot and bus in Henry's.

4 *Consider what times will accommodate other people involved in the work* 'Have you considered the use of other people's time?' Cathy and Henry had thought about the circumstances of individuals and their families when planning appointments. Nine in the morning might be convenient for the student to visit 83-year-old Mr Cook, but was not a time Mr Cook would welcome. Planning a first visit to a family around school collection time or meal times was not wise either. Cathy liked Henry's suggestion of an evening appointment to include a working parent, and both students had scheduled their diary to accommodate part-time and job-share staff.

5 *Anticipate the unanticipated by building dual-purpose times into the diary* 'How do you cope with unexpected work which disrupts your programme?' Cathy and Henry developed a metaphor which they had found useful in planning their diary time. A diary can be made of cast iron, netting or elastic. A cast-iron diary is unlikely to be able to respond to new demands; on the other hand, the holes in a diary made of netting are liable to allow appointments to fall through. Ideally, the elastic diary has a mix of firm appointments and dual-purpose times, which are scheduled for one purpose (for example, reading a policy paper or making non-priority phone calls) but can stretch or contract for other purposes if necessary.

6 *Anticipate the 'imprint effect'* 'What effect is the experience of one event likely to have on the next?' After the first few weeks of the placement, events in the working week are more familiar, so students can anticipate their after-taste. For example, Cathy and Henry could say whether the working party was likely to leave them feeling stimulated/bored, appreciated/isolated, calm/angry. It is often possible to anticipate how you will feel when visiting clients you already know. Using this information it is possible to obtain the most 'helpful mix' of diary entries – in theory!

7 *Appointments with myself* 'What helps you to keep your batteries topped up?' The most difficult aspect of the diary for Cathy and Henry was planning a regular hour's break each day and setting aside time for professional development, when they could pursue their own research interests and keep abreast of developments in social work. These tended to be given the lowest priority and were readily swallowed up. Yet things like a midday swim and time for professional development were crucial to survival and avoiding burn-out. They both agreed to pen, not pencil, appointments with themselves.

Perfect timing is an ideal to aim for. If students use these principles clearly, coherently and consistently, you can feel confident that they are gaining command of their workload and helping to reduce the stresses of the job.

It is much more important to *work smart, not hard*.

Notes for students

Loose ends

'Perfect timing' develops skills in managing a tight time-budget, by gaining an understanding of the principles you might use to fill a week's diary. These principles will help you to manage the stress which often comes with a full workload. You might also like to look at other examples of how social workers spend their time: see, for example, Barclay (1982, pp. 2–32) – does this 'fit' with current views of how social workers spend their time?

It is just as vital to be able to make use of unstructured time. Perhaps your placement setting allows for a great deal of informal contact with service users: for example, a drop-in centre for people with mental health problems may use a mix of planned individual and group sessions and unplanned contacts around the unit. You may find it more difficult to judge whether you are managing your time well when the boundaries are loose and your day is not stacked with prearranged appointments and meetings.

A good way of learning how to use this kind of time is to keep a personal log for a week (use a small pad and pencil which you can carry around with you conveniently). Make a brief note of the contacts you have made during the week: include those conversations you probably wouldn't normally record, such as chance encounters with people in the kitchen or in the hallway. Review the week's notes with your practice teacher to discuss what happened during these encounters and what follow-up, if any, there was. You will begin to see a network of contacts building up, and be able to discuss ways in which you can create opportunities for these informal conversations. When are the best times during the routine of the day at the centre to 'catch' informal contacts? These are the times when it is important to be visible and available, and not drinking coffee in another room.

The culture of time

We often joke about the way different people seem to have a different conception of the 'speed' of time. This is very evident in groups, where some individuals keep reminding the group of the pressure of deadlines, whilst others look as though there is all the time in the world. It is as though people's clocks go at different speeds.

The experience of time and time-keeping is shaped by our prior experiences and by the culture in our community: for example, we often talk about urban time being faster than rural time. Do the clocks of different cultures move at different speeds and, if so, how should we all take account of this? Is African-Caribbean time slower than Anglo-Saxon time, or is this

Reproduced from *The new social work practice* by Mark Doel and Steven Shardlow, Arena, Aldershot

crass, cultural stereotyping? How does a group of people with different ideas of time and time-keeping negotiate a way of working together, and how do you negotiate the ground between your client's sense of time (they might like to chat for a couple of hours) and your sense of time (you may have five other people to see)?

Reproduced from *The new social work practice* by Mark Doel and Steven Shardlow, Arena, Aldershot

12 Running a meeting

About Activity 12: Topical islands

'Topical islands' represents twelve stages of the meetings process, mapping the stages that meetings need to pass through if they are to be successful. The map represents a journey, with the overland trek from 'Purpose' to 'Punctual start' leading to a sea voyage through the 'Sea of Collaboration', back to the landing point of 'Closure' and the conclusion of the journey, 'Circulating the minutes'. Students use the map, first to analyse the progress of meetings, and then to help them plan and participate effectively in the conduct of a meeting.

Purpose

Meetings are a vital forum for the exchange of information and ideas. Decisions made in meetings have a considerable effect on students' work. A meeting is an opportunity for the student to make an impact, but it can also feel frustrating and intimidating if it is not run properly (see *Meetings, Bloody Meetings*, Video Arts, for a graphic example of this). 'Topical islands' introduces the student to a twelve-point framework for running a meeting: as a participant or as a chairperson, the student is given a basis to judge good practice.

Method

- Ask the student to list meetings attended during the last week. There may have been gatherings which the student has not perceived as meetings as such, so it is useful to look at different kinds of meeting. Take the student through the 'Topical islands' schedule, checking understanding and discussing what it can mean in practice. (Allow 15–20 minutes.)
- Arrange for the student to be an observer at a meeting, using the 'Topical islands' schedule to evaluate the meeting. Repeat this process in a meeting where the student is a participant, and again – ideally – where the student has a chance to chair a meeting. In the latter instance, it helps to video the meeting, with the consent of participants.
- Use the practice tutorial to review the student's use of the schedule. How has their experience of using the schedule influenced the way they think about meetings? Has it changed what the student actually *does* in meetings? (About 30 minutes.)

Variations

The definition of 'meeting' is not clear-cut and there are many links with groupwork. Team meetings, case conferences, residents' meetings, support groups – all have elements which relate to the 'Topical islands' schedule. There may be great variations in the climate of different meetings (for example, the degree of formality or informality), but the essential steps from preparation to closure remain the same. It is interesting for the student to experience different kinds of meeting and to see if the purpose of a meeting is reflected in the way the meeting is run.

Activity 12   TOPICAL ISLANDS

The map shown below represents twelve stages to help a meeting achieve its purposes. The map does not necessarily show the relative size or importance of each stage in any particular meeting. The islands follow a rough sequence, but most meetings are characterized by both *linear* movement from topic to topic, and *circular* movement, with eddies of discussion around each topic explored in detail.

Use 'Topical islands' as a kind of board game to analyse the progress of a meeting. Try it out first in a meeting where the practice teacher is a participant and where the student is an observer. This way, both of you experience the same meeting, with the student able to focus on the 'Topical islands' activity rather than having to contribute to the meeting. Once familiar with 'Topical islands', students can use it in meetings where they are active participants.

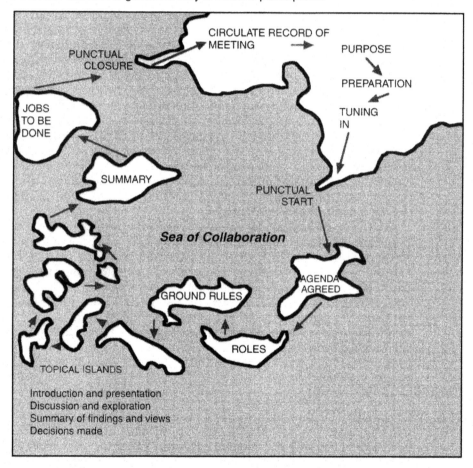

When you are familiar with the way this activity works, construct a 'Topical islands' sheet for a meeting where you are a participant or, better still, the chairperson.

Reproduced from *The new social work practice* by Mark Doel and Steven Shardlow, Arena, Aldershot

Notes for practice teachers

'Topical islands' is designed to help the student to conceptualize what happens in meetings. It also provides a graphic checklist for students to use when they are responsible for chairing meetings, and an illustration of how to help people work effectively together, which is an essential skill for effective chairing of meetings (Douglas, Etridge et al., 1988).

Preparation phase

Preparation begins with the essential question, 'What is the purpose of the meeting?' Inevitably, this leads to a consideration of who should be involved and whether their purposes are likely to be similar or different. Ironically, these are often least clear in well-established meetings, where original purposes may have become obscure. Is the meeting necessary?

Practical arrangements such as timing and venue give messages about the importance attached to the meeting and the amount of consideration given to participants. Minutes of any previous meeting and an agenda for the forthcoming one should be available well in advance. One-line items on agendas are common, but they are often misleading and uninformative. Each topic should have an explanatory sentence or two, including who will address it and what the meeting is being asked to do (a reflective wide-ranging discussion? new resources? more work? a final decision?). If the matter is complex and there is a great deal of information to consider, relevant papers should be available before the meeting, with a digest to help participants to come prepared.

The chairperson should estimate the time needed for each of the items; cramming too many topics into an agenda is demoralizing and irresponsible. A priority order for each item should also be suggested, checking this with participants at the beginning of the meeting. Always assuming that the meeting is finite, with an agreed time to end (not always a safe assumption), the time spent on each topic is also finite. Extra time spent on one topic means less time spent on another. More time spent in one meeting means less time spent in another. These simple mathematical truths are not always appreciated.

Travelling the islands

Starting the meeting on time is necessary in order for participants to know what being late means! It helps no-one to be unclear whether 9.30 means 9.30, 9.45 or 10.00. The welcome and introduction to the meeting should include a statement of purpose and a review of the agenda; if there are disagreements, uncertainties or confused purposes, it is better for them to emerge at the beginning. Rules and roles should be clarified at the beginning: who will take minutes? is smoking allowed? how are decisions going to be taken, by consensus or majority voting?

Once the meeting has established its own ground rules, it can begin work on the agenda. Thinking of the agenda as a map to guide people through the meeting, we can see that movement is both linear (moving from topical island to topical island) and circular (exploring each of the topical islands in more detail). If the movement feels unbalanced, the meeting is probably not working well. Often, the chairperson seeks linear progress, a quick inter-island hop, whilst individuals in the meeting dwell on circular motion, travelling around a topical island a number of times, landing on it and mapping it! If a major expedition to an unexpected location looks likely, the chairperson should ask the meeting to consider additional work on this item outside the meeting.

Closure

Ending the meeting at the agreed time is as important as beginning it punctually, and the chair needs to give regular reminders about how much time is left for the meeting. Each time the meeting leaves one topical island for another, the chairperson should summarize what has been discussed and decided in relation to that topic. It should not be revisited, unless this is essential for work on later items.

In closing the meeting, the chairperson should thank people for their work and give a brief summary of what has been achieved. If this is one of a sequence of meetings, it is useful to have comments on how this meeting has contributed to the overall progress. Decisions should be recorded, along with any action required by individual people before the next meeting: these should be included in the minutes of the meeting, with a record of who attended and any persons who gave their apologies.

Meetings in group care and cooperative living settings

People who live together need to have a forum where problems and aspirations can be aired. However, it is often difficult to step from one mode to another (for example, from informal group living with implicit roles to purposeful gatherings with more explicit roles; see Harris and Kelly, 1991). When people see each other on a daily basis – eating, watching television, socializing – what need is there for a *meeting*? Whoever heard of a family having a meeting, for example?

Yet a meeting is an essential gathering for people whose lives touch each other significantly. Where else are decisions going to be taken? A meeting, properly managed, brings power from behind closed doors into the open, with the opportunity for challenge.

Calling a meeting does not, in itself, guarantee that participation in decision making will be broadened (Tropman, 1980). Meetings can be oppressive and tokenistic with only a semblance of participation. This is not just a question of authoritarian leadership; more insidious is the oppressiveness which comes from *laissez-faire* meetings, where the loudest voices set the agenda because there is no structure to allow quieter voices to be heard. Grumpy talking-shops, with much huff and puff and little action, are a poor substitute for meetings. All members of a meeting share some responsibility for the conduct of the meeting – often groups who meet regularly can benefit from joint training or collaborative work to improve effectiveness and communication (see, for example, Woodcock, 1989).

Welsh, Johnson *et al.* (1989) describe a practical procedure for training chairpersons for meetings in cooperative living groups. The training was considered worth pursuing because of complaints about the length of meetings, lack of productivity and negative tone. The training procedures were developed over three years and they have been maintained successfully for five years. The trainees declared themselves feeling 'better prepared', 'calmer' and 'more confident' in relation to the meetings they ran after their training.

The researchers found that *having a go* was not sufficient to develop skills, and meetings suffered when chairpersons improvised and did not follow the procedures outlined by the checklist. They found that 'practice alone will not produce the levels of performance achieved with training' (Walsh, Johnson *et al.*, 1989). This is a message for practice teaching and learning as a whole.

Notes for Students

Negotiating skills and the 'secret' organization

There are many different kinds of meeting in most organizations, not all of them as open and accessible as the kind guided by the 'Topical islands' map. Meetings are one way of getting things done in an agency, but there are times when the alternative, unwritten procedure manual is more useful. Usually it is as important to know about the unspoken rules in an organization as it is about formal relationships: the secret 'Treasure Island' map often explains behaviour which previously seemed inexplicable.

Bringing the hidden, unspoken agendas into the open requires skill (see Chapter 7, in particular). What Fisher and Ury (1983) describe in *Getting To Yes: Negotiating agreement without giving in*, is an important ability at both interpersonal and organizational levels.

The process of looking at your organization as a focus for change, and the different kinds of skill required to produce this kind of change – open and covert – has been called 'intrapreneurial'. The intrapreneur moves around and between existing bastions of power in the agency, whether this power springs from profession, union, management or a combination of the three. Figure 12.1 shows the intrapreneur's ten commandments (adapted from Pinchot, 1985).

Now ask yourself the following:

- What are the forces for change and stability in your placement agency?
- What is your response to the intrapreneur's ten commandments?

Further ideas

Make of note of each meeting you have been to in the last week or two, and describe what you think were the purposes of the meeting in each case. Were all the participants in agreement with these purposes, or do you think they had other ideas?

Are there any practices in your agency where the informal procedure is markedly different from the formal one? How would you explain the gap between the two, and what is the effect on your work with clients?

Reproduced from *The new social work practice* by Mark Doel and Steven Shardlow, Arena, Aldershot

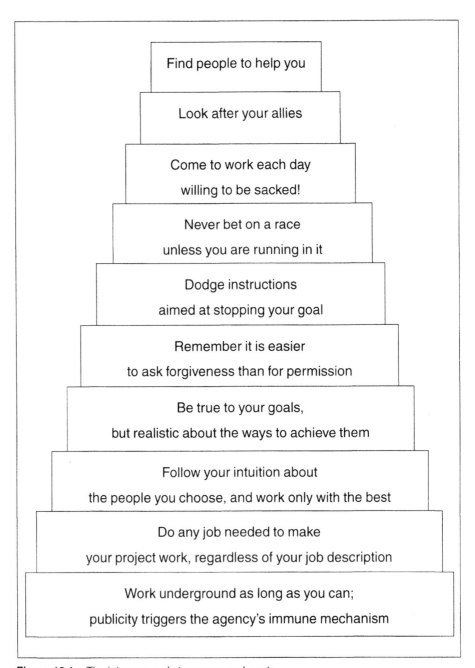

Figure 12.1 The intrapreneur's ten commandments

Reproduced from *The new social work practice* by Mark Doel and Steven Shardlow, Arena, Aldershot

13 Purchasing and providing services

About Activity 13: Travel agent

'Travel agent' invites students to consider buying one of a number of different holidays, the purchase of a holiday providing an analogy for the purchase of social services. The student is asked to consider factors such as high, medium or low season, the price of the holiday, and the remaining monies available for spending.

Purpose

'Travel agent' is designed to encourage students to consider some of the factors involved in making choices about services – in this case a service they might wish to obtain for themselves. Thinking about the factors that are important in making decisions about a holiday helps us to a better understanding of the decisions that must be made in the provision of other services. However, although it is possible to survive without a holiday, it may not be possible to continue living in the community without adequate services.

Method

- 'Travel agent' is best undertaken by a group of three or four students. It can also be undertaken by two people, such as the practice teacher and student.

- Students should read 'Travel agent' and, independently, consider the options for holidays. Ask the students to decide their first choice. In making this selection, students may want to find out if others in the group are considering the same package. If two or more students take the same holiday package they are entitled to a 20 per cent discount on the price, thus increasing their available spending money. However, there is no need to seek consensus. The discount is only one factor to take into account when deciding which holiday to select.
- Once students have decided on their holiday package, ask them to review the reasons for their selection, including the following factors:
    - Type of holiday; overall cost; balance of costs (meals/accommodation, and so on); time of year; location and facilities offered; whether the holiday is 'protected' and facilities inspected; available spending money; other factors.
    - Students should compare the relative importance of different factors in making their preferences.
- In the practice tutorial, students should be encouraged to consider the differences and similarities between the purchase of a holiday and the purchase of services to help an individual remain in the community.

Variations

This simulation can be modified to affect the issues considered by students in a variety of ways. Different factors can be introduced into the holiday, such as the safety or reliability of the travel agency. (You might introduce dice to make some holidays riskier than others – students could lose part or all of the holiday for which they have booked and paid if it is not protected.)

The parameters of the students' choices can be altered. Often, the user of social services has little real or effective choice, and students can experience this by having one student choose a holiday for another, without consultation.

Activity 13   TRAVEL AGENT

Read the following extracts from holiday brochures and decide which holiday you would like to take. Your choice will be influenced by a number of factors, such as the proportion of your budget you wish to spend on price and the proportion this leaves you for spending money.

Decide which holiday you would like to choose, taking account of your income and other commitments.

DISCOUNTS

Holidays are cheaper if you can share with another; if you want to negotiate with a fellow vacationer to share a holiday, you will both benefit from a 20% reduction (i.e. there will be a commensurate increase in your spending money – indicated in italics).

Note that Holiday G is a half-chance lottery – a 50% chance of your name coming up.

(A) Access for people with disabilities

(G) Guaranteed by the International League of Travel Agents

Holiday A

Two weeks in a self-catering cottage near Snowdonia in the heart of North Wales at the height of the summer season. You travel in your own car.

Travel:	EC$* 50
Accommodation:	EC$450
Meals:	EC$250
Spending money	EC$250
Spending money with discount:	*EC$400*

(A)

Holiday B

Ten days' cycling in Brittany, Northern France. Accommodation is provided in farmhouses and small family-run chambres d'hôte. You buy your own lunches. Travel to France is by train and a six-hour ferry.

Travel:	EC$200
Accommodation:	EC$500
Meals:	EC$150
Spending money:	EC$150
Spending money with discount:	*EC$320*

Holiday C

Two weeks in a caravan site in April on the coast of Northumberland. Travel to the campsite by own car. The campsite includes leisure complex with indoor heated pool, bars and theatre. A full programme of entertainment is provided.

Travel:	EC$ 50
Accommodation:	EC$150
Meals:	EC$250
Spending money:	EC$550
Spending money with discount:	*EC$640*

(A)

Holiday D

Three weeks' camping in the South of France during August. The campsite is located by the beach and also has its own outdoor swimming pool, tennis courts, crazy golf, etc. Travel by your own car and through the channel tunnel.

Travel:	EC$300
Accommodation:	EC$150
Meals:	EC$250
Spending money:	EC$300
Spending money with discount:	*EC$440*

(G)

Holiday E

A fly-drive one-week holiday at DisneyWorld in Florida. Accommodation is in one of several different themed hotels with meals included. This holiday can be taken at any time of the year

Travel:	EC$850
Accommodation:	included
Meals:	included
Spending money:	EC$150
Spending money with discount:	*EC$320*

(A) (G)

Holiday F

A two-week cruise on the Nile, visiting the Pyramids. All meals are included and travel is by charter flight.

Travel:	EC$950
Accommodation:	included
Meals:	included
Spending money:	EC$ 50
Spending money with discount:	*EC$240*

(G)

Holiday G

A 50:50 chance of a once-in-a-lifetime trip to Australia for three weeks, which includes stopovers in Sydney, Adelaide and Canberra, as well as a chance to explore the bush with Australia's aboriginal peoples. You pay the all-inclusive price and have *a one-in-two chance* of being selected from the draw.

Travel:	EC$800
Accommodation:	included
Meals:	included
Spending money:	EC$200
Spending money with discount:	*EC$360*

(G)

Holiday H

An Easter-break holiday of ten days in the Greek islands, staying in small hotels. Cost is all-inclusive of flights, but meals are separate.

Travel:	EC$600
Accommodation:	included
Meals:	EC$150
Spending money:	EC$250
Spending money with discount:	*EC$400*

*EC$ = Euro

Reproduced from *The new social work practice* by Mark Doel and Steven Shardlow, Arena, Aldershot

Notes for practice teachers

'Travel agent' is an activity that simulates some aspects of choosing a holiday. At first sight, this seems far removed from social work practice; however, the factors which influence the selection of a holiday are similar to aspects of choice about services for those living in the community. By thinking about those factors involved in a personal holiday, students can empathize with similar choices that confront the person living in the community about the services they receive. It is important, therefore, to encourage students to recognize these parallels and the common features between themselves and service users.

Process of choosing a holiday

People choose holidays in many different ways: as a result of the recommendations of others; for historical reasons (your family has always visited Regularville, the original reasons being long forgotten); through a quiet perusal of holiday brochures at home; or by seeking the advice of professional agents in a travel shop. None of these is preferable in itself, but it is important for the people making the choice to be satisfied both with the process and with the outcome.

Students can think about the similarities and differences inherent in the process of selecting a holiday and 'choosing' a care package. The person choosing a holiday is able to decide independently, to book directly with a holiday company and to purchase the service they require; they are not obliged to consult a travel agent. Compare this with the process of gaining access to social services when the person has to consult an 'agent' (a social worker or care manager). This agent will usually have privileged knowledge of services, in the sense that there is often very little published by way of a brochure about the availability of different services, and be charged with the responsibility of deciding the needs of the customer.

Some key elements that influence holiday choice

No matter what route we take to choose a holiday, certain factors are likely to influence our decisions about the kind of holiday we eventually take. The importance of each of these factors will vary from individual to individual and family to family. A person with disabilities might first look at accessibility, then have to take their budget into consideration. A well-to-do family might look at available entertainment for the children, with less concern for price. Below are some of the factors that may apply when choosing a holiday; these should be discussed with the student during the practice tutorial

- Access
- Availability

- Budget
- Climate
- Convenience
- Diet
- Entertainment
- Facilities
- Lifestyle
- Location
- Price
- Quality of service
- Time of year.

Encourage students to think about the relative importance of these factors in making their decision about the holiday they have chosen, broadening the discussion so that students consider the importance of holidays relative to a service that you may depend on for your well-being on a day-to-day basis (such as home care, meals at home, washing and bathing, or permanent residential care).

Students should also consider the possible kind of information they would expect to have available to guide their choice:

- choice of travel agents for independent advice;
- information direct from holiday companies (the providers of holidays);
- on-line information services to provide updated information about availability and price (Ceefax, and so on);
- ability to negotiate directly with the holiday company;
- information available at no charge;
- detailed brochures available about a variety of holidays throughout the world;
- availability of many different types of holiday;
- varying levels and packages of insurance (for the individual, concerning cancellation, theft, loss and medical costs; and for the holiday, itself, concerning the company's liability, and so on);
- procedures for complaints.

How far are similar facilities and options open to the person who is making choices about care in the community?

Oliver, recasting Titmus's ideas, has argued that it should be possible in principle to create a social services system to provide choice for people:

> It should be possible to allow for choice and control in service provision within a universal infrastructure if consumers have social rights to these services and if there are mechanisms whereby the needs of groups and communities, whether local or interest communities, can be articulated by them, themselves. (Oliver, 1990, p. 99)

Similar themes are expressed in the 1975 UN Declaration of Rights for Disabled People, which emphasizes the importance of being self-reliant, to have choice over how to live, and to be able to participate in social, recreational and creative opportunities of communities. However, the real question is not one of principle about desirability, but how to achieve the UN Declaration of Rights or Oliver's prescriptions in practice, within existing political and social structures.

Making 'care in the community' work

According to the Social Services Inspectorate, care management can be understood as a number of processes:

Stage 1

Prospective users and carers receive information about the need for which care agencies accept responsibility to offer assistance and the range of services currently available.

Stage 2

If an inquirer requests more than information or advice, basic information is taken about the need in question, sufficient to determine the type of assessment required.

Stage 3

A practitioner is allocated to assess the needs of the individual and of any carers in a way that also recognizes their strengths and aspirations. In order to take account of all relevant needs, the assessment may bring together contributions from a number of other specialists or agencies. The purpose of the assessment is to define the individual's need in the context of local policies and priorities and agree on the desired outcome of any involvement.

Stage 4

The next step is to consider the resources available from statutory, voluntary, private or community sources that best meet the individual's requirements. The role of the practitioner is to assist the user in making choices from these resources, and to construct an individual care plan.

Stage 5

The implementation of that plan means securing the necessary finance o other identified resources. It may involve negotiation with a variety of service providers, specifying the type and quality of service required, and ensuring that services are coordinated with one another. The responsibilit of practitioners at this stage will vary according to the level of their delegated budgetary authority.

Stage 6

Because circumstances change, the implementation of the care plan has to be continuously monitored, making adjustments, as necessary, to the services provided and supporting the users, carers and service providers in achieving the desired outcomes.

Stage 7

At specified intervals, the progress of the care plan has to be formally reviewed with the user, carers and service providers: first to ensure that services remain relevant to needs and, secondly, to evaluate services as part of the continuing quest for improvement.

Within this process there are many necessary social work skills, some of which are detailed in other chapters of this book (for example, Chapters 6–9). The essence of the process of care management as stated by the Social Services Inspectorate is located in the assessment of people's needs, the construction and purchase of a care plan to meet those needs, and the review of the effectiveness of this plan. Hence the so-called 'purchaser–provider' split in agencies has developed, where some staff will be entirely concerned with assessing people's need for services and purchasing those from within a limited budget, while others may be concerned with the provision of services.

Care in the community provides considerable opportunities for the involvement of the user. The question is, how to achieve involvement for users in the process of care management? Breeforth (1993, p. 23) characterizes traditional professional attitudes to the involvement of users in relation to an example drawn from the provision of mental health service as follows:

> The officials' view
> > we're the providers of mental health services
> > we know what is best
> > we have to organise services
> > we must have user participation
> > let's set up a users' group
> > do we know any users we can ask?

Breeforth suggests instead that social workers must adjust the way that they think about the involvement of users as follows:

> How to involve users
> > get users together
> > leave us alone to talk

> invite us onto your committees
> listen to what we say
> give us information
> pay our expenses

Involving service users in the process of community care is not a simple process. Lindow and Morris (1995), reviewing published research, found evidence of several barriers to the involvement of service users:

- the division of people into service user groups (for example, older people, people with sensory impairment);
- consulting with carers rather than service users;
- exclusion of service users' views because of perceptions about the incapacity of the user to understand or communicate (for example, due to dementia);
- differences of culture and language;
- the marginalization of some groups (for example, older people);
- the difficulties of being clear who is representative of whom and to whom are people accountable.

Notes for students

Caring for people in their own homes entails a set of complex tasks. These tasks are ostensibly for social workers, yet there are those who do not regard this as a part of social work at all. For instance, many local authorities in the UK are appointing people without social work qualifications to undertake the assessment of need and the planning and reviewing of required care. There have always been debates about 'what is' and 'what is not' social work (see Chapter 20). In the UK, in the 1990s, government has defined probation practice as different from social work. We would assert most strongly that the provision of care in the community is a definite and central part of social work practice.

'Care in the community' is laden with a whole host of ideological associations and a variety of terminologies has developed to refer to the provision of care for people living in the community. Some of these are given below, along with some key associative ideas. See which words convey which ideas.

Key terms	Associations
community-based work	care at home
care in the community	care provided by family
community care	care provided by men
community work	care provided by neighbours
community action	care provided by women
domiciliary care	empowerment
informal care	involvement of the local community
locally based work	mobilization of resources
neighbourhood work	participation
patch-based work	practical services
voluntary work	radical action
accessibility of service providers	value for money
	volunteers

What other associations can you find?

Consider which of the associations are positive and which negative.

Reproduced from *The new social work practice* by Mark Doel and Steven Shardlow, Arena, Aldershot

History of community care

The development of care in the community is difficult to describe briefly, especially since the origins of the term 'community care' are indeterminate. As long ago as the 1960s Titmus (1968) stated that he had unsuccessfully attempted to identify the genesis of the idea. According to Means and Smith (1994), community care originally referred to the notion of a policy shift from the provision of hospital-based care to care in the community for people with either learning difficulties or mental health problems. The scope of the term community care (or care in the community) now encompasses a wide range of people and is applied to all vulnerable adults who need some form of care – where that care is provided by means other than the removal of that person to a residential unit on a permanent basis.

A strong influence on the development of models of care management in the UK has been the case management approach (see Moxley, 1989), developed in the US and the work of the Personal Social Services Research Unit (PSSRU). Case management evolved in the US as a method to organize, manage and review a complex range of services provided by various organizations in the community. Similarly, concepts of assessment, planning, delivering and reviewing services were extensively researched in the Kent Community Care Scheme, which explored the abilities of a specialist team of social workers to prevent admission of older people into residential care by the provision of alternative services (Davies and Challis, 1986). The seminal Griffiths Report, incorporating ideas derived from both case management and from the PSSRU, stated that action should be taken to enable people to stay in their own homes for as long a period as possible, and that 'residential, nursing home and hospital care is reserved for those whose needs cannot be met in any other way' (Griffiths, 1988, p. 28).

Government was receptive to the clear ideological message behind this statement, that it is desirable wherever possible for people to live in their own homes and that there should be services available to people to help them continue to live at home. Through the White Paper, *Caring for People* (Department of Health, 1989) and the NHS and Community Care Act of 1990, a legal and procedural framework for the provision of care in the community has been established. The White Paper proposed six key objectives for the successful development of care in the community:

- the development of domiciliary, day and respite service to enable people to live in their own homes;
- provision of services for those who care for others, so that they are helped to continue to provide care;
- increased importance of high-quality and detailed assessment of need, leading to the construction of a care plan for individuals who need care;

Reproduced from *The new social work practice* by Mark Doel and Steven Shardlow, Arena, Aldershot

- encouragement of a mixed 'economy of care', so that there should be an independent sector of private and voluntary services in addition to state services;
- clear differentiation of the roles of respective agencies;
- to secure better value for the money spent by the taxpayer on community care.

It has, therefore, been recognized by government that most people who live in the community and who need help with the tasks of daily living receive that help from family, friends and neighbours (DoH, 1989). For those who receive help from social workers, the development of systems for care management has substantially altered the way in which services are provided. Many different systems of care management are evolving in different parts of the UK and elsewhere (Challis, Davies and Traske, 1994).

A brief guide to key concepts in care management

Care management has introduced a new range of ideas and terminology into the social work lexicon. You need to survive in this brave new world, so here are a few key concepts:

Assessment

There is an established literature about the assessment of clients from a variety of different perspectives. Care management has introduced the idea of a 'needs-led assessment', implying an integrated assessment for all services which does not presuppose the outcome at the point of assessment and which provides access to a range of services. For example, an assessment for meals in the home should not lead to the assessment for this service alone, but to an identification of the dietary and other needs of the person requesting help, and the planning of the best way to meet the identified needs.

Care planning

After the assessment of need, the social worker will draw up a care plan which will detail how the needs are to be met. Care plans should involve all the relevant people – service user, relatives, carers and professionals – who will be involved in the provision of care. The social worker or care manager has the responsibility for purchasing the services to meet these needs. It is from this point in the process that the 'purchaser–provider' split emanates. To ensure that the care manager does not merely link clients to pre-existing services in the care manager's agency, there is an organizational split between the purchaser of services for the client and the provider of those

Reproduced from *The new social work practice* by Mark Doel and Steven Shardlow, Arena, Aldershot

services. To return to the holiday analogy in 'Travel agent', this means that the organization purchasing a holiday on your behalf (the travel agent) would not be the same as the organization providing the holiday (the travel company). Plans must be sensitively organized and flexible:

> A package of care is not like a basket of goods and services; it is a fluid set of human relationships and arrangements. The care manager's main tasks will be to make the efforts of the people involved coherent; to ensure that the care of a dependent person is not dropped like the baton of a badly co-ordinated relay team. (Smale, Tuson *et al.*, 1994, p. 4)

Care planning is a detailed process, not merely a single event. It involves monitoring of the quality of services and reviewing the continuing need for those services. For more detail about the nature of care planning, see Orme and Glastonbury (1993) and Payne (1995).

Contracts

There is an established body of literature about the use of contracts in social work, and much of this relates to agreements between the social worker and the client. In care management, the social worker contracts with a service provider for a particular service to be supplied to an individual. Meredith (1995) identifies three different types of contract:

- *Block contracts* refer to a given amount of service purchased in advance (for example, all the places in a day centre for six months). If this is the sole provision, it may reduce choice, or the places may not be fully taken, which increases the costs per place for the purchaser.
- *Spot contracts* apply when a 'unit' of service is purchased (for example, so many hours of home care for one person). The provider may be very vulnerable to fluctuations in demand, but this type of contract can provide the purchaser with choice if there are many providers.
- *Cost and volume contracts* represent a compromise between block and spot contracts: the purchaser agrees to purchase either a minimum level of service or contributes to the fixed costs of the provider.

Inspection

Social workers have always been concerned with the quality of services that people receive. The process of care management has introduced and strengthened the notion that all services should be inspected by independent inspection units. Such inspections should be concerned not only with the basic physical standards of service provision but also basic values. For example, the Social Services Inspectorate has stated that the maintenance of values such as privacy, dignity, independence, choice, rights and fulfilment should be evaluated when inspecting residential homes.

Reproduced from *The new social work practice* by Mark Doel and Steven Shardlow, Arena, Aldershot

There is a great deal of published guidance about care management, much emanating from government. To develop your own understanding of these complex processes and how these might best be operated, try talking to groups of service users about how they experience the process.

Reproduced from *The new social work practice* by Mark Doel and Steven Shardlow, Arena, Aldershot

IV

Themes of practice

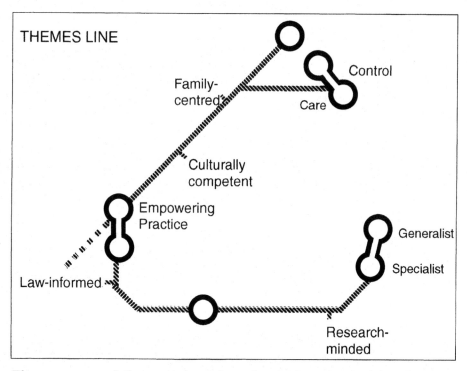

There are several themes in social work which are essential to learning good practice. These make up the core elements which run throughout the whole curriculum for practice learning. They change only slowly in response to new social circumstances and they constitute the fundamentals of practice.

We have chosen seven aspects, which we think provide the bedrock for social work practice. Although these aspects constitute Part IV of this book, it has been difficult to know where best to place them. They should come both before *and* after the learning which takes place in the other Parts, or perhaps they should come neither before nor after, but *through* the other chapters. As themes of practice, they offer different perspectives on each of the other chapters in this book: if these others run 'north–south', then the seven in Part IV run 'east–west'.

Care and control (Chapter 14) has been a continuing and enduring theme in social work practice, and this chapter helps students consider the issues when assessing danger, balancing risks and contemplating intervention.

Family-centred practice (Chapter 15) looks the family squarely in the face and, for better or for worse, places it centre stage. Students and practice teachers are asked to use their own experiences to think about power and decision making in families: partnership with the wider family means developing an understanding of the various *protocols*, or ways of acting, which different families develop, and the skills to work with them.

The continuum of Culturally competent practice (Chapter 16) is a measure for students to understand their own cultural inheritance and that of others. In particular, it deals with the impact of race, gender, class and creed on behaviours, customs, values and institutions. Students learn to recognize cultural incompetence in individuals, agencies and systems, and aim to challenge it.

In Chapter 17, Empowering practice, students focus on themes which have been running through other chapters in the book – issues of power, inequality and anti-discriminatory practice. This chapter guides students in their struggle to make notions such as empowerment and partnership a reality in their practice.

In Law-informed practice (Chapter 18), students examine their own response to the law and learn the importance of understanding a legal framework rather than memorizing the details of countless laws. The notion of *practice dilemma* is introduced to help demystify the law and legal processes.

Research-minded practice (Chapter 19) focuses on the student's attitudes towards research. The aim of this activity is to help the student to see parallel processes in social work and research, and to include research in the student's frame of reference.

Finally, is it strange that a profession should continually be asking itself what it is? Social work's identity crisis is not new to our times, and the final chapter in Part IV focuses on an enduring theme, Generalist and specialist practice. It places the tension between generic, general and specialist practice in its historical context and suggests a framework to help students (the future standard-bearers for the profession) understand the common base of social work.

Chapters 14–20 isolate the themes of practice for the purpose of teaching and learning, but these themes are not confined to these chapters and activities alone. We have been mindful of the need to include material throughout the book which resonates with these seven themes.

14 Care and control

About Activity 14: Dial 'D' for Danger

'Dial "D" for Danger' consists of six different scenarios which students rank according to how dangerous they consider the situations to be for the individual client or others. By taking account of this 'risk ranking', students indicate their propensity to intervene.

Purpose

'Dial "D" for Danger' is intended to help students explore the complex issues involved where social work practice is at the crossroads of caring for people and/or seeking to control some aspects of their lives.

Method

Before undertaking this activity you will need to copy the dials on page 150. This consists of six 'dials of danger' and six 'dials of intervention'.

- 'Dial "D" for Danger' is best completed by a group of students and a practice teacher working together, though it can be used by a practice teacher and student pair. Give the students the list of scenarios (page 149), and ask them to rank them according to the 'dial of danger' (about 10 minutes). Then, ask the students to indicate their propensity to intervene (a further 10 minutes).

- If you are working with a group of students, you can encourage them to discuss why they have made their particular risk-ranking decisions, and to explore the reasons for their propensity to intervene in any given situation. (Allow 30–40 minutes.)

Variations

You may find it is better to devise your own distinctive scenarios to fit with the nature of practice within your own agency. For example, if the student is placed in a children and families team, you may wish to create scenarios that relate only to these kinds of situation.

'Dial "D" for Danger' can be completed independently by students and used as an exercise for discussion in a practice tutorial.

Activity 14 DIAL 'D' FOR DANGER

Think about the following six scenarios and consider:

1   how dangerous the situation is for the client or for others;
2   your own willingness to intervene in each case.

Scenario 1

Gillandi is a 49-year-old woman who is a chronic alcoholic (and has been for at least 10 years). She has a husband (who is self-employed as a painter–decorator) and two children, young women aged 17 and 19. Recently she has been drinking particularly heavily. There has been a series of incidents where she has almost injured herself or others. A week ago she was nearly run over by a car; two weeks ago she allowed food to burn on the cooker, causing a small fire in the kitchen.

Scenario 2

Winston, a British African-Caribbean male aged 19, has been found guilty of several different crimes (including burglary and taking and driving cars) by the court. He has been sentenced to six months' home-based curfew between the hours of 8 p.m. and 8 a.m. for six nights per week. During the first three months he does not seek to break the curfew and spends the one night that his curfew is not in force working at a youth project for offenders. He is very well liked by all at the youth project. In the second part of the sentence Winston continues with the work at the youth project and maintains his curfew except for one night each week. He is evasive and will not tell you what he is doing during that time. In all other respects Winston is conforming to all the court's expectations.

Scenario 3

Howard is a well-educated white man in his 30s. About two years ago he lost his job – one carrying considerable responsibilities with a large commercial enterprise. Since then, he has experienced financial difficulties leading to the break-up of his marriage and loss of family home. He now lives on benefit in social housing. He is adamant that he can care for the two children, a boy aged 6 and a girl aged 8. The school has expressed some concern about the children not being fed properly and arriving at school hungry.

Scenario 4

In the area served by your office there is a large block of high-rise flats run by the local authority. These flats are in a poor state of repair and decoration. Many of them are damp. No facilities exist for children to play and there have been many muggings and attacks on local residents in the lifts and communal areas. There are several residents who wish to take action to improve the state of the flats. One of the residents asks you to organize a public meeting to bring people together to take action about the condition of the flats, but some of the other residents are not enthusiastic about involving social services.

Scenario 5

Bob is a white 85-year-old, living on his own in a small flat provided by the local authority. For the last year he has encountered difficulties in living on his own. Neighbours have complained to the local authority that his flat is smelly and that there is rubbish accumulating inside and outside the flat. On a visit to his flat, he allows you to see the inside: it is in a chaotic and filthy condition. Bob is obviously not eating properly, and the state of the kitchen is bad. His clothes are dirty and he smells. In conversation, his memory appears to be failing. Yet he says he is content.

Scenario 6

Two people in their 20s, Robert and Sally, with moderate learning difficulties, have married and set up home together in a local authority flat. They are both determined to be as independent as possible. They decide to have a baby and just before the baby is due state that they do not need the help of social services any longer now that they are to become parents.

Reproduced from *The new social work practice* by Mark Doel and Steven Shardlow, Arena, Aldershot

Dials of danger

Without consulting any of your colleagues, complete the following rankings for each of the scenarios.

The more dangerous you consider the example, the higher the ranking on the dial of danger (minimal risk = 1; mild risk = 2/4; moderate risk = 5/7; considerable risk = 8/10, maximum risk = 12). The numbers in the centre of the dials refer to the scenarios.

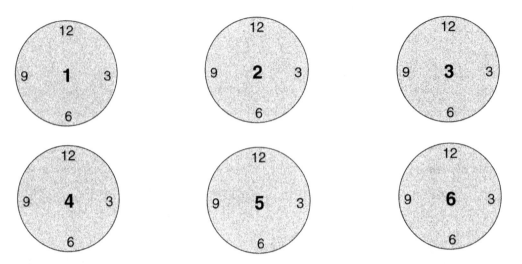

Propensity to intervene

Taking account of the dangerousness of the situation, you should now grade your willingness to intervene, by rating from 1 = no inclination to intervene to 12 = no choice but to intervene.

Reproduced from *The new social work practice* by Mark Doel and Steven Shardlow, Arena, Aldershot

Notes for practice teachers

'Dial "D" for Danger' presents students with an apparently simple task: to categorize their propensity to intervene according to their perception of the degree of danger in a range of situations involving service users. The 'propensity to intervene' and the 'degree of danger' encourage students to compare two different dimensions of response to these situations. It might be assumed that a high degree of danger would have a correlation with a high propensity to intervene, and therefore lead to intervention. However, we know that this is not the case (many women are in situations of extreme danger in domestic disputes, but this does not necessarily lead to a police presence), and there are many other factors which come into play. Encourage students to explore the reasons for their responses, which are likely to be bound up with a range of factors, including:

- attitudes to taking control;
- cultural views about acceptable behaviour;
- fear of making mistakes;
- fears about own safety;
- beliefs about the role of the social worker in society;
- confidence about professional judgement;
- knowledge of the legal context of social work practice.

Example

Sue Shuk Wan had achieved a high level of competence on her first placement with children and families. Her second placement in an adults' team was proving a little more difficult. Sue's Chinese parents had moved to Britain when she was only two. Brenda, her practice teacher, noticed that Sue found great difficulty in deciding when to intervene in the lives of older people. When Sue completed 'Dial "D" for Danger' she gave a very high danger ranking to Scenario 5, yet demonstrated a very low propensity to intervene. In discussion she was reluctant to discuss her reasons, but it was clear to Brenda that Sue had difficulty with this scenario. No more was said at this point. A few weeks later Brenda asked Sue to repeat the exercise with some specially created scenarios, all about older people. One of these concerned the situation of an older Chinese woman living alone, which by chance mirrored Sue's grandmother's situation. Using this example she found it possible to discuss her own attitudes to old age, and intervening in the lives of older people, which were located in her own personal and cultural identity.

Intervening in the lives of other people may curtail their rights to live independently and may challenge a central notion of social work practice – the commitment to promoting empowerment. Stevenson and Parsloe (1993) identify three categories where intervention may be required:

- *Physical risk* Circumstances where the individual may harm themselves or cause harm to others. In these cases social workers may have to decide, either alone or in conjunction with others, on the extent of that risk as in the case of somebody who is mentally ill and threatening harm.

- *Social risk* Individuals whose behaviour isolates and alienates them from others should be encouraged to behave in a more socially acceptable fashion; in addition neighbours and family can also be encouraged to understand and manage these behaviours.
- *Emotional risk* Circumstances where the physical health or emotional well-being of people is put at risk by the role that they occupy; for example, where a person has the sole care of another highly dependent individual.

Identification of level of risk

Ascertaining levels of risk is always a complex issue (Singleton and Holden, 1994; Adams, 1995). Students may identify that a situation has a high level of risk for one or more individuals but may be unsure of the grounds on which they might intervene. Usually, powers of intervention will be defined by statute (see Chapter 18). Students can be encouraged to think about whether intervention in these situations is likely to be perceived by others as a demonstration of care or the imposition of control over the way that individuals conduct their lives – or a combination of both.

If it is possible to estimate the level of risk with some degree of accuracy, then a professionally balanced decision about whether it is necessary to intervene is also possible. The estimation of level of risk depends on detailed knowledge about the potential causes of risk and how to apply that knowledge to a particular situation. Corby (1996) notes that in the field of child protection there has been a considerable growth, especially in the US, in the number of risk assessment instruments: the most widely used is P. Milner's (1986) Child Abuse Potential Inventory for which a very high success rate is claimed. For a review of some of these assessment instruments see Doueck, English et al. (1993).

Assessing risk is very difficult when people have a number of different risk factors in their lives: the identification of risk that a child might be abused by its parents requires different knowledge from the estimation of risk that people with mental illness will harm themselves or others, and different again from the associated risks for some people with physical disabilities in performing certain tasks (Kemshall and Pritchard, 1996). However, in each case there are common questions to be considered when making a judgement about risk:

- What is the nature of the risk – is it life-threatening or a minor inconvenience?
- What is the level of risk – is it high or low? There is some risk attached to crossing the road, yet for many people it is a risk taken every day because the incidence of accidents is low relative to the number of people crossing roads.
- Is there a risk to a minor or a vulnerable person?

Care and control

- Is it a risk to a person who is able to judge the level of risk for themselves, or are they prevented from doing so?
- Is this a subjective or an objective definition of risk – is there agreement among those involved about the determination of the risk?
- What protection can people take for themselves against the risk?
- Are there risks if you do intervene, and how are these weighed against non-intervention?

The answers to these questions help to determine whether or not intervention is suggested.

Notes for students

Debates over whether social work is an activity that promotes care or control are long-standing. Consider the following apparent contradiction:

> Professional codes of practice for social workers tend to affirm a core professional value that social work is about helping other people to achieve their aspirations, in other words, to empower them (see BASW, 1986; IFSW, 1988; NASW, 1996). Yet, social work also has a duty, often enshrined in law, to protect certain categories of vulnerable people, such as those who by virtue of age or infirmity are unable to protect themselves.

Balancing care and control

Social work has a duty to do both: to control certain forms of behaviour and to care for vulnerable individuals. For example, it would be unthinkable to allow children in group care to behave as they pleased, yet there must be acceptable limits to the ways in which behaviour is controlled (Department of Health, 1993). A problem may arise when social workers have almost complete control over the lives of vulnerable individuals, as in group care, and there have been several well-reported examples where that power has been abused (Clough, 1996). There is no reason to suppose that care and control cannot be balanced. Being a parent involves both caring for and controlling a child's behaviour, and successful parents are able to demonstrate love and control – if not without tensions!

> It seems as if there's no happy medium. You either let them out and you're careless, or you keep them in and you're over protective, and your lad's gonnae have a accident because you cannae teach it to be street wise if you've got him in the house. (Roberts, Smith and Bryce 1995, p. 66 – from a study by Brown and Harris)

This parent expresses well some of the dilemmas implicit in both caring for somebody and seeking to put limits on their behaviour. A similar dilemma can be seen in the following example from social work practice:

> John Newton was a likeable chap – twenty two years old, not steadily employed, but always willing to help. Even before Ray Dunkirk, the community worker, had arrived on the scene, Newton had organized a number of young adults into a club. This club was well known in the neighbourhood for the many helpful services it provided. The community's elderly population was especially appreciative of the security service this group gave them. Thefts, holdups, and even murder of older people had ceased ever since the club began to operate in the community. But Dunkirk also became aware that Newton intimidated local store owners and obtained small payoffs from them in return for promising them 'protection'.
> What was Ray to do? He considered various options, including the following:
>
> To overlook Newton's protection racket in view of the many positive things he was doing that were benefiting the community.

Reproduced from *The new social work practice* by Mark Doel and Steven Shardlow, Arena, Aldershot

> To report Newton's protection racket to the police, since illegal activities should never be condoned.
>
> To strengthen his relations with Newton with the view of helping to guide him away from the illegal activity, but in the meantime not to report the law violation to the police.
> (Loewenberg and Dolgoff, 1988, p. 118)

What would you do?

The protection of one individual, whether child or adult, may entail a restriction on their rights to behave as they choose or it may restrict others. In such situations social workers are placed in an invidious position in having to fulfil two contradictory imperatives. This is exemplified by the cartoon (Figure 14.1) in which the social worker cannot win.

A difficulty for social work is to determine when to intervene, even if there are legal grounds for so doing: in other words, what standards of behaviour are acceptable and what standards prompt social workers to intervene? The practice method described in Chapter 8 guides students in deciding what sanctions their involvement and whether they have a 'mandate' for intervention. Even so, the problem of determining socially and culturally acceptable standards for intervention remains a complex problem for society in general and social work practice in particular.

At the level of sociological analysis, social work may be seen by some to be a force for the social control of deviant behaviour and social minorities: for example, a Marxist view of social work would identify such control as being exercised in the interests of maintaining the power of the ruling élite (see Chapter 2). Social work may be experienced by individuals as an unwelcome interruption of the way they choose to live their lives, or as a positive and caring experience.

Reproduced from *The new social work practice* by Mark Doel and Steven Shardlow, Arena, Aldershot

Figure 14.1 'The social worker cannot win?' by Kevin Kallaugher

15 Family-centred practice

About Activity 15: Whanau

'Whanau' is an activity which puts students in touch with the family dimension of social work practice, by looking at decision making and power in their own families. The activity is inspired by Maori practices in New Zealand, where a radical approach to decision making in the area of child welfare has put the wider family centre stage. The approach is called *whanau*, from the Maori word for family.

Purpose

For good or bad, the family is a major influence on the lives of children and adults, and it is important to be able to work with the idea and the reality of family. This chapter aims to put students in touch with their own feelings about families and develops the theme of partnership in work with families.

Method

- You need a blank sheet of paper on which to draw your family tree, starting with yourself towards the bottom of the page. Use the model in the 'Whanau' example (page 159), with the symbols described. Discuss your family as you draw it. Next, ask the student to go through the same process. (You need to check beforehand that the student is comfortable with this request.)

- When you have both completed family trees and you have an idea of who is who, discuss the three questions (to be found on page 159), about power and decision-making in your respective families.
- Discuss your views of families – positive and negative responses – and the political context of 'the family'. Are the student's thoughts and feelings concerning families likely to prevent or help working in partnership with families? (Allow 30–60 minutes.)

Variations

If 'Whanau' is used with a small group, it is best for one of the group leaders to model the process on a flipchart and then ask the group to work in pairs, sharing as much as they wish with the large group. Professionals are often particularly hostile to the idea of their relatives having any say in their family's decisions. If they have 'escaped their background', they may emphasize friendships rather than kinships, but this may not reflect the values of the people they work with. When the chips are down, many people rely on the wider family in a crisis, and given the choice between decisions made by professionals and those made by the broader family, many – perhaps most – prefer the latter.

Activity 15 WHANAU

Whanau is the Maori word for family. The Maori perspective on family decision making is having an impact on services to both Maori and Pakeha (white) populations in Aotearoa (New Zealand). The professionals act as facilitators to bring family members together to make a collective decision about the care and welfare of children in the family. (Decisions about prosecution in child protection cases are made by the courts.) Relatives come from great distances, from overseas if necessary, to be included in the family decision-making meeting, which can sometimes take all day (Wilcox *et al.*, 1991).

To begin to appreciate this perspective we need to understand our own families and understand how each family develops its own 'protocol', or ways of doing things.

Using symbols (circles for females and squares for males), draw a family tree going back as far as your grandparents, if you can. Make sure you include all the branches and off-shoots: cousins, step-aunts, and so on. If you have children, you may wish to draw the tree from their point of view, to include their other parent's branch of the tree. Put a line through any symbol which represents a person who has died.

Below is an example family tree.

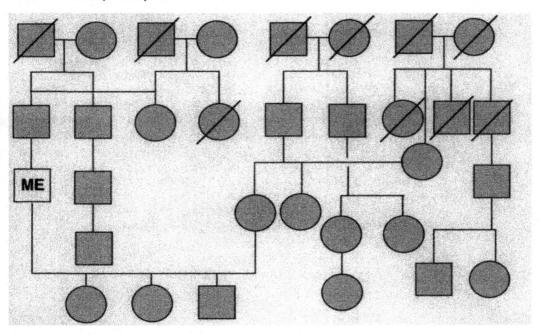

Consider these questions

- Who makes the decisions in your family and home?
- If there were a family conference whom would you want invited? Whom not?
- Who is powerful in your family?

Maori dissatisfaction with Pakeha (white European) ways of doing things led to a reassertion of their idea of family decision making. It is interesting that both Maori and Pakeha populations are now using the *whanau* system successfully.

Special thanks to Larry Monu, Judy Moore, Maraea Ropata and Harry Walker

Reproduced from *The new social work practice* by Mark Doel and Steven Shardlow, Arena, Aldershot

Notes for practice teachers

The 'Whanau' activity is designed to put people in touch with their own experiences of family. Whether the student's feelings towards their own family are shrouded in a warm, misty glow or are pushed to a fractured, frosty distance, it is important that they gain some understanding of the impact this has on their general attitude to families. Professional practice begins with an ability to draw on these experiences without generalizing from them.

Deficits model and strengths model

Of all the paradoxical and ambivalent feelings which we bring to our social work practice, those attached to the idea of the family are probably the strongest. The notion of the family has had a bad press, coming under fire from many directions. The influence of psychodynamic theories on early social work emphasized parental responsibility for dysfunctional families. Later developments in existential psychiatry (the anti-psychiatry movement) saw families as the oppressive tool of a sick society, with powerless individuals scapegoated by powerful others in the family (Laing and Esterson, 1964). Ironically, both psychiatry and anti-psychiatry had the same effect: to pile blame and guilt on the family and to confirm professional distrust of families. How can the family be part of the solution when it is part of the problem?

The family has also been a political football, too often exploited by the Right as a cheap source of care for increasing numbers of citizens, young and old. Professionals have been properly suspicious of a definition in which 'the family' equals 'unsupported female carers at home'.

Stated baldly, it is paradoxical that most abuse occurs by family members on their own kin, yet the best protection is offered by the family, in its wider sense.

Families as allies

The deficits model of the family is being challenged by the strengths model. Instead of dwelling on pathology, the social worker concentrates on the family's capacities and builds on these. It can be surprisingly difficult for some practitioners to identify any strengths. This is partly explained by the legacy of training in pathology spotting, but also results from a tendency to define the family in a narrow, nuclear way. The wider family is often unknown to the practitioner, and even a father can be excluded from the picture, especially if he is not around during the daytime.

The deficits in the care system as an alternative source of protection for the child are becoming clear. If a child has suffered abuse by an individual or individuals in the family, the child's removal can compound this abuse

As we discovered in Chapter 14, the balance of risks – inside and outside the family – is difficult to estimate.

The family is its own best expert. Family members have far more knowledge of themselves and contact with each other than professionals can ever hope to achieve, and decisions can only be effective if family members are allies in those decisions.

In addition to the history of mistrust already described, many professionals have trouble setting aside their training and background to take a fresh look at the contributions families can make. The Families as Allies Project (Portland, Oregon) has pioneered training events for families and professionals together, in equal numbers, to help them take an honest look at each other and to develop collaborative methods of working. This kind of collaboration has spawned wider participation by families as *advocates* in policy making.

Whanau: family decision making

Whanau decision making is a process which recognizes the central role of the family:

> The history of all peoples includes models of families (in their widest sense) accepting responsibility for their own children and, indeed, exerting control over their own members. They do this in a way which cannot be accessed by non-family members. (Wilcox et al., 1991)

Wilcox *et al.* (1991) describe the family group conference as the culmination of a process in which a coordinator brings together the broadest possible range of family members – aunts, uncles, grandparents and cousins, as well as parents and children. Distance is no obstacle, so family members come from the length and breadth of the country, financed by the social services: in British terms, cousins from Cornwall and Kent would have a conference with family members in Caithness.

The *whanau* decision-making process separates the investigation process from the family decision-making process. Decisions about who will be prosecuted in abuse cases are taken by the police, and decisions about the care of the child are taken by the wider family. A key factor in the success is the social work department's willingness and ability to give financial support for the family's decisions, where reasonable and where necessary. Even so, 'it was discovered that families almost always needed fewer resources than state care systems ... the remarkable thing is that most families ask for nothing' (Wilcox et al., 1991).

Parents often say that there is no-one else in their family willing to take any responsibility for their children, but practice has shown that this is just not true for almost all the families with whom the New Zealand social workers have worked. Parents may say the matter is no business of their mother, brother, aunt, and so on, yet those same parents would want to be involved in decisions affecting the care of their nephew, niece or cousin.

What parents are most frightened of is disapproval and anger over present or past events, and it is essential that the family has private discussion time away from the professionals, because there are always things they will not say in front of professionals and these things may be crucial.

The decision about the child's care is made by family members (including the child) on their own, with the professionals *outside* the room. The decision can take anything from 15 minutes to three or four hours, and occasionally all day. It is important that all the family stays until a decision about the child's care is agreed, and the coordinator keeps the family fed, watered and comfortable. In the rare event that the family makes a decision which the professionals simply cannot work with, the matter is referred to court. However, trusting the family's decisions has resulted in an extraordinary 90 per cent of children previously in sole guardianship of the state now placed successfully with their wider families (Wilcox et al., 1991).

If the decision doesn't work, the *whanau* decision-making process is repeated to review and broaden the options. It has proved to be a rare experience that there is no-one in the wider family able and willing to care for their child relatives.

For a discussion of family group conferences in the British and North American contexts see Marsh and Crow (1996).

Family protocol

What has this system to offer the student's learning? One of the most important lessons from the *whanau* approach is the notion of family protocol. Each family has a different way of doing things, its own culture. This is related to the broader, 'tribal' culture, but with features unique to each family. It is essential for students to comprehend and work alongside each family's protocol if they hope to be successful in working with the family.

Notes for students

Decision making with families

Social workers are asked to make decisions in controversial circumstances, and the public inquiries of the past two decades have not made this environment feel any safer for the decision maker.

Sometimes a family's protocol (see earlier) is so far removed from the general view of the 'norm' that the social worker comes under pressure to break up the family. The news story (Figure 15.1) is typical of this kind of situation, where such pressure was resisted.

Read the news story, then discuss the four questions raised below.

BOY WILL STAY WITH MOTHER

An 11-year-old boy found living with his mother in a house full of dead and dying pets will not be taken into care, Westshire's social services director said yesterday.

Marian Sellars said the boy and his 31-year-old mother are fit and well, and working through a plan to rehabilitate them into normal life.

Following an initial case study, it was decided it would be in both their interests to stay together. They are staying in a council residence while further assessments are carried out.

Comprehensive medical, social, emotional, and psychiatric assessments have already started, and are expected to last a few months.

Police were shocked by the squalor when they broke into the house where the boy and his mother lived, to investigate theft claims.

The boy had never been to school or allowed to mix with people, and social services did not know he existed.

There was no sign that he had been neglected or ill-treated.

Although social workers say his educational development is normal for his age, and he has adjusted well to the home where he was moved with his mother, it is still not clear how they came to be in the situation they were in.

'We still have a long way to go to build up a clear picture, and will need to do much more work with them,' Marian Sellars said.

Figure 15.1 A typical news story

- What kind of involvement do you think social services should have in these circumstances?
- If the family's neighbours were aware of the situation, should they have alerted the social services?
- Would you try to involve the extended family? How hard would you try to find them?
- What, if anything, would you want to happen before the boy and his mother were returned home together?

Reproduced from *The new social work practice* by Mark Doel and Steven Shardlow, Arena, Aldershot

16 Culturally competent practice

About Activity 16: Ethnic realities

'Ethnic realities' is designed to trigger discussion about the notion of ethnic-sensitive practice and the fine line between useful generalizations and destructive stereotypes.

It leads on to a discussion in the 'Notes for practice teachers' of insider and outsider groups, which in turn develops into a wider consideration of power and oppression.

Purpose

This chapter is designed to sensitize students to cultural differences by understanding more about their own assumptions. The student learns that cultural competence is not an absolute quality and that 'culture' is not something which is limited to certain groups, classes or races. The chapter also introduces students to the idea of the ethnic reality, a powerful combination of class and ethnicity.

Method

- Consider the eight statements in 'Ethnic realities'. Have a copy for each person participating.

- Keep the discussion focused on the four questions at the beginning of the statements.
- If you are guiding the feedback, you will find it useful to read the 'Notes for practice teachers' first.

Variations

'Ethnic realities' can be completed as an individual activity by the student, or in a practice teacher–student pair, or in larger groupings.

If you have time, consider adapting 'Ethnic realities' by collecting statements in relation to other groups (gender, sexuality, age, ability, and so on).

Activity 16 ETHNIC REALITIES

Below is a set of eight statements taken from *Ethnic-Sensitive Social Work Practice* (Devore and Schlesinger, 1991). They suggest that social work practice needs to take account of the 'ethnic reality' – that is, the combination of class and ethnicity – for a person's view of the world.

- What is your response to the eight statements below?
- What fundamental notions do you think they spring from – ideas of privacy, concepts of shame, and so on?
- How might they influence your work in specific ways?
- Do you have any reservations about these ethnic realities, or the idea of ethnic reality in general?

---

1 Many **Eastern Europeans** feel particularly ashamed at having to ask for help.

2 Many **Jewish** and **Italian** people are quite voluble and seem ready to express discomfort and pain publicly.

3 **Asians** are likely to consider eye-to-eye contact as shameful. This is particularly true for women who believe that 'only street women do that'.

4 Some **Chinese** clients are unlikely to ask for help with emotional problems without at the same time asking for concrete assistance.

5 There is increasing evidence that social agencies minimize the role of the **black*** male, both as service user and as provider ... [it is important to adjust] agency hours and service delivery patterns to facilitate the key part black men can and do play in helping their families to cope with problems.

6 The Ignazios are **Italian**: therefore, it is likely that the importance of being a good mother was something Mrs Ignazio heard about all of her life.

7 **Black*** men are disproportionately unemployed and underemployed, contributing to negative self-image and interpersonal problems ... the relatively high levels of depression found among black men may be related to the frequency of stressful events they are more likely to encounter. These include changes in residence, job changes, physical illness, and arrests – all found with greater frequency among black men.

8 Groups respond differently to deviant behaviour by their members. While all experience some sense of shame or of being disgraced, some **Poles** [and] **Asians** ... find it particularly difficult to deal with the assault to group pride represented by delinquency or crime.

*Black is substituted for African-American.

All of the above are quoted from Devore and Schlesinger (1991) (page number given below), and refer to particular pieces of research:

1 Giordano and Giordano, 1977 (p. 195)
2 Zborowski, 1952 (p. 196)
3 Toupin, 1980 (p. 199)
4 Chen, 1970 (p. 204)
5 Leashore, 1981 (p. 206)
6 Gambino, 1974 (p. 208)
7 Gary, 1985 (p. 210)
8 Lopata, 1976 (p. 216)

Reproduced from *The new social work practice* by Mark Doel and Steven Shardlow, Arena, Aldershot

Notes for practice teachers

If 'race' is about socially constructed definitions of groups based upon a belief in differences in physical characteristics, 'culture' is about behaviours, customs, values, rites and institutions. An understanding of culture is the key which translates meaningless activities into meaningful interactions. Culture is not confined to people of colour and it is not limited to artistic or spiritual life: the way we eat a meal, the way we shape our physical environment, our orientation to time, our feeling about where control and responsibility are located, all are expressions of our culture.

Ethnic-sensitive practice

> Ethnic-sensitive practice is first and foremost good social work practice. (Devore and Schlesinger, 1991, p. 188)

Wynetta Devore and Elfriede Schlesinger's book, *Ethnic-Sensitive Social Work Practice*, is seminal. Though written in the North American context, it is a useful text for students and social workers elsewhere. Devore and Schlesinger bring together what they see as repeatedly identified strategies and procedures in social work practice, and suggest how these might be adapted in keeping with what they term the 'ethnic reality', which is a combination of class and ethnicity. They look at four overlapping stages:

- The work prior to involvement
- The work on finding out what the problem is
- Working on the problem
- Termination

Developing a community profile is a first step to conducting a study of the needs of ethnic groups and available informal resources (see page 170). In the first encounters with service users, Devore and Schlesinger counsel a 'level of cultural awareness ... that surpasses the usual injunctions about patience, genuiness and honesty' (1991, p. 52).

The notion of ethnic-sensitive practice is a general one, not limited to a person from a dominant ethnic group working with a person from a minority one. For example, a Jewish hospital social worker doubted that the doctors' concern that an infected rash on the leg of a child was exacerbated by dirt: as an insider she knew that 'Jewish mothers fuss and bathe their children a lot'. However, in this case it turned out that the child's rash was indeed, worsened by lack of hygiene. The worker's insider knowledge of 'proper Jewish behaviour' misled her, and she subsequently described herself as feeling insulted by this mother's behaviour. Her assumptions as an insider slowed the process of helping the mother come to grips with the problem (Devore and Schlesinger, 1991, p. 191).

Practice approaches

How open to ethnic sensitivity are the various approaches to social work practice? Devore and Schlesinger reviewed six approaches:

- psychosocial;
- problem-solving;
- social provision and structural;
- systems;
- ecological;
- approaches specifically focused on cultural awareness and ethnic-sensitive practice, which includes Devore and Schlesinger's own model (1991, pp. 123–61).

Whereas many of these approaches, such as the task-centred model (in the problem-solving school), do not contradict prevailing understandings of cultural, class and ethnic diversity, Devore and Schlesinger's summary highlights the point that 'for a long time, limited attention was paid to modifying or generating procedures that heighten the practitioner's skill in working with sensitivity with people who are members of various ethnic, class and minority groups' (1991, p. 161).

It is important, therefore, to consider which methods are most open to ethnic-sensitive practice, and – whatever approach is used – to adapt it in such a way that ethnic-sensitive practice is uppermost.

Systemic source of problems

The student should be aware of the harm caused by attributing to individuals problems which are, in fact, systemic (Devore and Schlesinger, 1991, p. 210). In other words, racism, poverty and prejudice cause problems for individuals and add to their burden, but the problems should not be attributed to the individual. Workers who do not experience racism, poverty or prejudice on a personal basis have to be especially careful to find out what impact it has, and to confront it.

One of the most powerful weapons which insider groups use against outsiders is guilt and blame. To the practical burden of poverty add the moral burden of guilt for not being able to find work or support a family adequately. It is important for social work to help people to untangle responsibilities, and to challenge ideas of blame which the in-groups (in work, in money, in luck) attribute to the out-groups (see Chapter 18).

One of the most virulent examples of blaming out-groups is found in attitudes to people with positive HIV/AIDS status. Blaming somebody for catching a disease through sexual contact is as ridiculous as castigating a cholera victim for drinking contaminated water. With more knowledge of risks, individuals have increasing responsibility for their own behaviour, but the moral dimension is one which the insider group decides to attribute.

Relationship of race to ethnicity

Race and ethnicity are not synonymous. Racial judgements are based on perceptions of physical appearance, whereas ethnic identity is composed of some, if not all, of the following:

- Ideas of 'peoplehood' – a shared homeland
- A language or distinctive dialect
- Identification with a particular religion
- A distinctive culture (way of life)

(taken from Blakemore and Boneham, 1994, pp. 6-7).

Defining your own racial and ethnic identities is a subjective activity. Asian and African Caribbean people may be discriminated against on the basis of both race and ethnicity.

Continuum of cultural competence

Cultural competence, as described by Cross *et al.* (1989) is a set of behaviours, attitudes and policies which enable individuals, agencies and systems to work effectively in cross-cultural situations. It should be understood as a continuum, a process of becoming culturally competent. Cross describes six phases along the continuum, from cultural destructiveness to cultural proficiency.

Cultural competence is not just about an individual's ability. There is *institutional culture*, and agencies should also assess their cultural competence along the continuum. Cross reminds us of the need to develop systems of care which are culturally competent and encourage the dynamics of difference: 'the ability to adapt practice skills to fit the client's cultural context'. Valuing diversity, making cultural self-assessments and adapting to diversity are essential elements of cultural proficiency.

A cultural inventory

Flood (1988) describes the development of a cultural inventory in his work in Lincoln City, a community on the Oregon coast of North America. Such an inventory engages local people in identifying their cultural attributes, including the perceived strengths and weaknesses of the community. The inventory is a resource to help communities develop neighbourhood projects, and the process of developing the inventory brings people together with the specific aim of making local improvements.

The plan to develop a cultural inventory of Lincoln City included the history and traditions of the people in the region, and ways to help people to recognize the unique resources which made up their cultural commonwealth:

> This cultural commonwealth included: initially, Native Americans and later several Finnish families; a small neighbourhood park full of a wonderful range of art designed by a neighbour; the people's close physical relationship to the ocean; a successful problem-solving project which imported grass carp to clean up Devils Lake, a unique natural resource; a physically disabled member of the community who has taken photographs of construction in Lincoln City over the last 30 years; and a growing elderly population.
> (Flood, 1988)

For the student's purposes, the community can be as broad or as narrow as time allows. For example, an elderly persons' home, a village or an urban neighbourhood can all be considered as communities for the purpose of the inventory. It is the common identity, the cultural commonwealth, which defines it. The student should consider the following questions which could help to stimulate people at a gathering in 'Ourplace' to think about their unique culture (adapted from Flood, 1988):

- What are your favourite places, buildings, events, festivals in Ourplace?
- Where are the places which bring people together or allow a person to be alone?
- What do you want to tell the rest of the world about Ourplace?
- What are you proud of about Ourplace?
- What are you not proud of?
- Who are the different groups of people living in Ourplace?
- What organizations in Ourplace contribute to the community's needs?
- What changes have you seen in Ourplace – do you like them?
- Imagine you are a visitor walking through (or driving through) Ourplace for the first time and you lost your way (or your car broke down). What would happen to you? What would you see? How would you be treated?

After the cultural inventory has been articulated, the community should be encouraged to take action on its ideas.

Mentor system

How culturally competent is your agency? Does staffing reflect the cultural diversity of the agency's clientele? Wilcox et al. (1991) describe the establishment of a bi-cultural management structure in social welfare departments in New Zealand. A mentor system was used in which staff already in management positions had Maori staff placed alongside them in equal acting positions. Maori staff selected whom amongst them would be placed alongside the mentors.

> Maori were questioning why there was a disproportionate number of Maori children and young people in Department of Social Welfare institutions and why they were also heavily over-represented on the caseloads of social workers. Together with this there developed a challenge to the placement of Maori children and young people with

> Pakeha (white European) foster parents. Later there was also the question as to why there were virtually no Maori social workers employed by the Department of Social Welfare. (Wilcox et al., 1991)

Eventually Maori managers were being appointed to senior positions on the basis of merit and a bi-cultural management system was developing.

Together with the student, explore the cultural competence of your agency and the implications of a mentor-type system.

Notes for students

People all over the globe have basic needs which must be met. Satisfying hunger by eating food is one of those needs, and when this is coupled with the need for companionship, the act of eating is transformed into the cultural experience of a meal. Different cultures have developed various rituals and meanings associated with meals. The sights and smells of our childhood and the routines around meal times are a rich seam in our culture, but one we often take for granted. The section below, 'You are what you eat', is designed to put you in touch with your cultural background, as expressed in the making and taking of food.

'You are what you eat'

To prepare for this exercise, put these meals in order for a typical day and add any meals which are not named (for example, some South Walesians eat *tea-tea*, a meal of cold, sweet foods taken in the late afternoon):

DINNER   BRUNCH   TEA   BREAKFAST
LUNCH   ELEVENSES   SUPPER

- As a child, which of these meals did you eat?
- What image does the word to describe each meal bring to mind?
- We only need to eat two meals a day, so why so many possible meals?
- Were there any periods of fast in your family?
- What was the main meal of the day in your family? Who was present?
- On weekdays, was your main meal of the day at school or at home?
- Was there any special day of the week with a different meal pattern?

Smells

- What are your earliest memories of food smells?
- What, if any, smells greeted you as you came home from school?
- Are there any smells which have special memories for you?

Tastes

- What was your favourite-tasting food? Was it associated with a family meal?
- Did your family encourage you to try unfamiliar foods and tastes?
- If you didn't like the taste of something on your plate, what happened?

Reproduced from *The new social work practice* by Mark Doel and Steven Shardlow, Arena, Aldershot

Touch

- Did you have to wash your hands before coming to the table?
- What foods could you eat by hand at the main family meal?
- Were you ever hit for misbehaviour at the table? If so, what had you done?

Sounds

- Did your family make any blessing before eating?
- Were family meals times for conversation or silence?
- If conversational, were these happy, argumentative or a mix?

Sights

- Who prepared the meal, set the table and served the food?
- How was the table set – did you have a tablecoth, napkins, and the like?
- Would you often or seldom see guests eating with you at the family table?

How have the habits of your childhood meals influenced your adult meals? If you share meal times with a partner, what similarities and differences did you notice in your meal-time behaviours? Have other cultures influenced the way you take the main meal of the day now, or is it very similar to your childhood experience?

Cultural self-awareness

Culture is both an individual and collective expression of common values and experiences. As individuals we need to get in touch with our own culture so that we can begin to understand other people's. 'You are what you eat' explored food and the rituals around eating as a fundamental expression of culture. There are other avenues which you might like to explore with colleagues and clients in order to get a better mutual understanding of cultural influences.

'When I was ill ...' is a powerful sentence starter for people to reflect on how they were looked after as children at vulnerable times, such as sickness. 'As a child, when you had a cold, how were you treated?' This helps people with mental health problems or chronic physical difficulties to gain more understanding of present attitudes to caring and ill-health.

'When I was punished ...' is another strong sentence opener. 'As a child what would you be punished for and how would you be punished?' An understanding of past experiences of control can help to understand present behaviours.

Reproduced from *The new social work practice* by Mark Doel and Steven Shardlow, Arena, Aldershot

The medium should be as evocative as possible for the individual or group of clients. For example, music or touchable artefacts from the past can help reminiscence groups of elderly people get in touch with cultural memories.

Useful generalizations or destructive stereotypes?

How do ethnic realities relate to stereotypes? For example, is there a difference between this kind of statement (no. 4 from the 'Ethnic realities' activity on page 167:

> Some **Chinese** clients are unlikely to ask for help with emotional problems without at the same time asking for concrete assistance

and this kind of statement:

> Chinese people look after their own.

Chiu (1989) describes the breakdown of traditional support for Chinese elders in their communities caused by the working hours in the catering industry:

> Consequently, the number of elderly Chinese who have little ongoing family support, little familiarity with British systems of welfare and who are unfamiliar with the English language create a social need which goes largely unnoticed. (CCETSW, 1991)

This might in large part explain what appears to be a 'factual' generalization such as 'Chinese people look after their own'.

What is your response to the following two statements – useful generalizations or destructive stereotypes?

1. In connection with the interplay of age, race and ethnicity:

    > The acquisition of a 'Caribbean' or 'black' identity is relatively recent, and older Afro-Caribbeans were brought up in societies in which island distinctions were of primary significance. (Blakemore and Boneham, 1994, p. 4)

2. In relation to the linguistic and cultural barriers to cross-national groupwork:

    > Let us take a light-hearted example. In no matter what culture they find themselves, the English tend to form a queue for anything: the French do not. The Dutch, like the French, greet strangers when they enter the confined spaces, for example, of a shop, a lift or an office: the Belgians do not, be they French or Flemish speaking. Austrians on foot wait for green before crossing a main road: never the Italians. Swiss drivers and even pedestrians are voluble if you mistake a road sign or impede the flow of traffic: Swedish people are much more tolerant and forgiving. (Taylor, 1994, p. 11)

Reproduced from *The new social work practice* by Mark Doel and Steven Shardlow, Arena, Aldershot

How many English people would recognize their culture from this advice taken from a current Far Eastern tourist guide to England:

> When invited to tea, no matter what your host's station in life, you should observe a certain etiquette. Do not clank your spoon vigorously. Always pour milk in first, then add sugar. Sip quietly. Any clumsiness will be indulged with amusement.

Have you heard the one about ...?

The desire to confront cultural incompetence is not always matched by the skills to do it, and the situation is complicated if a helping role with a client suddenly looks as if it is changing into a challenging role.

An additional complication is uncertainty about where you stand on the matter. This is particularly true of humour, where you may find your laughter turning to doubt about how correct your response was. Use the notion of the continuum from cultural destructiveness to cultural proficiency to discuss your reaction to the following jokes:

- How many social workers does it take to change a light bulb?
  One; but only if the light bulb really wants to change.
- How many Irishmen does it take to change a light bulb?
  Ten: one to hold the bulb and nine to move the room round.
- How do you get a blonde to laugh on a Saturday?
  Tell her a joke on a Tuesday.
- What do you call the useless bit of skin at the end of a penis?
  A man.
- My mother made me a homosexual.
  If I gave her the wool would she make me one, too?
- What do the Royal Family and a bowl of pea soup have in common?
  They're both rich, thick and hard to swallow.

Reproduced from *The new social work practice* by Mark Doel and Steven Shardlow, Arena, Aldershot

17 Empowering practice

About Activity 17: Steps

'Steps' takes nine principles of partnership practice and asks the student to consider their relevance to a particular piece of work, and how they have been put into practice.

Purpose

Issues of power, oppression and discrimination have permeated the teaching and learning associated with all the work in this book. This chapter brings these issues together under the single notion of 'empowering practice', focusing on empowerment and partnership as essential aspects of the student's anti-oppressive practice.

Concepts such as partnership and empowerment are easily voiced, but less easily made specific and put into practice. This chapter aims to explore these notions in more detail and encourage students to apply them in a practical way to their work.

Method

- Use the nine 'Steps' as a trigger to help the student consider what empowerment and participation mean. Are these principles which the student agrees with, or do they want to make some changes to them?
- When the student is satisfied with their own 'Steps', ask for an audit of

a piece of the student's work, applying these principles in a practical way.
- Later in the placement, ask the student to review the principles, perhaps adding any which have been triggered by their experiences on the placement.

Variations

Are the 'Steps' universal to all aspects of social work? It is illuminating to work on this activity across settings if you have the opportunity to join with other practice teachers and students (for example, a practice teacher and student from a child protection team and from a community care setting). How commonly applicable are these principles?

Activity 17   STEPS

Take a piece of work you have been involved in and measure it against these nine practical steps to partnership and empowerment.

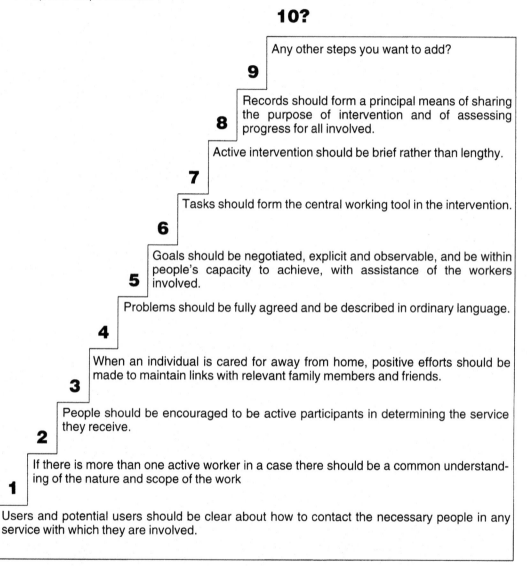

10? Any other steps you want to add?

9 Records should form a principal means of sharing the purpose of intervention and of assessing progress for all involved.

8 Active intervention should be brief rather than lengthy.

7 Tasks should form the central working tool in the intervention.

6 Goals should be negotiated, explicit and observable, and be within people's capacity to achieve, with assistance of the workers involved.

5 Problems should be fully agreed and be described in ordinary language.

4 When an individual is cared for away from home, positive efforts should be made to maintain links with relevant family members and friends.

3 People should be encouraged to be active participants in determining the service they receive.

2 If there is more than one active worker in a case there should be a common understanding of the nature and scope of the work

1 Users and potential users should be clear about how to contact the necessary people in any service with which they are involved.

The principles above are taken from P. Marsh and M. Fisher, *Good Intentions: developing partnerships in social services*, 1992.

Reproduced from *The new social work practice* by Mark Doel and Steven Shardlow, Arena, Aldershot

Notes for practice teachers

Power: insider or outsider

Perhaps the most chilling of Margaret Thatcher's expressions was to ask if a person was 'one of us'. What makes it particularly unsettling is not just that it came out of the mouth of the most powerful person in the land, but that we also recognize a truth to which it pointed: we do identify insiders and outsiders, groups to which we belong and groups to which we do not.

What is important with this knowledge is how we act on it. Margaret Thatcher used it to increase the power of an already powerful in-group, the haves. Social work is perhaps unique amongst professions in that it works largely with people who, in some way or another, are outsiders. Often, it is their very status as outsiders which brings them into contact with social work.

Some groups you can choose to identify with; others you cannot. As a gay person you can choose whether to identify with the gay community; as a black person, by and large but not always, you are immediately identifiable as black. Identification can come as a surprise, like the 65-year-old woman who was resting in an easy chair and overheard one person tell another not to disturb 'that old lady there'. It took her a while to work out that they were referring to her.

Identification is often felt most strongly by outsider groups. We hear little about 'a white perspective' or 'the heterosexual community'. A black researcher working in a predominantly white agency in a predominantly white town explains that whenever he enters a meeting and there is another black person present, his first thought is, 'What are they doing here?' White people are often only aware of their whiteness if and when they experience an all-black environment.

People who resist or bend their identification arouse strong feelings in others. This is especially true for gender and sexuality, as witnessed by the heated controversy over 'outing' homosexuals, the ridicule which transsexuals experience, and the public fascination for transvestism as an entertainment. The strength which both in-groups and out-groups derive from identifying themselves in relation to each other (that is, heterosexual as 'not gay', homosexual as 'not straight') is shown by the particular hostility reserved for groups which challenge this polarization, such as bisexual people and people with dual heritage.

When you have established your own status as insider or outsider in relation to a number of different groups, the relative power of these groups is significant (see *Who Am I?* in Doel, Shardlow, Sawdon and Sawdon, 1996 p. 50). You may be an insider of a group which is an outsider in society (often labelled with the inadequate term, 'minorities'). It is important for us to be aware of our own status as insider and outsider of different groups and how this is similar to, or differs from, the people we work with.

Power is in danger of becoming a dirty word in social work, yet its use is essential to anti-oppressive practice. Like money, those who do not possess it want and need it. Dalrymple and Burke (1992, p. 14) correctly identify 'the legitimate use of power is ensuring that service users are treated as equals in decision-making processes concerning their lives, such as case conferences, ward rounds and planning meetings'. It may not be possible or desirable for students to help people cross boundaries from out-groups to in-groups, but the student can and should develop practices which identify and address imbalances of power and strategies which redistribute it.

Oppression is multi-dimensional

Different levels

Thompson (1997, p. 19) describes the way inequalities of power and opportunity operate at three levels – personal, cultural and societal. The personal includes individual practice and personal prejudice. The cultural relates to commonalities, consensus and conformity; and the structural refers to social divisions and oppression at a socio-political and institutional level (for example, the fact that women are more likely than men to be imprisoned for a first offence).

Double jeopardy

The term 'double jeopardy' has been used to describe the vulnerable position of older black people, though it might as easily refer to others who are doubly vulnerable (for example, children with a sensory impairment who are abused). Blakemore and Boneham (1994, p. 38) quote American research which groups the different indicators of inequality between ageing black and white people as inequalities in:

- income;
- life expectancy and disease;
- social support by family, neighbours and friends;
- life satisfaction, self-esteem, morale and psychological well-being.

Moreover, material and health inequalities tend to widen between black and white people as they age. In some other respects, however, age may be 'a leveller': for example, American research suggests that white people have the lowest frequency of contact with relatives in old age, and life expectancies 'cross over' after the age of 75. In other words, black people can expect to live longer than white people if they reach the age of 75, whereas in middle age they have a much higher probability of death than white people (Blakemore and Boneham, 1994, p. 42).

'The term "triple jeopardy" has been used to refer to people at risk because they are old, because of the physical conditions and hostility under which they have to live, and because services are not accessible to them'

(Norman, 1985, p. 1), though the term more usually refers to the combination of age, race and social class.

Rather than attempting to construct a hierarchy of oppressions (which is divisive and ultimately futile), students need to develop an awareness of the multiplicity of oppressions, and the complex ways in which they interact. This means achieving a careful balance between meaningful generalizations (about 'men' and 'women' for instance) and destructive stereotyping (see Chapter 16). Blakemore and Boneham (1994) provide an interesting summary of the very mixed experiences of older African-Caribbeans and Asians in Britain, which suggests that the differences in the experiences of black elders makes it difficult to generalize about 'black elders'.

Anti-oppressive practice addresses issues of power and oppression in a complex web, interweaving in various ways. However, the student's understanding of, and feeling for, anti-oppressive practice is incomplete without the practice skills to convert good intentions into effective action. The principles and practices of partnership are a first step in this direction.

Partnership

> Partnership has become the dominating principle in welfare provision (and legislation).
> (Marsh and Fisher, 1992, p. 9)

A core aspect of the student's practice learning is how to develop a partnership in their work. Marsh and Fisher (1992) identify the user's voice as paramount in the drive to give greater emphasis to this perspective, from which two clear messages emerge:

- Users have relevant things to say about both their own experiences and the wider aspects of services: greater participation in service decisions and planning would both meet users' demands and produce more effective services.
- Users' views show the chasm between the expressed intentions of social services workers and the users' experiences of their actions, especially where legal authority for intervention has exacerbated a lack of ability to *negotiate* with users. This chasm arises not because workers intend to alienate users, but rather because practice skills are insufficiently developed to translate good intentions into effective practice.

The 'Steps' activity explored some practical ways of creating and sustaining partnerships. In what ways do different social work practice methods live up to the partnership ideal? Marsh and Fisher (1992, p. 10) claim that 'effectiveness studies, user views, partnership orientation, practical use and a developmental stance which suits the changes now under way in social services come together in the task-centred approach'. Their project, *Social Work in Partnership,* set out to identify the implementation problems for a partnership practice based on the task-centred model, and it revealed

> a lack of clarity about how far workers had authority to protect people against their wishes, sometimes resulting in coercive practice, lack of information to help older people play an active role in service decisions, narrow service-led assessments, and problems in recognizing and negotiating with carers. (Marsh and Fisher, 1992, p. 10)

The project developed five principles and a number of implications for direct practice skills. The principles are not designed as statements of intent, but as yardsticks to evaluate how well partnership is being applied.

> Principles of partnership practice
> 1 *Investigation of problems must be with the explicit consent of the potential user(s) and client(s)*
> Where there is not explicit consent, investigation should be kept to the minimum consistent with statutory responsibilities and the assessment of risk with a view to the use of statutory intervention.
> 2 *User agreement or a clear statutory mandate are the only bases of partnership-based intervention*
> All active intervention with users should be on the basis of a clear statement of the problems, specifying which parts of the intervention are agreed, and which are mandated by statute.
> 3 *Intervention must be based upon the views of all relevant family members and carers*
> Individuals within a family may have their own agreement or there may be a family agreement covering common and individual problems.
> 4 *Services must be based on negotiated agreement, rather than on assumptions and/or prejudices concerning the behaviour and wishes of users*
> This principle particularly addresses the assumptions and prejudices deriving, for example, from sexism, racism or ageism, which may substitute agency or worker-assumed definitions for those of the user.
> 5 *Users must have the greatest possible degree of choice in the services they are offered*
> Users have the right to an explanation of any limits imposed, for whatever reason, on the choice of service (including choice of worker). (Marsh and Fisher, 1991, pp. 13–14)

Partnership practice is not always possible to achieve. It may not always be possible for the student or practitioner and the client to agree on the nature of the work, which may be an unwelcome intervention as far as the client is concerned (see Doel and Marsh, 1992, pp. 10–22, for more discussion of work with 'unwilling' clients). However, even if partnership practice is not the result, it is always possible to take a partnership *approach*, following the above principles.

What do these principles mean in practice for the student's work (and, indeed, your own) in your agency?

Empowerment

If partnership is the vehicle, empowerment is the route. The partnership between social workers and the users of their services should be harnessed in such a way that, at the end of the work together, the user feels more powerful rather than less.

Ahmad (1990, pp. 29–73) devotes a chapter to a presentation of the notion of empowerment from a black perspective. She asks us not to enumerate a long list of ways in which black people are disadvantaged, but to see how they are oppressed; to move away from an analysis of the symptoms of black people being disadvantaged, towards the causes, which are rooted in oppression. She acknowledges that this is difficult, because it requires an acknowledgement of social work's role as oppressor.

Ahmad (1990, pp. 46–50) discusses empowerment in relation to a radical social work agenda, with a checklist comprising these four headings:

- *Empowerment as social work ideology and ethos*   This includes an understanding of power as a central element in social work practice, and a commitment to equal access for all citizens.
- *Empowerment as social work resource and service*   This includes mobilizing professional power to influence policy, recognizing the strengths of oppressed groups and communities and bringing them into policy making.
- *Empowerment as social work practice*   This includes a 'firm outcome orientation' – in other words, that people are seen to gain self-power and control.
- *Empowerment as monitoring social work*   This includes identifying and logging specific changes resulting from the commitment to empowering practices and policies, and service users' evaluations of these changes.

What do these mean in practice for a student on a placement in your particular agency?

Barriers to empowerment

Even if we have a clear idea of what empowerment is, there are many barriers to it becoming a reality. In particular, Ahmad's radical agenda has a long journey to make in most social work agencies.

Together with the student, make a list of the blocks and barriers to empowerment likely to be encountered by you and the student, under the headings 'personal', 'agency' and 'structural'.

One of the potential barriers you might identify is a conflict of interest between the people using a service and the people employed by the service – between users and workers, clients and professionals, and so on. The appropriate exercise of professional authority is a skill which students need to develop, but how is 'appropriate' to be defined, and when users' and practitioners' interests do conflict, how might you maintain a commitment to the principle of empowering practice?

The power relationship is not one which ends at the level of service user and service worker. Workers themselves can feel a lack of power in relation to their organizations, where decision-making power and policy making can feel remote. Students undertaking a placement with you need to consider the question of empowerment – the barriers and the opportunities – in relation to workers in the agency as well as the users of the services.

Representativeness

Empowerment is a question not just of practice, but also of policy. Important though it is for individuals to have more involvement in the kind of service available, empowerment is also a matter of wider representation in the way in which services are developed and delivered.

Students are unlikely to have the opportunity to be active in this arena, but they ought to be aware of the 'openings' and 'closings' in the agency where they are placed (see 'Notes for students').

The organizational response to representation by user groups is often to question the processes or technicalities, in particular how to achieve the appropriate 'representativeness'. In reviewing the use of panels as part of a strategy for user involvement, Barnes and Wistow (1993, p. 56) explore the question of how representative individuals can or should be. They usefully remind us of three different meanings of the term 'representative':

- An elected representative is chosen to speak on behalf of a particular constituency.
- The selection of a representative sample is obtained by the application of statistical rules to a known population.
- An individual, or individuals, may be considered representative by sharing typical characteristics of a homogeneous population.

Give the student an opportunity to explore the structures which exist within the agency to empower service users by hearing their voices. If these structures are not in place, it will be useful for you both to discuss why this is the case.

Notes for students

Empowerment as full participation in society

Empowerment and user involvement can be seen in terms of 'openings' and 'closings', where some developments seem to be creating opportunities for empowerment, and others to be cutting us off from them. Beresford (1993, pp. 10–13) identifies the following:

> Examples of 'opening'
> The National Health Service and Community Care Act (with reservations); the massive growth in the number, strength and significance of organizations of people who use services; the Independent Living movement; an increasing number of professionals who want to work in partnership with service users; the increasing number of services under the control of the users; the emphasis on people's rights brought about the consumer view of services; the increasing strength of the citizens' rights movement.
>
> Examples of 'closing'
> The cuts and restrictions in expenditure for public provision; services which people value, such as home care, are being reduced or changed; the Independent Living Fund has been closed; charges are increasingly being made for services; increases in the number of older people and people with learning difficulties in institutional accommodation.

What examples of opening and closing are evident at your local level (for example, in the agency where you are placed, or in the unit or neighbourhood)?

In his analysis of the ways in which people can be involved, Beresford identifies two approaches:

- 'Supermarket' or *consumerist*, which is service-centred and concerned with asking people what they want, in order to get better managed and more responsive services.
- *Control*, better understood as the democratic or empowerment approach, which is people-centred, in that people are in charge of what happens to them.

> People want more say in their lives, not just in services. Services aren't their primary concern ... Having a say in separate welfare services doesn't make up for being restricted to them. (Beresford, 1993, pp. 15–19)

Beresford makes a strong case that involvement should go beyond the narrow world of services to having a say in mainstream life, using the analogy of the difference between living in a separate state of Welfare – a 'homeland' – and living in the country proper. Access and support are the two key factors which make it possible for more people to become involved. In order to ensure that involvement is real and not token, it is necessary to audit involvement:

Reproduced from *The new social work practice* by Mark Doel and Steven Shardlow, Arena, Aldershot

- where is the cash spent on it* going?
- who is being involved?
- what redistribution of power if any is there?
- what changes is it leading to in people's lives?
- how is it helping people secure and safeguard their rights? (Beresford, 1993, p. 25)

* It is not clear from the text whether the 'it' is the process of involving people, or the services themselves. Either way, it is a question worth answering.

For further readings on empowerment see Adams (1996), Ahmad (1990), Stevenson and Parsloe (1993) and Braye and Preston-Shoot (1995).

Reproduced from *The new social work practice* by Mark Doel and Steven Shardlow, Arena, Aldershot

18 Law-informed practice

About Activity 18: Spirit and letter

'Spirit and letter' consists of nineteen situations in which there is a possibility that a law has been broken. Students are not being tested on their knowledge of the law, but are asked to judge how *confident* they are that a law has been broken or not, and to consider their own attitudes to the law.

Purpose

This chapter is designed to help students to develop a legal framework for their practice. In speaking of law-informed practice, the activity recognizes that it is not possible to have detailed knowledge of all the laws which are significant to social work practice, and that students need to be as aware of what they don't know as what they do. The activity aims to start a process which demystifies the law and legal processes.

Method

- 'Spirit and letter' can be undertaken either by a practice teacher and student together, or in a small group. Make the exercise available beforehand, so that answers to the questions on the sheet can be prepared. Students should indicate against each item those situations where they are confident that a law has been broken; those where they are confident that it has not; and those where they are uncertain.

Activity 18 SPIRIT AND LETTER

Has a law been broken?   Yes   No   Unsure

7-year-old Amy has been left unattended at home for an hour in the evening. □ □ □ A

16-year-old Brian has been sniffing glue in the toilets at school. □ □ □ B

Care worker Chris has locked a door to stop Mrs Cargill (who is demented) from leaving the Centre. □ □ □ C

On the way to an urgent call, probation officer David drives at 37 mph in a 30 mph zone. □ □ □ D

Social worker Eve claims 50 extra miles on her car allowance to subsidize a trip for the members of her substance abuse group. □ □ □ E

Landlord Mr Finch has locked a tenant out of a furnished bedsit complaining of 'filth and squalor'. □ □ □ F

The local authority has failed to provide a stair-lift to Ms Garthwaite, who suffers from multiple sclerosis and lives in her own two-storey house. □ □ □ G

18-year-old Howard, who is severely disabled, requests his key worker to masturbate him. □ □ □ H
His key worker Ian agrees to do this. □ □ □ I

The Jahnus are denied attendance at the case review of their daughter who is in residential care with the local authority. □ □ □ J

Keith reveals he had sexual intercourse with a 14-year-old girl three years ago. □ □ □ K

Mrs Lehry is not registered as a child minder, but she minds two children after school twice a week. □ □ □ L

Martin tells a group for young offenders that his parents grow marijuana on their allotment. □ □ □ M

Mrs Nyczeski was not informed when her granddaughter was fostered. □ □ □ N

Reproduced from *The new social work practice* by Mark Doel and Steven Shardlow, Arena, Aldershot

Has a law been broken?   Yes   No   Unsure

Fearing for Mr Old's safety, his warden Olga breaks a kitchen window in order to gain entry.	☐	☐	☐	O
Probation officer Pat is told that the Patels have reconnected their electricity.	☐	☐	☐	P
There is no leaflet available in Sanskrit for Mr Quereshi to read about social services in his area.	☐	☐	☐	Q
Mrs Rose is denied access to her case file by her care manager.	☐	☐	☐	R
10-year-old Sam has stolen a chocolate bar from the sweet shop.	☐	☐	☐	S

- If a law has been broken, should it be invoked?
- If so, what steps would you take to invoke it?

Note: Answers are not given, both because the law does change – it applies differently in different countries – and also because, in not providing answers, further opportunities for students to undertake follow up work to check the current legal position becomes possible. (For those who wish to test their legal knowledge and have the answers provided, see page 197.)

Reproduced from *The new social work practice* by Mark Doel and Steven Shardlow, Arena, Aldershot

- Discuss each item in turn, looking at the further question, if a law has been broken, should it be invoked? Follow the student's own interest in pursuing two or three of the situations further. Ask the student to do some follow-up work in relation to a couple of the scenarios which relate to the kind of work done during the placement.
- Small groups can each work on five or six of the situations and share their findings. A deliberately wide range of situations is included so that the student gets an understanding that law-informed practice is significant in a variety of settings, not just probation, child care or mental health specialisms. (Allow about 1 hour.)

Variations

Once the student has been sensitized by this activity to the importance of law-informed practice, it is helpful to provide case material tailored to the placement setting as examples of the ways specific laws can influence, guide or determine practice. A case example which is set at different stages in its development helps the student to look at the legal options at various steps in the 'career' of the case, and the consequences of choosing or not choosing particular paths. An example of this kind of build-on exercise is provided by Braye and Preston-Shoot (1990). CCETSW Paper 7 (1991b) also has examples of exercises to use with students.

Notes for practice teachers

The 'Spirit and letter' activity has two main purposes. The first is to sensitize the student to the importance of the legal context of social work practice; the second is to dispel some of the mystique about the law offering clear, hard and fast rules. These two purposes may seem paradoxical – the one elevating the profile of law and the other diminishing it. In fact, the activity is an opportunity for the student to develop law-informed practice, tuning in to the connections between social work and a legal framework. Ball, Harris *et al.* (1988) compare the social work student who does not understand the legal framework to 'a bricklayer without a plumbline'. The law offers not one, but many plumblines, which can be used to very different effects: guaranteeing clients' rights; securing clients' protection; enforcing social control.

Students need to be honest with themselves about their attitude towards the law. For example, where would the student rate these statements on a scale of 1 to 10 (strongly disagree to strongly agree)?

The law is:

- a weapon the powerful use to keep the powerless in their place;
- a safeguard for the individual against the state;
- relatively arbitrary in the way it is applied;
- a reflection of social tensions and dilemmas;
- an intrusion into the lives of individuals;
- slow to catch up with social changes;
- white, male and middle class;
- an ass.

Practice dilemmas

The teaching of law for social workers has come under considerable criticism, and added fuel to the fire which carried probation education and training out of social work (Ball, Harris *et al.*, 1988; Ball, Roberts *et al.*, 1991; Blom-Cooper, 1985). Section 2.1 of CCETSW Paper 30 (1991a) outlined the core areas of legal knowledge to be studied by all students, and the Review of the Diploma in Social Work built a working knowledge of legal and statutory requirements into the Core Competences for the professional qualification (CCETSW, 1995). The critics of law teaching as it stands say that law must be a central part of social work teaching and pivotal to professional practice.

However, there are also critics of the prescriptive approach to teaching law. Braye and Preston-Shoot (1990; 1992) assert that teaching law and its subsequent application 'must be considered in a conceptual frame of practice dilemmas which confront every practitioner and create role conflict, uncertainty, ambiguity, and insecurity'. These dilemmas, 'posed by taking account both of the law and the ethical duty of care in professional practice, lead social workers into the eye of the storm'. The authors look at the tensions between rights versus risk; care versus control; needs versus resources; duty versus power; legalism versus professionalism, amongst others. They suggest that it is not just knowledge of the law which must be conveyed, 'but the problems and the dilemmas in applying it'.

Of particular interest to practice teachers are Braye and Preston-Shoot's findings about ways to help students learn, retain and apply law teaching. The group of students with whom they worked had reservations about the lack of practice opportunities, feeling that it is difficult to retain knowledge of the law without putting it to use. Practice-led methods of learning were preferred by two-thirds of the student group, where a case example was used to trigger discussion and subsequent teaching inputs linked directly to concerns arising from the discussion. It is interesting that Braye and Preston-Shoot (1992) saw evidence of 'an unsettling effect' as some of the students moved from a state of blissful ignorance to a realization of what they did not know.

The scenario approach

Eadie and Ward (1995) took this approach further, focusing all the learning around students' work on case examples presented to them. This 'scenario approach' arose out of the findings of an earlier study (Hogg, Kent and Ward, 1992) of law teaching on placements, which they describe as 'profoundly disturbing':

- a widespread lack of accurate substantive knowledge of legislation, precedent and legal structure, processes and concepts;
- a confusion about the nature of the law – what is a legal issue? – and the relationship of the law to social work activity;
- an inconsistent approach to teaching both in college and on placement;
- little awareness of how gender and race issues affect teaching and learning.

The law scenarios enable small groups of students to develop their inquiry and investigative skills to find out what they need to know in a number of different areas, such as 'Through-care' in Probation. At the end of their investigations, the students give presentations, so that they can all learn from each other's researches (Eadie and Ward, 1995). Although the different areas produced different details, the processes of the research were very similar, as were themes such as issues of racism and discrimination institutionalized in legislation.

It would be possible to use a scenario approach on an individual basis with a student, or perhaps by gathering a small group of students placed in your agency. As an approach which focuses as much on the processes of learning about the law and the context for its application as on the content of the law, it has more likelihood of 'sticking'.

Seeking legal expertise

CCETSW Paper 7 (1991b) lists 37 different Acts relating to social work practice in England and Wales, 44 in Northern Ireland and 44 in Scotland. It would be a feat to remember the titles of these Acts, never mind the details of their provisions. Even when the details of Acts are learnt and tested, it is questionable how much of this detail is retained. How much legal knowledge have you retained from your own qualifying training?

Stevenson (1988) doubts whether it is desirable or feasible to acquire factual legal knowledge in basic training, and questions its reliability. Inaccurate legal advice given to a client is worse than no advice at all. The most important knowledge students can cultivate is an understanding of what they don't know, and the skills to know when and how to seek additional expertise.

Initially, students need to develop a clear picture of the practice goals in a particular piece of work, with the people involved and *within a legal framework*. Once they have this picture, they need to know how and where to seek the advice which will help them to achieve those practice goals; detailed legal advice will, in turn, reshape some aspects of those practice goals, but it is a myth to believe that 'application of the law' will by itself bring clarity to the picture. The law is not cut and dried: it seldom offers concrete conclusions, because – like social work practice – it, too, reflects the dilemmas in society. Braye (1995, p. 31) exposes other myths about the law: that it is helpful, neutral, confers substantial powers, and provides good and right solutions.

In conclusion, knowledge probably sticks when it is related to specific practice examples, and when the student has used it personally. It needs consistent reinforcement. It is unrealistic to expect the student to gain detailed legal knowledge; better that students develop law-informed practice, so that they know which questions to ask and where and how to seek legal expertise to provide the detail.

Notes for students

Approval – disapproval continuum

> Social workers have been criticized for being over-zealous in their use of the law and for failing to use available legal powers. (Preston-Shoot, 1993, p. 65)

In addition to a knowledge of the legal framework, it is also important for you to be aware of your own feelings about how the law should be invoked. Return to the nineteen scenarios in 'Spirit and letter'. How strongly do you feel about each of them? Take your three lists (one where you think a law has been broken, one where you think it has not, and one where you are uncertain), and draw a *continuum* line for each list. Using one end for strongly approve of the action taken (1) and one end for strongly disapprove (10), place each scenario on its continuum (Figure 18.1).

A LAW HAS BEEN BROKEN		
strongly approve	neutral response	strongly disapprove
(1)	(5)	(10)

A LAW HAS NOT BEEN BROKEN		
strongly approve	neutral response	strongly disapprove
(1)	(5)	(10)

UNCERTAIN WHETHER A LAW HAS BEEN BROKEN		
strongly approve	neutral response	strongly disapprove
(1)	(5)	(10)

Figure 18.1 Approval–disapproval continuum

Reproduced from *The new social work practice* by Mark Doel and Steven Shardlow, Arena, Aldershot

Are there situations where you are confident that a law has been broken, but where you feel less disapproval than for situations where a law has not been broken?

Categories of legal activity

Ball, Harris *et al.* (1988), describe these categories of legal activity:

- Enforcing the rights of clients
- Protecting the vulnerable
- Protecting society
- Enforcing compliance.

Which category do you think each of the situations in 'Spirit and letter' might fall into?

Sanction

Perhaps the greatest legal sanction is related to age, in society's attempts to define when its citizens move from childhood to adulthood. See how many of these questions you are able to answer correctly (answers available as of 1994 on page 199).

In Britain, at what age can I, or do I do the following?

1. Buy a pet
2. Become of 'compulsory school age'
3. Leave school
4. Open and draw money from a National Savings Bank account
5. Open a Post Office Girobank account (but you will need a guarantor who will be liable for your debts)
6. Open and draw money from a Trustee Savings Bank account
7. Open a bank account or Post Office Girobank account without a parent's signature
8. Drink alcohol in private – for example at home
9. Go into a pub, but not buy or drink alcohol there
10. Have beer, cider or wine with a meal in a restaurant
11. Buy and drink alcohol in a bar
12. Apply for a licence to sell alcohol
13. Vote in general and local elections
14. Become an MP
15. Be convicted of a criminal offence in England and Wales if it is proved you knew what you were doing was wrong

Reproduced from *The new social work practice* by Mark Doel and Steven Shardlow, Arena, Aldershot

16. Be convicted of a criminal offence in Scotland if it is proved you knew what you were doing was wrong
17. Marry with parental consent in England and Wales
18. Marry without parental consent in Scotland
19. As a female, consent to sexual intercourse
20. As a male, consent to a 'homosexual act' in private with a partner of this age or older
21. Work in a part-time job (with certain restrictions; for example, not work more than two hours on a school day or Sunday)
22. See a U or PG category film at a cinema
23. See a category 15 film
24. Drive an invalid carriage
25. Drive a moped
26. Hold a licence to drive most vehicles
27. Hold a licence to drive a large passenger vehicle or heavy goods vehicle
28. Be trained to appear in dangerous public entertainments subject to the grant of a local authority licence
29. Be employed as a street trader by your parents, subject to local authority bye-laws
30. Become a street trader
31. Serve on a jury
32. Have to pay a child's fare on trains, and on buses and tubes in London
33. Possess a shotgun, airgun, air rifle or ammunition
34. Buy or hire any firearm or ammunition
35. Buy cigarettes and tobacco
36. Be allowed to enter or live in a brothel
37. Reach the age of maturity, an adult in the eyes of the law
38. As a boy, under certain circumstances, be sent to a prison to await trial
39. Be given a community service order if convicted of an imprisonable offence
40. Have criminal charges dealt with in an adult court
41. Be detained 'during Her Majesty's pleasure' for a specific period, including a life sentence, if guilty of homicide
42. As a male, be convicted of rape, assault with intent to commit rape and unlawful sexual intercourse with a girl under 16
43. As a male, join the armed forces with parental consent

Reproduced from *The new social work practice* by Mark Doel and Steven Shardlow, Arena, Aldershot

Appendix

Answers (as of 1994):

Age 5: 2, 8, 22, 32
Age 7: 4, 6
Age 8: 16
Age 10: 15, 41
Age 12: 1, 28
Age 13: 21
Age 14: 9, 29, 33, 42
Age 15: 5, 23, 38
Age 16: 3, 10, 17, 18, 19, 24, 25, 30, 35, 36, 39, 43
Age 17: 26, 34, 40
Age 18: 7, 11, 13, 20 (since 1994), 31, 37
Age 21: 12, 14 (20 until 1994), 27

(Taken from *The Guardian*, 5 January 1993.)

Reproduced from *The new social work practice* by Mark Doel and Steven Shardlow, Arena, Aldershot

19 Research-minded practice

About Activity 19: Signposts

The journey from observation to action is often made quickly, instinctively and – more riskily – often without reflection. 'Signposts' is a way of slowing down that journey, to inspect the component parts and to consider how research-minded the practice is.

Purpose

This chapter is designed to dispel the mystique associated with research and the question of 'integrating theory and practice'. It scrutinizes the processes which affect the practitioner's judgement in turning observations into action. Formal research is only one of these many processes, and it is likely to take a minor role compared to action based on the observer's past observations, feelings, value base and so on.

The meeting-point of research and practice is one of the most fraught locations on the social work map. All too often, practitioners' complaints that research findings never tell them what they do not already know are matched by researchers' criticisms that practice is based on professional folklore. The chapter aims to bring these two 'camps' together and put research on the student's map.

Method

- Both you and the student should consider (independently) one specific

observation which you made during a mutual contact with a client. This need not be the one which you thought was the most striking, but it should be one which influenced your subsequent action. It should be a very specific observation.
- Make notes around the eight panels signposted as leading from 'Observation' to 'Action' in the 'Signposts' activity. Comments should be brief and specific to the one observation which you are focusing on. End with the specific action taken.
- When you have completed the exercise, compare notes. This kind of scrutiny enables you both to reflect on factors which influenced your actions which you were not necessarily aware of at the time. In particular you should focus on the Research panel – how prominent was it? At what stage in the process did it have an impact, if at all?

Variations

The journey from Observation to Action is not as linear as in 'Signposts'. For the purposes of the activity, the eight processes headlined in 'Signposts' are shown as following one from the other, but the journey itself is made in a much more circuitous way, revisiting some stages and probably neglecting some of the others.

It is not possible to subject every action to this kind of detailed scrutiny but if students can do this exercise a few times, they become aware of their own 'profile'. This helps them to develop their capacities as reflective practitioners and to develop a practice base which is research-minded.

The student who struggles with this activity might benefit from discussing the illustration on pages 203–6, but it is better not to begin with an example, because this taints the student's responses.

Activity 19 SIGNPOSTS

Practice theories are an assemblage of signposts which social workers have accumulated in the course of their work. These signposts are made up of a combination of explicit theoretical knowledge, practice wisdom, experience, feelings and observations. But the *process* by which all these ingredients are employed is little understood and it might be useful to think provisionally in terms of a cartographical analogy. (Curnock and Hardiker, 1979, p. 160)

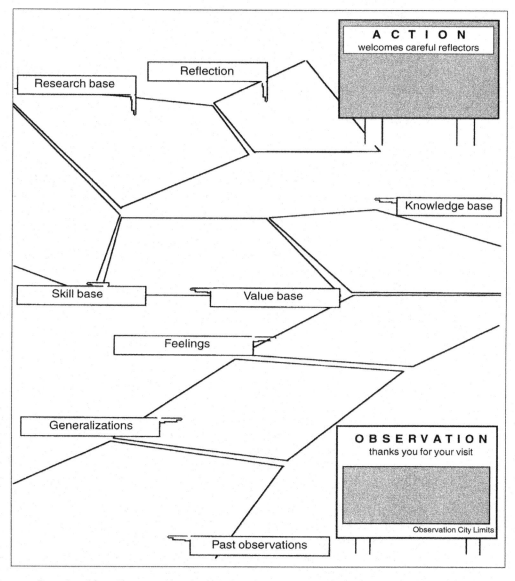

Reproduced from *The new social work practice* by Mark Doel and Steven Shardlow, Arena, Aldershot

Notes for practice teachers

The steps from observation to action

Selected observation

For the purpose of this exercise the student is asked to focus on one particular observation from recent direct work. This selected observation should be briefly described and not analysed at this stage.

Example: 'In visiting Mrs Jackson with her daughter Mrs Turner, I saw that Mrs Turner had a different view of the situation from Mrs Jackson and this led to conflict between them.'

Past observations

When we observe a situation we are not looking at it for the first time. Even at a basic physical level our eyes and brains are making sense of what, without previous observation, would be an incomprehensible image – upside down and highly selective, so the brain inverts the image once more and fills in the details for us. This physical 'tampering' with the image to make more sense of it is a good metaphor for the psychological and social meaning which we put into our observations. They are influenced and made understandable by relating them to past experiences. It is important to be aware of what these are: if we scrutinize them in this way, we can begin to see how relevant they are.

Example: 'In my own family there is a lot of conflict between the generations.'

Generalizations

As we discovered in Chapter 16, generalizations have a very powerful effect on the way we interpret our observations, but we are often inclined to deny that we make generalizations because they are seen as a 'bad thing'. Generalizations are, in fact, essential as a way of grouping thoughts and avoiding an incomprehensible mental clutter. At a very basic level, wherever we use a word ('bird') we are using a generalized concept which brings together a number of associated ideas ('birdness'), which allow wide diversity (an ostrich and a swan). At a more complex level, we rely on generalizations in social interactions, too. However, if we do not keep these generalizations under scrutiny, they can become stereotypes and we can act on a false grouping.

To deny a generalization is to avoid the opportunity to scrutinize it, so do not let students pretend they do not make any. We all make them and rely on them: are we prepared to be aware of them so that we can challenge them?

Example: 'I think there tends to be conflict between the generations in western societies – your power is based on your economic productivity, so elders have very little power and the next generation are keen to keep their economic power, which leaves little time to look after their elders.'

Feelings

Feelings are a powerful mediator in the journey from observation to action. Indeed, the strength of our feelings can influence what we observe and what we choose not to observe in the first place.

Some feelings, such as sympathy and warmth, are easier to acknowledge and handle than others, such as disgust or mistrust. Students need to develop the habit of being honest about their feelings, so they can assess the likely impact on subsequent action (see Chapter 4).

Example: 'Mrs Jackson reminded me a bit of my grandmother and I felt sorry for her; I felt angry at her daughter, Mrs Turner, for butting in all the time.'

Knowledge base

Linked closely with generalizations, the knowledge base which even an inexperienced student draws on is potentially enormous. In order to act quickly, we make forays into our knowledge base in a highly selective way; so, what were the first associations relevant to this particular observation?

Example: 'I know that family conflict is destructive and that a time of crisis is an opportunity for change and realignments in relationships. I don't know if this is the kind of work this agency expects or allows me to do.'

Value base

The action which is taken is influenced by what students think *ought* to happen. The emphasis which they place on individual rights or community responsibilities, on private, family obligations or public, welfare provisions, are all guided by their particular ethical awareness and value base.

Example: 'Mrs Turner is in a more powerful position than her mother, Mrs Jackson. It is not right for elders to be oppressed by their more powerful children, and it is right for me to try to redress this balance.'

Skills base

The adage says 'If you only have a hammer in your tool kit then you treat every problem as a nail.' Students need to be aware of their strengths, and they also need to be aware of their limitations, to prevent them defining situations to fit their skills. What particular skill strength influenced the move from observation to action?

Example: 'I am able to use some of the techniques in family conflict to allow different members to participate and begin to listen to each other.'

Research base

There is some evidence that the research base is the area likely to be most neglected by practitioners. Later in this section we look at why formal research is neglected, and whether we should worry about this. For the moment, the student might not have made any comment in this box. The student whose example we are following here wrote this:

Example: 'The concept of jeopardy has been a useful one to look at the position of older people in Britain, and there is evidence that black elders, like Mrs Jackson, experience "double jeopardy".'

Reflection

How does the student reflect on all this? What sense do all these areas make, in converting the observation into action? How much weight does the student give to one area as opposed to another, and is the student aware of how these judgements are made? The practicalities, in terms of what is possible and what obstacles might get in the way, are part of this reflective process.

Example: 'I realized that I was putting all my emphasis on Mrs Jackson's position, and that I needed to consider Mrs Turner's situation, too; her support will be essential if I am to work successfully with Mrs Jackson.'

Specific action

What was the specific action, or decision, which the selected observation led to?

Example: 'I decided to see Mrs Jackson and Mrs Turner separately.'

These 'Signposts' from observation to action are intended to demystify a process which too often has felt false and obscure by students who are required – somehow – 'to integrate theory with practice' and to bring research findings into their work.

Practice exemplars

A document published by the (then) DHSS in 1978, *Social Service Teams: The Practitioner's View*, found that few of the social workers interviewed were able to give any indication that they were consciously applying any theoretical knowledge to their work. The situation is probably unchanged now, with an added dimension that practitioners may feel they are using a specific method of work even when many of the significant elements are missing (for example, the *We Do All This Already* effect described in respect of partnership practice by Marsh and Fisher (1992, p. 48) and by Doel and Marsh (1992, pp. 95–6) about task-centred work.

The conventional view of social work practice as the selection of appropriate theory and research, and its application to the particular case and context, is criticized by Gould (1989) in an article on reflective learning in social work practice. This traditional approach to integrating theory and practice is visible in the tendency to see a period of class-based learning in the college as 'preparation' for putting this into practice in the agency.

However, Schön's (1987; 1995) view of reflection-in-action is taken as a more accurate way of describing what actually happens. Schön considers that theory used in practice is practitioner-led, implicit and developed through experiential learning. Gould (1989, p. 10) quotes Schön's findings that professionals' theory is actually revealed and transmitted through practice exemplars, not explicit 'espoused theory' or formal research findings. In other words, there is no process by which the practitioner looks at a situation and decides 'Theory P' supported by 'Research Q' is the one to apply.

Instead, the practitioner has mental maps of good practice – practice exemplars – which become refined by experience of what works. Reflecting on practice can develop these exemplars and free people from habitual ways of thinking and acting. Practice teachers should, therefore, focus on helping students to become reflective practitioners.

Central to Schön's belief is that practice is a form of artistry, and that improvisation is a central feature of successful practice. This does not mean that practice 'happens' or is necessarily *ad hoc*, but it underlines the importance of developing ways of reflecting on practice and learning from it. The 'Path' in the 'Signposts' activity is one way of breaking out of habitual patterns to develop explicit practice exemplars which are accessible to challenge and change. In this way research-minded practice can be developed.

What does 'research-minded' mean?

Students may become research-minded in two respects:

1 They are willing and able to make use of existing research, and interested in the implications of research findings for practice and policy.
2 They are willing and able to undertake research, formulating a research purpose and design, conducting and evaluating the research.

The first aspect requires the student to be open to knowledge and skills which come from sources other than doing the job. This does not mean abandoning practice wisdom, nor does it mean unquestioning acceptance of 'Research'. It does require a willingness to make practice wisdom less private and implicit and put it to the test.

The second aspect requires an openness to the notion of a researcher as a *role*, rather than as a *speciality* (Reid and Smith, 1989). Research is not something confined to ivory-tower academics; students need to see their practice as akin to research, each piece of work posing its own research questions. Although there are often differences in the time-scale of practice and research, there are remarkable similarities in the processes. Whitaker and Archer (1989) quote Norah Dixon's parallel processes:

SOCIAL WORK PROCESSES	RESEARCH PROCESSES
1 Social worker/project worker is presented with a problem.	1 Researcher is presented with a problem or question.
2 Social worker collects facts which illuminate the nature and purpose of the problem.	2 Researcher searches the literature on the problem or question.
3 Social worker makes a plan of action.	3 Researcher designs a study.
4 Social worker attempts to carry out action plan noting progress.	4 Researcher collects material and collates it.
5 Social worker reviews work and may make new plans.	5 Researcher analyses material and produces conclusions and possibly recommendations for future action.

Much of the knowledge and the technology in social work practice is created to solve immediate problems; a practitioner–researcher aims to preserve it to *build* research knowledge and to add to our understanding of what is sometimes called 'intervention technology'. The practitioner-researcher's activities can also help to combat practice fatigue and the dangers of work becoming routine.

The student will find it useful to read examples of small-scale research studies by practitioners (Fuller and Petch, 1995; Whitaker and Archer 1989). For example, a study of the experiences and needs of carers of the demented elderly found that some carers were reluctant to use services available, and that the reasons for this included

> feelings of guilt at placing relatives in the care of others ... and concerns that a mentally infirm relative could return from a period away even more disoriented than before [and some rejected the idea that anyone else could possibly provide adequate care ... On the basis of the findings it was possible to suggest ways of working with carers which could help them to think through and resolve some of their feelings about utilizing services. (Whitaker and Archer, 1989, p. 13)

So far, we have been considering the individual response to research, but it is also important to consider how research-minded your organization is (Everitt, Hardiker et al., 1992, p. 82). Does it collect information in a systematic fashion in order to evaluate its services, and how do agency staff participate in this process? Although 'the demand for social workers and their managers to identify the effectiveness of their work is now very great' (Cheetham, Fuller et al., 1992, p. 3), the extent to which staff are active participants in this and the proper dissemination of findings, varies considerably.

Different purposes of research

Research is often categorized by design (single case experiments, surveys, and so on), or by who participates in designing and conducting it (participatory research, for example). Whitaker and Archer (1989) give a useful description of different kinds of *purpose*, as expressed within these five general questions:

1 How can a complex process or phenomenon which is incompletely understood be better understood? (Exploratory research)
2 What is accomplished by a particular procedure, policy or practice approach, and is it effective and efficient in achieving its intended goals? (Evaluation or outcome research)
3 What processes and experiences are involved in a particular programme, policy or practice approach which accounts for its outcomes? (Process–outcome research)
4 How can I find out, while a programme is going on, whether and how it is working, and how if at all I ought to modify my approach? (Action research)
5 How frequently does a problem or situation occur, what are likely future trends, and what are the implications for service delivery and the allocation of resources? (Survey research)

In addition to Whitaker and Archer (1989), see Cheetham, Fuller et al., 1992; Everitt, Hardiker et al., 1992; and Fuller and Petch, 1995, for examples of how it is possible for practitioners to plan and conduct research on practice issues, and the impact which practitioner-led research can have.

Strengths rather than weaknesses

The hostility of the social work profession towards research has to be faced squarely. As a practice teacher, you need to reflect on your own response to research. In a study which predated the changes in practice teacher training in the UK, Brodie (1993, p. 81) explored the content of supervision sessions, and found that practice teachers were reluctant to consider the application of theory to practice as part of the supervisory task. Specifically, the frequency with which the practice teachers in Brodie's sample alluded to theory was 1.05 per cent and the frequency with which they referred to theory was 0.35 per cent (this compares with a frequency of 33.75 per cent for offering opinion). However, the full-time practice teachers in Brodie's study made significantly more use of theory than the singleton teachers.

Reid and Smith (1989) describe how 'the use of tests, structured observations and the like was seen as impeding the formation of a therapeutic relationship'. For those occasions when research is allowed through the door, it has tended to concentrate on pathology, on discovering what is wrong and what does not work. Yet it would be useful to know more about what factors help people to change, to cope, to be assertive. Reid and Smith sum up: 'we cannot help people use their strengths if our knowledge is limited to their weaknesses'. In a similar vein, discussing the experiences of black students on social work courses, Aymer and Bryan (1996) assert the need to 'accentuate the positives'.

If students are to become research-minded, we as practice teachers must confront our own hostility towards research and consider how we are to help the student to learn from positive experiences by looking at what works, and why.

Notes for students

Did you know?

The exercise which follows is designed to help your awareness of the way your beliefs influence your receptiveness to new information. How do you respond to those parts of the report which confirm your beliefs and how do you handle those which challenge them? Are you able to develop a number of different hypotheses, or do they all fall within a narrow range of explanation? An ability to look critically at your responses is the first step to converting prejudices into well-informed beliefs.

The exercise also provides an opportunity to continue to put your attitudes towards research under the microscope. A negative view of the research endeavour is probably a greater barrier to research-minded practice than lack of skills or understanding.

Below are two reports of research findings. Each has three panels. Read a panel at a time and formulate your own hypotheses as possible explanations for what you have read. How do your hypotheses change in response to the new information in the next panel?

(A) FEWER TRANSPLANTS FOR BLACK PEOPLE

PANEL 1

Black Americans who need kidney transplants are significantly less likely to receive them than whites.

The conclusion, published in the *New England Journal of Medicine* by a group of transplant physicians, is the latest effort to address a trend that has troubled the medical profession for several years: although black people are four times more vulnerable than whites to kidney failure, studies have shown that when transplants become available, they tend to go to white patients.

In 1985, only 21 per cent of all kidney transplants went to blacks, even though they accounted for 28 per cent of the patients with serious kidney disease, according to the Health Care Financing Administration. Figures from the United Network for Organ Sharing indicate that although blacks make up a third of the nearly 18 000 people on the national waiting list, they received only a fifth of the kidney transplants last year.

Before you read Panel 2, write down your hypotheses which might explain the findings in Panel 1.

Reproduced from *The new social work practice* by Mark Doel and Steven Shardlow, Arena, Aldershot

Then continue by reading Panel 2:

PANEL 2

Previous studies have theorized that subconscious bias might account for the inequity in transplant rates.

But Thursday's report – a review of existing data by a committee of the American Society of Transplant Physicians – concluded that 'it is likely that both biological and socio-economic differences between blacks and whites contribute to this inequality'.

'We never found anywhere that there is any wilful discrimination against blacks or other minorities,' said Dr Jaroslav Havel, a co-author of the study and a professor of medicine at the University of California, Los Angeles.

Rather, Havel said, the little hard evidence available points to a variety of complex factors, ranging from a lack of health insurance among blacks to differences in blood types that make many black patients incompatible with the majority of organs in the donor pool.

For example, the study found that white families are two or three times more likely than blacks to donate a deceased relative's organs for transplantation. Blacks have a much higher incidence of hypertension and diabetes that can result in kidney failure and thus are over-represented on the waiting list for kidney transplants. But because of genetic differences in blood and tissue types, many black people cannot accept organs taken from whites; they have to compete for a much smaller organ pool.

'We strongly feel that the differences could be improved if we could encourage donations by racial minorities,' Havel said.

How do the statements and findings in Panel 2 confirm or challenge the hypotheses you made after Panel 1?

Make a note of any new hypotheses made at this stage, before moving to Panel 3:

Reproduced from *The new social work practice* by Mark Doel and Steven Shardlow, Arena, Aldershot

PANEL 3

Another possible factor, the study found, may have to do with variations in insurance coverage. Although Medicare pays much of the cost of transplants for most people, it does not offer complete coverage in every state. Poorer blacks may be unable to afford the remaining costs, and may therefore be considered less suitable candidates for transplants, the study noted.

Other factors may have to do with whether a patient is a good risk for a transplant, the physicians found. For example, the study noted, doctors may not offer transplants to black patients because they may suspect them of alcohol and drug abuse, which would undermine surgery.

'The prevalance of heroin abuse may be higher in blacks than in whites,' the authors explained.

Adapted from Shawn Hubler, *The Oregonian*

What conclusions have you reached as a result of reading all three panels? To what extent have the hypotheses which you made after Panel 1 been confirmed or challenged?

(B) EMILY ASSERTS HER MANHOOD

PANEL 1

Parents who name their daughters Sophie or Emily in the hope of encouraging a feminine personality may instead turn out gender rebels who will reject conventional sex roles, psychologists said yesterday.

For parents with sons, avoiding the name Nigel makes good psychological sense as people cannot agree whether it is has macho or wimp associations.

Psychologists Carol Johnson and Helen Petrie, of Sussex University, surveyed the perceived masculinity and femininity of names and whether these could influence personality.

Before you read Panel 2, write down your hypotheses which might explain the findings in Panel 1.

Reproduced from *The new social work practice* by Mark Doel and Steven Shardlow, Arena, Aldershot

Then continue by reading Panel 2.

PANEL 2

For women, but to a much lesser extent for men, names appeared important in shaping personality. Women either embraced the feminine stereotypes suggested by their names or rebelled, shortening them to 'unisex' versions, such as Chris for Christine, or adopting male versions, such as Alex for Alexandra or Charlie for Charlotte.

Ms Johnson told the annual conference of the British Psychological Society that 255 students had found little difficulty in assessing the masculinity or femininity of 86 names – with the exception of Nigel.

'The lack of agreement on Nigel surprised us. There are two different stereotypes in Great Britain about Nigel,' says Ms Johnson. 'One is very upper class such as the actor Nigel Havers, and the other is an Essex Man figure such as racing driver Nigel Mansell.'

The researchers found that the most feminine name was seen as Sophie, and the most masculine as John. Lee was judged the most unisex.

The students were given personality tests to assess masculine and feminine attributes. Women with highly feminine names had more feminine personalities, while those who had abbreviated their names showed more masculine characteristics.

How do the statements and findings in Panel 2 confirm or challenge the hypotheses you made after Panel 1?

Make a note of any new hypotheses made at this stage, before moving to Panel 3.

PANEL 3

'Our study suggests that it is women who refuse society's sex role orientation who are using their diminutive names as one way of indicating this rejection.

'Giving a daughter a highly feminine name may have an enduring effect on her personality. Amongst our subjects there were no boys named Sue but there were girls named George, Cecil and Jack.'

From Chris Mihill, *The Guardian*

Reproduced from *The new social work practice* by Mark Doel and Steven Shardlow, Arena, Aldershot

What conclusions have you reached as a result of reading all three panels? To what extent have the hypotheses which you made after Panel 1 been confirmed or challenged?

Practice wisdom

When you hear a generalization being made by a colleague, note it down as soon as you can. In this way, you will build a small dossier of practice wisdom relevant to the agency where you are placed. An example of this kind of generalization is: 'After a short period in care, demented people often go back home more confused than ever.'

Resist the temptation to comment on them; at this stage recognizing them as generalizations is useful because it helps you be aware of the impact that these hypotheses have on people's actions, including your own. You could be surprised at the number of pieces of practice wisdom you accumulate during the placement.

Take one of the generalizations which most teases you. It may be one that you have arrived at yourself during the placement; certainly, it should be one which interests you, but which you have no firm opinion about. For example, one court officer said: 'I'm sure that a lot of the kids who get into trouble with the law seem to be "middle" children in their family.'

How would you go about finding out more information, either to confirm or refute the generalization, and how useful would it be for practice?

Reproduced from *The new social work practice* by Mark Doel and Steven Shardlow, Arena, Aldershot

20 Generalist and specialist practice

About Activity 20: Essence

'Essence' is designed to trigger a consideration of what is different about, and what is common to, the various manifestations of social work. In this chapter, students are encouraged to look for the 'core' of social work practice.

Purpose

One of the major sea-changes in social work practice is the ebb and flow between generic and specialist practice. This chapter explores the historical development of these practices and explores differences between 'generalist', 'generic' and 'specialist' practice.

Method

- Read the advertisements in the 'Essence' activity. They are all taken from the back pages of the same issue of *Community Care* (4 December 1996). The names of employing agencies have been changed, contacts and addresses have been omitted, but in all other respects the advertisements are unaltered.
- What do you consider are the main similarities and what are the main differences in the work which these job adverts reveal? What is the 'social worker' in them?

Activity 20   ESSENCE

West Hollisshire NHS Trust
PRIORITY ENHANCED CARE MANAGER

£17,282–£19,372 pro rata per annum

A highly motivated person is required to manage a service providing quality Community Care to the people of West Hollisshire.

You should have a business background, be computer literate and familiar with Microsoft Word and Excel packages. You must also be flexible and prepared to accept responsibility outside working hours.

The hours are 22.5 per week worked in the main over three days based at Park Hospital. Car driver essential.

Perlman House Adolescent Unit
SENIOR PRACTITIONER

£25,092–£26,969 p.a. inc.

Perlman House is an NHS tertiary inpatient, daypatient and outpatient unit for adolescents. It provides multiprofessional assessment and therapeutic services for young people with a wide range of problems. Referrals come from both health and local authority services.

We are looking for a senior practitioner with substantial operational experience with child care and child protection to join as a senior member of the multiprofessional team. Within the Unit you undertake assessments as a care manager, coordinate discharge packages, compile court reports and provide specialist advice in child protection. Externally you will liaise closely with local authority social work, education and probation services. Expertise in group work and interest to develop and run outpatient group programmes are desirable.

Meyer and Timms County Council
WORKING TOWARDS EQUALITY

Social Workers (Part-time)

Salary £14,436–£20,766 pro rata

At Coping, 18.5 hours each post. An opportunity has arisen to join our Older Adults Team, for qualified Social Workers (CQSW, CSS, DipSW).

The responsibilities of the post will include individual and care assessments of need, as well as the arrangement and monitoring of complex packages of care. This will involve using a range of provider services including independent and voluntary agencies, both in a hospital and community setting. The work is intensive in nature and experience of work with physically frail elderly people and people with dementia is desirable.

The team is committed to providing good support and supervision and developing staff through training initiatives. A formal appraisal and development scheme is actively used. In addition there is the opportunity for information technology use.

A full driving licence is essential. A casual car user allowance is attached to these posts.

City of Younghusband
Social Services Department

Fostering and Adoption Officer
£20,229 to £21,975

We offer the opportunity of undertaking a variety of both fostering and adoption work, as part of a skilled and innovative but busy team. At present we are continuing to develop a Short Break Scheme and other services for children with disabilities, and would particularly welcome applicants with an interest in this area.

You should be a qualified Social Worker and have substantial child care experience. Family placement experience would be an advantage.

Experience and previous skills are recognized by this Unit and are built upon through regular supervision and opportunities for further training and development.

Reid Community Mental Health NHS Trust and Epstein Hospice
Bereavement Counsellor
£16,024–£18,747 + Allowances (A+C Grade 6)

Younghusband Trust is looking to appoint a full time family counsellor to provide support to families and carers facing bereavement.

Based in two palliative care units, you will work closely with Volunteers and Nursing staff in the delivery and ongoing development of a high quality Bereavement Service.

If you have background as a Social Worker and have experience of bereavement care, we would like to hear from you.

BIESTEK SOCIAL SERVICES

Senior Outreach Day Centre Worker
£17,097–£18,837 p.a. inc. (2 posts)

To enable people with a high level of need to access and obtain appropriate services, including working in service users' own homes. You will need to hold an RMN, CSS, DipSW, CQSW or other relevant qualification. You will need to have experience at a supervisory level of working directly with people who have mental health support needs, have a knowledge of community outreach work and of relevant legislation relating to mental health.

Reproduced from *The new social work practice* by Mark Doel and Steven Shardlow, Arena, Aldershot

DEVORE SOCIETY
giving children a chance

African Planning Scheme
Social Worker

£16,700–£23,000 2 year contract

'Positive Options' provides practical support to parents living with HIV/AIDS who wish to make long term plans for the future care of their children. You will work directly with families and children from a wide range of cultures and backgrounds, providing advice and support. In order to maximise the resources available to them, you'll need to liaise with a range of statutory and voluntary agencies, in both the UK and Africa. You will also build links with the African community, who comprise 75% of our users.

Training, consultancy and co-work with other professionals, such as family finding social workers in the Boroughs will be an important aspect of this role. You will also need to keep yourself well informed with regards to legislation and information on HIV and AIDS, and keep this and other important information in an organized manner.

With a minimum of two years in a local authority childcare setting, you communicate well with children, young people and families and are well-versed in legislation affecting children.

You are self-motivated, committed to anti-discriminatory practice and possess the confidence, common sense and personal strength to work with families facing bereavement and other complex issues. A good standard of written and spoken English, a knowledge of African languages and a recognized social work qualification are essential. Section 5.2(d) of the Race Relations Act applies.

London Borough of Barclay
Specialist Social worker with Deaf People

£17,097–£21,978 p.a. inc.

We are seeking a qualified Social Worker and a qualified (or Stage 3) BSL user, based within the Physical and Sensory Disabilities Team at the Community Care Advice Centre, Hadleigh Road, Pinker Park.

Barclay has an informed and active deaf community where groups work alongside local voluntary groups and agencies.
You will be based within an established Community Care Team, which undertakes assessments and care management with disabled people.

Direct work with deaf people and development work within the Borough are the focus of this post, therefore candidates should be suitably experienced.

This post is available for job share.

South Richmondshire
WORKING TOWARDS EQUAL OPPORTUNITIES

Independent People

We are looking to set up a pool of independent people who could be asked to help investigative complaints or sit on a complaints Review Panel as part of our borough's complaints procedure.

You will need to have:

- excellent inter-personal skills, tact and sensitivity
- a social work qualification (although exceptional people without qualification will be considered)
- knowledge and experience of social care, Social Services Departments and complaints
- investigative, organizational, analytical and report writing skills
- independence from the County – which means you must not have carried out any work (paid or unpaid) for the County before.

We will provide full administrative support as necessary.
Investigation and Review Panel work will be contracted out individually dependent on the case and will be time-limited.
We will pay £150 per day, all inclusive.

CITY AND COUNTY OF MINAHAN
CO-ORDINATOR – DEMENTIA TEAM

Salary £20,247–£23,925

Unitary Dementia Team is a joint initiative between the City and County of Minahan and Pincus Healthcare NHS Trust, and offers a comprehensive, multi disciplinary service. The Co-ordinator will be responsible for the leadership and management of the team of social workers, nurses, care managers and specialist home carers and night settlers. The ideal candidate will have a sound awareness of the issues involved in working with persons with dementia, their relatives and carers; proven assessment, communication and organizational skills; and knowledge and preferably working experience of the NHS and Community Care Act and Care Management process. Recognized qualification essential (CQSW, CSS, DipSW).

Octavia Hill School
Head of Care

Salary Scale NJC PO Range

The Headteacher and Governors seek to appoint a suitably qualified and experienced person to fill this post as soon as possible. The successful applicant will be a member of the Senior Management team, responsible for the residential staff. Octavia Hill caters for approximately 40 Statemented boys with emotional and behavioural difficulties. The postholder need not be resident, but accommodation is available on site.

North Bartlett Council
Social Work Department

Community Worker
£13,977–£18,180
(7.5% Irregular Hours Allowance)

You will promote, implement and support community development in priority areas of Sainsbury Social Work Area Team.

You will undertake analysis of social needs and provide support and practical assistance to a variety of groups within the area. As a result, there may be a requirement to work evenings.

It is essential that you have a Degree or Diploma in Youth and Community Work. Possession of a relevant social work qualification and a driving licence is desirable.

Reproduced from *The new social work practice* by Mark Doel and Steven Shardlow, Arena, Aldershot

- What do you think the job adverts tell you about current social work practice? Try asking five people who are not connected with social work (friends and relatives, for instance) what social work is.

Variations

Five or six detailed job descriptions from your own agency might draw out the commonalities and differences even more clearly. Try comparing these with adverts from other non-social work journals for related posts (for example, health visitors) – how different and how similar are they?

In order to begin to understand the great diversity in the way specialist practice is represented (see 'Notes for practice teachers' for more details), students could be asked to make a note of all the different specialist social work practice they are aware of. The harder task is to identify what is the 'social worker' in all of these.

Notes for practice teachers

The note on the flysheet of Zofia Butrym's book, *The Nature of Social Work*, was written in 1975, but remains apt today:

> This book argues that the present lack of consensus about the nature and the functions of social work constitutes a serious problem which, if allowed to continue, will result in loss of purpose and usefulness by social workers. It therefore attempts to answer the question: 'What is social work?' (Butrym, 1975)

Twenty years on, the title of Malcolm Payne's book asks *'What is Professional Social Work?'* His narrative, which runs through the book, 'implies that being involved in education and management, being in the voluntary and statutory sectors and doing community, policy and development work can all be regarded as social work' (Payne, 1996, pp. 9–10).

If experienced social workers in educational and practice settings are asking 'what is social work?', students can be forgiven for pondering the same question. In this chapter we take one abiding tension in social work practice – that between general and specialist practice – as a specific illustration of the quest to define social work. We will root this central tension in its historical context; an understanding of the recurring nature of these themes will help students to understand the present state of social work and better anticipate its future.

The common base of social work practice

> The common base of social work practice consists of concepts, generalizations, and principles relating to knowledge, values and intervention – i.e. abstract ideas. (Bartlett, 1970, p. 129)

Writing in 1970, Harriet Bartlett made a distinction between generic practice and the common base of social work practice which is as useful now as it was then. Bartlett warns against what she refers to as 'bipolar thinking'; in other words, a division which separates people from their contexts. She sees the need to direct attention to the nature of the exchange between individuals and their environment as a way of eliminating this separation.

Bartlett considers that the early focus in social work on 'feeling and doing', though useful in developing the skills base of the individual practitioner, deflected attention from 'thinking and knowing', so there was no equal momentum toward a comprehensive view of social work. 'Thus the relation between the practice of the individual social worker and the broad essentials of his [sic] profession's practice was not faced' (Bartlett, 1970, p. 134). Bartlett proposed the concept of social functioning as providing a common base for social work practice. Later, in the 'Notes for students', we shall describe how – just at the time Bartlett was writing – methodologies were being developed which would be forces for integration rather than division in social work practice. These forces continue to provide a conceptual map, both for the social work profession as a whole and for individual practice as a part.

What is a specialism?

Going further back, almost half a century ago, Hollis and Taylor (1951) pointed to the 'lack of adequate criteria for determining what is *basic* and what is *specialized* in social work', and considered this to be the main reason for the inability to develop a satisfactory social work curriculum. Bartlett (1970, p. 194) noted that the concept of specialization is only valid 'when there is a concept of a whole that can be divided into parts' and that social work's peculiar origins as 'a profession growing *through* its parts' led to premature concepts of specialization. An aggregation can just as soon become a disaggregation. She declared that 'practitioners not long in practice cannot be regarded as specialists because specialization rests on extended study and experience from which true expertise develops' (1970, p. 195). Bartlett would have considered the idea of developing a particular or focused area of practice in the second year of study as a social work *student* as very premature. Perhaps this rush to specialist practice, in advance of the testing and integration of a sound base, explains social workers' difficulty in resisting agency definitions of what social work practice is.

Bartlett argued for greater discrimination in the use of the terms 'generic' and 'specific', and of 'basic' and 'specialized'. Papell (1996) reminds us that the term 'generic' first appeared in North American social work in the report of the Milford Conference in 1929, though only a single method (casework) was then involved:

> The recommendation was that education presented in the university was to be generic while the specialized knowledge needed in settings wherever casework was practised – such as psychiatric, medical, child welfare – was to be taught in the field. (Papell, 1996 p. 16)

The division between specialist and generic, specialism and generalism, remains far from clear. The distinctions can be drawn along many different lines, depending on time and place. A quarter of a century ago, Bartlett noted that social workers were accustomed to think of their practice in terms of agencies, fields and methods. She mused why it was proving so difficult for 'social workers to take the necessary steps toward a perception of their practice as no longer fragmented' (Bartlett, 1970, p. 131). A quarter of a century later the movement towards specialist practice in the UK is strong and is largely defined by age: children and families, or adult services. Traditionally, lines have been drawn according to client groups defined by the nature of the 'problem' – mental health worker, child protection worker, mobility officer, and so on.

The setting in which the practitioner is based can also be seen as a specialism: field social worker, residential worker, day centre worker. Historically, setting has been an important definer of salary and status, bu the trend has been for settings to be merged in the education of social workers (in the 1960s there were Residential Child Care Officer courses, but a recent attempt to establish a Residential Child Care 'pathway' on a Diploma in Social Work programme was not considered viable and it merged with the Child Care pathway).

In addition to setting, 'field' has also been used to demarcate areas of specialist social work practice: hospital, school, court, and so on. In these circumstances, social work is a secondary activity to the principal profession – medicine, education, the law, and the like.

Specialism by territory

In these views of specialism, social work is a land of many territories (defined by age, client group, nature of problem, setting, and so on) and specialist workers become knowledgeable about their territory in more detail, rather like consultants carve up the territory of the human body – foot; heart; ear, nose and throat, and so on (see Figure 20.1). However, in North America, the concept of specialist practice (sometimes called 'concentration' in the curriculum) is concerned more with depth, so that one can have a generalist knowledge or a specialist knowledge of the same territory, the difference being the depth of knowledge, not the territory itself. In this construct, 'the generalist practitioner is defined as one who works with a variety of systems' (Tolson, Reid and Garvin, 1994, p. 396). We shall explore these ideas in more detail later.

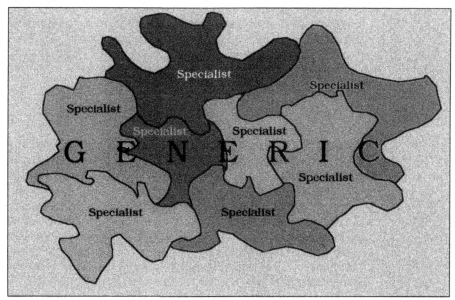

Figure 20.1 The territorial model

Reproduced from *The new social work practice* by Mark Doel and Steven Shardlow, Arena, Aldershot

Specialism by method

In addition to the territorial approach to medical specialisms, there are other kinds of demarcation. Acupuncturists, chiropractors and homoeopaths specialize in alternative *methods* of practice. By contrast, social work does not have a strong base in practice methodology. It seems that everyone is either eclectic (code for agnostic), or claims to practise in a task-centred way (despite the absence of all the formal elements of the task-centred model!). Indeed, agencies would be suspicious of practitioners declaring themselves to be method specialists: seeking a position as a Brief Solution specialist or a Cognitive Behavioural specialist would carry little weight.

Practitioners, too, often show scepticism towards the idea of models and methods as suspect and restrictive. The nearest approach to a methodological specialism is groupwork, which some probation services have adopted as the preferred method of service. However, groupwork is as much a context for practice as it is a single method of practice (there are, for instance, as many methods of groupwork practice as there are individual practice).

Interestingly, some areas of specialist practice are seldom considered specialisms. Is social work management a specialism? Neighbourhood work, long associated with 'generic practice', could – paradoxically – be considered a specialism in a particular geographical locale as well as being a method of working.

In conclusion, the notion of specialization, though fashionable at present, is far from clear-cut. The terms of debate have been all but closed off by the assumption that the meaning of specialist work is defined by the current organizational practices of social work agencies.

What is generalist practice?

Ironically, exploring the notion of generalist practice with students can provide them with a clearer view of what specialist practice is. At the core of all social work practice are the knowledge, values and skills which make that practice 'social work'. This is the basis of social work, and it is generic because it is what underpins all social work practice. 'It' is disputed; 'it' is not transparent; but whatever 'it' is, it is common to all settings, fields, methods and client groups. For example, the reflective process described in Chapter 19, from observation to action, is a process which is generic. It lies at the heart of all social work practice (or *should* lie at its heart) whatever the setting. Indeed, most of the activities which begin the chapters in this book are 'generic' – appropriate and applicable to all forms and settings of social work practice.

Generic and generalist

There is an important distinction between generic and generalist practice. In Britain, the term 'generic' has become equated with an ability to work with a range of people in a variety of different settings and circumstances (see Figure 20.1). However, this is an unfortunate equation, since genericism can therefore be interpreted as 'the sum of many specialisms'. This leaves the generic worker open to the (gender-specific) charge of 'jack of all trades and master of none', and very vulnerable to a retrenchment into the constituent specialist parts.

It is preferable to understand generic practice as the common and core knowledge, skill and value base at the heart of social work practice. *Generalist* practice, on the other hand, is a concept to refer to the breadth of systems with which the social worker is expected to work (it is a term more commonly used in North America). In this model, the difference between generalist and specialist practice is the number and level of systems with which the practitioner engages. There is no hierarchy, but a notion of both generalist and specialist practice building from a common generic core (see Figure 20.2). In fact, generalist practice is more complex than specialist practice, because it requires a broader knowledge of systems and the skills to move between them. Indeed, it is often the team rather than the individual worker which is generalist, a team constituting a generalist system of service (each member of the team specializing), rather as Seebohm saw the reorganization of British social work services in the early 1970s.

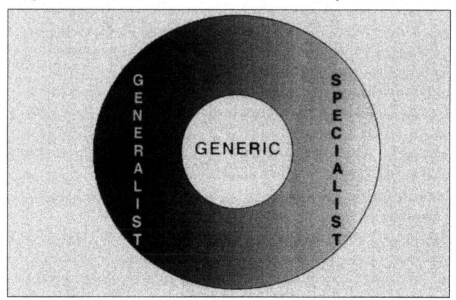

Figure 20.2 The systems model

Reproduced from *The new social work practice* by Mark Doel and Steven Shardlow, Arena, Aldershot

Thus, it is the idea of 'systems' which best helps us to conceptualize the generic/generalist/specialist debate. Tolson, Reid and Garvin (1994, pp. 397–9) propose a continuum from least to most generalist practice. 'Most traditional social workers ... specialize in work with one system – *either* individual or families or groups or organizations or communities'. In Figure 20.2 we present the continuum as a circle shaded from most generalist to most specialist. Without the generic core – the inner circle – all other practices, whether generalist or specialist, are ill-founded, and any headlong rush into a single specialist practice or a combination of specialisms (which, as we have seen, are sometimes misleadingly called 'generic') leaves social work practice vulnerable.

Because generalist practice is concerned with the ability to work at different levels with many different *systems*, it provides social work with an integrating concept. Unlike genericism, which in its manifestation as the sum-of-the-parts has no core text, generalist practice has an influential text in Pincus and Minahan's (1973) *Social Work Practice: Model and Method*, standard reading on training programmes in the 1970s, and more recently in Tolson, Reid and Garvin's (1994) *Generalist Practice: a Task Centred Approach*.

So, there are two reasons why it seems necessary to ask the question 'What is social work?' with such regularity:

- The profession is uncertain about how to conceptualize itself. The territorial approach leaves social work vulnerable to break up. We have advanced another possibility in this chapter, but this systems model is by no means generally accepted or understood – and has only been arrived at after some re-defining of existing terms. Our intent has been to demystify, but the result may well have been the opposite!

- Even when a conceptual map for social work has been agreed and understood, the generic core is by no means a given. What are the knowledge, values and skills common to all social work practice?

Notes for students

Generalist methods

The partnerships between agencies and educational institutions to deliver the Diploma in Social Work in the UK have given the social institutions and agencies which employ social workers a stronger role in determining what social work is. The new managerialism has also permitted these institutions to flex their muscles in ways which were considered less acceptable in former times. In these circumstances, we need to ask what is to prevent professional practice becoming occupational practice.

It is not the first time that social work has been vulnerable as a profession. Writing about the 1960s, Heus and Pincus (1986, p. 6) noted that

> in spite of the existence of a single professional association, social work remained fragmented by method (casework, groupwork, and community organization), fields of practice (e.g. medical social work, child welfare, corrections) and divided purposes (e.g. individual change versus environmental change, service versus reform).

The 1970s, however, were a time when the prominence of systems theory acted as a unifying process, with a broad view of the service users' situation, and the development of an integrated social work method. Social work became conceptualized as planned change rather than individual therapy, and systems theory helped to integrate the profession, with a focus on the interaction between people and their environment. To use the language of systems theory, 'the client was no longer automatically assumed to be the appropriate target of change' (Heus and Pincus, 1986, p. 7).

The creative generalist

Heus and Pincus (1986) develop a notion of the 'creative generalist'. They ally systems thinking and a problem-solving approach with knowledge from the interdisciplinary field of creativity, in an attempt to 'further understand the *art* side of practice'. They seek to ally intuitive and rational thinking. This approach supports the systems model of generic practice (Figure 20.2) rather than the territorial one (Figure 20.1).

As we have seen, the territorial model has led us to associate a generalist with an eclectic, 'master of none' approach, and a specialist with an expert. 'Since expertise is a hallmark of professionalism, the eclectic is [seen as] less than professional' (Heus and Pincus, 1986, p. 13). Similarly, the tendency in North American universities to offer generalist practice at a beginning, bachelor's level, has emphasized its place as a junior. Heus and Pincus emphasize the fact that 'what a creative generalist knows a lot about and is expert in, is simply different from what the specialist knows a lot about'.

Reproduced from *The new social work practice* by Mark Doel and Steven Shardlow, Arena, Aldershot

Martin (1992, p. 341) uses the term 'domain' to describe the territory occupied by a profession 'on the grounds of exclusive or superior knowledge, ... practice competence, or both'. She analyses the difficulties social work has faced in staking out its own territory in the Australian context. In particular, she highlights the interrelationship of gender and organizational issues, where a largely female profession has found it difficult to penetrate a bureaucracy in which senior positions are usually male. Social work has tended to rely heavily on a sole employer, and during the period when it had the greatest opportunity to occupy exclusive territory, it was severely short-staffed; unqualified staff had to undertake these functions thus undermining subsequent claims that they could only be performed by professional social workers.

At one time, social work's strongest claim to a unique terrain was its ability to occupy a large territory – in the absence of an exclusive domain, it could rightly claim to have an unmatched 'spread'. However, over recent years,

> as the boundaries of older professions expanded and there developed an increasing number of competing occupational groups and educational programmes related to welfare and what became known as the human services, the domain of social work became harder rather than easier to define. (Martin, 1992, p. 342)

It is possible to develop specialities in the territorial sense (probation, mental health, and so on) alongside a generalist orientation. Heus and Pincus (1986, p. 15) argue cogently that it does not require giving up one for the other. However, they are equally clear that

> specializations that emphasize treatment approaches (e.g. behaviour modification) or system sizes (e.g. family group, organization) are, in effect, specializations by *solution*. They are thus incompatible with the creative problem-solving orientation of the generalist.

High tide of specialist practice

In the UK in the late 1990s, the specialist tide is as high as it has ever been but there is no reason to suppose that the specialist–generalist cycle has come to an end. Social work's strength is, no doubt, its diversity and its ability to extemporize as society changes and evolves. However, the failure to conceptualize notions of generic, specialist and generalist practice continues to leave social work exposed. The territorial model is implicitly adopted by default in the absence of clear thinking about alternatives, and it leaves professions in general, and social work in particular, vulnerable to colonization or disintegration. A systems model (Figure 20.2) puts generalist and specialist practice on an equal footing, each with a common generic core.

Reproduced from *The new social work practice* by Mark Doel and Steven Shardlow, Arena, Aldershot

Finally, the following three criteria are suggested as indicating when employers may not be in the best position to define competences:

- when the profession is predominantly self-employed;
- where employers do not have precise knowledge of the requirements of the profession;
- where there are statutory training requirements.

(From a government position paper on Higher Vocational Qualifications, 1997)

From your experiences on placement in a social work agency, and as a person who will shortly be entering the profession, what safeguards do you consider these criteria offer for social work? How will you ensure that your practice in the future continues to be 'social work'?

Reproduced from *The new social work practice* by Mark Doel and Steven Shardlow, Arena, Aldershot

Exit: Comparative social work

About Exit Activity: Gulliver's travels

'Gulliver's travels' consists of an opportunity for students to think about social work practice in different countries. They are provided with brief details of an imaginary country and have to consider how to develop social work there, drawing on the experience of social work in their own country.

Purpose

The purpose of this activity is to help students to consider how social work differs across different countries or regions, and – as a result – to gain a greater understanding of social work in their own.

Method

- 'Gulliver's travels' is best undertaken by a group of three or four students. It can also be completed successfully with a single student and practice teacher working together.
- The students read the extract from the report on the imaginary country 'Gangnidborb' (about 5 minutes).
- Independently, they complete their own recommendation sheet (15 minutes) and then jointly discuss the reasons for their recommendations (about half an hour).
- In the subsequent practice tutorial, students discuss their views about

Exit: GULLIVER'S TRAVELS

- Read the information on the fact sheet about 'Gangnidborb', a country in Eastern Europe, then consider what recommendations you would make about the development of social work there.
- Complete the Recommendation section of the report.

Briefing information

On behalf of the Partnership of Nations Organization for Social Work Development (PONOSWOD), you have joined three other international observers to make a visit to Gangnidborb, in order to observe the level of social work development, and to work with the Gangnidborbs to advise about future needs. Some of the essential extracts from the reports your colleagues have prepared on Gangnidborb are given in the Gangnidborb fact sheet (next page).

Report to PONOSWOD on Gangnidborb

When you have considered the fact sheet, use the following questions to help you frame your report. The size of the boxes is not intended to be indicative; you may prefer to use a separate sheet.

Recommendations

We recommend that social work should be established and that it should seek to achieve the following:

-
-
-
-
-
-

To do this we suggest the following strategy:	It will also be necessary to identify the following resources:

Reproduced from *The new social work practice* by Mark Doel and Steven Shardlow, Arena, Aldershot

Gangnidborb fact sheet

Background...
A medium-sized country – 453 679 sq.k – located in Eastern Europe, with access to the sea. The population is 45 million people and has been declining for four years, Most of the population lives in rural communities. There are six large industrial cities with a combined population of 12 million.

The population...
is highly differentiated. There is a small minority, less then 5% with access to considerable wealth; the rest of the population lives in poverty. The principal minority group is the population which lives in the west of the country – the 'westerners'.

By tradition...
under the communist regime there were some homes for older people, but access to these was limited to those who occupied special positions in the party hierarchy, or for particularly favoured groups, such as farm workers or members of the army. In addition, there is a well-established tradition of sanatoria for all groups in society (for example, children with behavioural difficulties might be sent to a sanatorium for a few weeks' recuperation).

Housing...
is in severe shortage, and it takes many years' wait to be allocated a flat in an apartment block. Often, these apartments are overcrowded, with several generations of the family sharing the same room. In the countryside people live in small single-storey wooden houses.

Recently...
Since the overthrow of the communist state, there has been an attempt to establish a democratic political system and a free market economy. However, economic production has fallen by 50% in four years. The infrastructure (roads, telephones, etc.) is in a desperate state of disrepair.

Social work...
There has never been a social work profession. There is a large number of trained doctors, psychologists and psychiatrists (some of whom are keen to retrain as social workers). The previous regime took the view that there could be no social problems under a communist system and therefore no need for a profession of social work.

Previous structures and services...
The police have dealt with all forms of crime and families have been expected to cope with their own problems.

A network...
of psychiatric hospitals exists. In the past these have been used to incarcerate dissidents... and there are a few children's houses for orphans or children abandoned by their parents. These houses typically care for 60 or more children. Adoption and fostering are unknown in any formal, legal sense.

Current problems...
The country has been traumatized by involvement in a recent war, and many conscript soldiers have returned home wounded and psychologically distressed, often unable to find jobs. There is a growing range of problems: a rapid rise in drug abuse, an increase in crime (much of it controlled by Mafia-type groups), an increase in suicide and depression, and a growth in prostitution.

Finances...
The government's financial resources are severely limited and tax revenues are falling. There has been 10% inflation per month for the last two years. The government is committed to the establishment of social work as a profession to mediate the hardships that the population is experiencing.

---

if you were to compile a similar fact sheet on your own country or state, what recommendations would you be likely to come up with? How much would these differ from the actual organization of social work in your country or state?

Reproduced from *The new social work practice* by Mark Doel and Steven Shardlow, Arena, Aldershot

how to develop social work practice, paying particular attention to the reasons for their recommendations.
- In the practice tutorial, students should be encouraged to explore their views about the nature and form of social work practice in their own country. Students should identify those aspects of social work that reflect good practice and which could be used as models to develop practice in 'Gangnidborb'. However, models of practice are not necessarily directly transferable to another cultural context.
- Encourage the students to consider whether their views about good practice in their own country have been influenced by considering the development of social work practice in another country.

Variations

You may want to change the details of the example country, 'Gangnidborb', to reflect particular aspects of social work practice that you would like students to explore. There is no reason why students need to consider a country with little previous experience of social work. They could consider a country with a similar history to their own, but one which exhibits a different form of social work. Likewise, real examples serve just as well as imaginary countries. For example, if you are working within the UK you may wish to use the different constituent countries, England, Scotland, Wales and Northern Ireland, to explore differences in practice. For example, a comparison of Northern Ireland with one of the other UK countries allows students to explore the influence of sectarianism on social work practice (see for example Cairns, 1989; Smith and Campbell, 1996).

It is also possible to consider regional differences using a comparative approach: for example, to consider social work practice in two different states of the US, such as urban New Jersey and rural Oklahoma.

If you have access to the Internet you can easily obtain basic data on all countries to include in the information you prepare for students. This will give your simulations a sense of reality.

In the activity you may wish to set limits on the resources that a student can suggest are made available for the development of social work. You could suggest that a certain budget would be provided from external sources; in the case of an Eastern European state this might be from the European Union.

Notes

In learning about how to 'do social work' we can draw a parallel with learning how to drive a car. In the early stages of driving, many learners find that there are too many actions to perform in a very short time period and there can be a similar feeling of being overwhelmed when learning social work. In such situations learners may tend to focus on the minutiae of task performance rather than broader considerations about the meanings and significance of actions. The novice car driver may be unconcerned with asking questions about the mechanics of the car, the social symbolism of car ownership or the impact of the car on urban life. Likewise, the beginner social worker may be unconcerned with questions about the need for social work as an activity in society, the impact of social work on individuals and the state, or whether social work takes different forms in different countries, regions or societies.

Even so, students should be encouraged to ask these broader questions, and to consider social work in a comparative way is one way to achieve this breadth. When we examine the practice of social work in differing geographical locations we find that there are many significant differences as well as similarities in the practice and organization of social work (see for example Colton *et al.*, 1995).

Dimensions of difference

The student needs to consider ways in which social work might, and does, differ across national boundaries, and possible reasons for those differences. Asking such questions may lead students to speculate why there is a professional activity known as social work at all. Why, for instance, are all caring functions not left with families, or all forms of social control and social monitoring left with agencies such as the police? Consider the following example:

> Ukraine is now an independent state. Previously, as part of the USSR, no social work profession existed, and a branch of the local military police was responsible for detecting delinquent juveniles and bringing them to the courts, and also for the community supervision of those found guilty (and not given custodial sentences). Caring functions were often left to families; children with disabilities did not have the right to attend state schools and no other suitable educational provision was made available. Consequently, such children remained all day in apartments, cared for by parents or other family members. One reason for the state's refusal to recognize and make provision for such problems was ideological – the belief that there could be no such problems within a socialist society and that all social problems were a function of capitalism.

In the states of Eastern and Central Europe, previously under communist rule, there has been a rush to establish social work as part of the social and economic transformation of society (Deacon *et al.*, 1992; Hare, 1993). Social work is seen as an essential constituent of a modern industrialized state, to provide care for those in society unable to care for themselves and to protect those who are vulnerable. As such, social work is necessary to keep the machinery of society running smoothly (Davies, 1994). There are, of course, different views of the function of social work (see Chapter 2).

Forms of social work

Around the globe, social work is practised in a variety of different ways (in respect of Europe see Cannan, Berry and Lyons, 1992; Hill, 1991; Lorenz, 1994; Munday, 1993; Shardlow and Payne, 1998) and an awareness of some of these differences will help students to understand this wider context of social work and reflect critically on social work practice 'at home'. In the US, for example, there is a significant number of social workers who practise as private practitioners, offering their services to clients for direct payment (usually insurance payouts). So strong is this trend that the University of California has developed a programme to encourage students to consider working with the original clients of social work, that is those on the margins of society who are poor. As Grossman and Perry (1996) comment:

> From the late 1970's until recent years, the profession of social work in the USA has become disconnected from its traditional focus on the needs of the poor and the institutions that address these needs – typically the publicly-supported social services. Training for social work has increasingly meant preparation for careers serving middle class clients in private practice. As social work participation in private practice has increased, the profession's involvement in public and non-profit agencies has declined, to the extent that many key public institutions have become de-professionalized. De-professionalization is associated with increased bureaucratization, decreased individualization of services, and increased focus on maintenance and protection rather than prevention and rehabilitation. Moreover, lack of professional assessment increases the frequency of bad choices that may result in harm to children and other vulnerable client populations. (Grossman and Perry, 1996, p. 43)

This could not be more different than the position of social work in some other countries, such as Portugal, where there is considerable involvement of social workers in community development, with a particular focus on the alleviation of poverty (Rodrigues and Monteiro, 1998).

Boundaries of social work with other professional groups

Social work is one of many human service or helping professions that we might expect to find in a developed or developing society. Typically, social workers will have working relationships with medical practitioners (doctors, nurses and other clinical professionals), teachers, lawyers, the police and local and central government officials. We should not assume that the roles and functions of these occupational groups will be similarly defined in different states. There is potential for considerable overlap between social work and these groups according to the construction of social work within any state. Social work is an interesting profession in that it is shaped by the national traditions of the society in which it functions. Encouraging students to 'map' the boundaries, in terms of roles and functions, between social work and other professional groups in one national state or region provides the opportunity for comparison.

An example of differences in professional boundaries between human service professions is to be found within Europe. In some states (for example, Denmark, Germany and Italy) there is a profession unknown in other states, such as Eire and the UK: members of this profession are variously referred to as social pedagogues (taking an Anglicized version of the Germanic name for the profession). According to Cannan and colleagues (1992), social pedagogues

> play a major role in the provision of services for children and young people in both community and residential settings ... [Social pedagogy] can be seen as a perspective, including social action, which aims to promote human welfare through child rearing and educational practices to prevent or ease social problems by providing people with the means to manage their own lives, and to make changes in their circumstances.
> (Cannan, Berry and Lyons, 1992)

Social pedagogy is grounded in the notion of education, not for academic excellence but for social competence and citizenship, and it is a concept of 'education' not commonly understood in the Anglo-Saxon countries. (See Hämäläinen, 1989 for further discussion of the concept.)

Social pedagogy is just one very striking example of the differences between the professional boundaries of social work and other professional groups which exist across national boundaries. Another fruitful area you may choose to examine is the involvement (or not) of social workers in the provision of income maintenance.

In conclusion

Comparative social work allows consideration of fundamental questions about the nature of the discipline:

- Is there agreement in a society that there should be some form of social work provision?
- If there is agreement to provide social work, what form should it take?
- Who should be included and excluded in the provision of social work help?
- How should social work help be provided?

It is easy to become locked into our own society's response to these questions, without recognizing that others have reached different conclusions and are evolving diverse forms of social work practice, often based on quite fundamentally different premises. Sacco (1996) describes an African paradigm as a foundation for a spirituality in social work practice which is in strong contrast to the Western materialist basis. Indeed, one of the peculiarities of social work as a profession is the degree to which it is rooted in the historical traditions of the society in which it is found (for an account of those historical factors in the UK see Younghusband, 1981). What are the distinctive features of social work practice in your country and what historical factors explain its particular configuration?

Social work practice is different to a significant degree in various countries in that it occupies different professional space, has different organizational forms, is founded on diverse cultural paradigms and educates would-be social workers differently (Brauns and Kramer, 1986; Constable and Metha, 1993). We may, then, legitimately ask, 'What is common to social work practice across the world?' 'What is social work?'

Wherever you practise social work, wherever you are learning to become a social worker, we hope you have found some answers to these questions in the pages of this book.

Bibliography

[1-20] numbers in brackets refer to chapters
[P] refers to Preface
[N] refers to Entry
[X] refers to Exit

Adams, J. (1995), *Risk*, London: UCL Press. [14]
Adams, R. (1996), *Social Work and Empowerment* (second edn), Houndmills, Basingstoke: Macmillan. [17]
Ahmad, B. (1990), *Black Perspectives in Social Work*, Birmingham: Venture Press. [2,8,17]
Ash, E. (1992), 'Piggy in the middle', in 'Staff Supervision', *Community Care*, 30 July. [N]
Aymer, C. and Bryan, A. (1996), 'Black students' experiences on social work courses: accentuating the positives', *British Journal of Social Work*, **26**, 1–16 [19]
Baird, P. (1991), 'The proof of the pudding: a study of clients' views of student practice competence', *Issues in Social Work Education*, 10 (1&2), 24–50. [3,8]
Ball, C., Harris, R., Roberts, G. and Vernon, S. (1988), *The Law Report. Teaching and Assessment of Law in Social Work Education*, London: Central Council for Education and Training in Social Work, Paper 4.1. [18]
Ball, C., Roberts, G., Trench, S. and Vernon, S. (1991), *Teaching, Learning and Assessing Social Work Law*, London: Central Council for Education and Training in Social Work. [18]
Banks, S. (1995), *Ethics and Values in Social Work*, Houndmills, Basingstoke: Macmillan. [3]

Barclay, P. M. (1982), *Social Workers: Their Role and Tasks* (The Barclay Report), London: Bedford Square Press. [11]
Barnes, M. and Wistow, G. (1993), *Gaining Influence, Gaining Support: Working with carers in research and practice*, Working Paper no. 8, Leeds: Nuffield Institute for Health. [17]
Barnes, M. and Wistow, G. (1994), *Researching User Involvement*, Leeds: University of Leeds. [11]
Bartlett, H. (1970), *The Common Base of Social Work Practice*, Washington, DC: National Association of Social Workers. [20]
BASW (1983), *Effective and Ethical Recording*, Report of the BASW Case Recording Project Group, Birmingham: BASW. [10]
BASW (1996), *A Code of Ethics for Social Work* (rev. edn), Birmingham: British Association of Social Workers. [3,14]
Beresford, P. (1993), 'Current issues in user involvement and empowerment', in P. Beresford and T. Harding (eds), *A Challenge to Change: practical experiences of building user-led services*, London: NISW [17]
Berne, E. (1966), *Games People Play*, London: André Deutsch. [4]
Billington, S. and Paley, J. (1993), 'Gender, Language and Social Work: A Dialogue', *Issues in Social Work Education*, 13 (2), 4–36. [10]
Blakemore, K. and Boneham, M. (1994), *Age, Race and Ethnicity: a comparative approach*, Buckingham: Open University. [16,17]
Blom-Cooper, L. (1985), *A Child in Trust*, London: London Borough of Brent. [18]
Bogo, M. and Vayda, E. (1987), *The Practice of Field Instruction in Social Work*, Toronto: University of Toronto Press. [E]
Bourne, I. (1996), 'Groupwork Approaches to Social Work Supervision', unpublished Ph.D. thesis: Bristol. [N]
Brauns, H.-J. and Kramer, D. (1986), *Social Work Education in Europe*, Frankfurt am Main: Deutscher Verein. [X]
Braye, S. and Preston-Shoot, M. (1990), 'On teaching and applying the law in social work: it is not that simple', *British Journal of Social Work*, 20 (4), 333–53. [18]
Braye, S. and Preston-Shoot, M. (1992), *Practising Social Work Law*, London: Macmillan. [18]
Braye, S. and Preston-Shoot, M. (1995), *Empowering Practice in Social Care*, Milton Keynes: Open University Press. [18]
Breeforth, M. (1993), 'Users are people', in V. Williamson (ed.), *Users First: The real challenge for community care*, Brighton: University of Brighton, pp 19–27. [13]
Bristol Polytechnic (1982), *Putting It Together: no. 7, personal management and skills*, Bristol: Management Learning Productions. [9]
Brodie, I. (1993), 'Teaching from Practice in Social Work Education: a study of the content of supervision sessions', *Issues in Social Work Education*, 13 (2), 71–91. [N,19]
Brown, A. and Bourne, I. (1996), *The Social Work Supervisor*, Buckingham: Open University Press. [N]
Butrym, Z. (1975), *The Nature of Social Work*, London: Macmillan. [20]

Cairns, E. (1989), 'Society as a Child Abuser: Northern Ireland', in W. Stainton Rogers, D. Hevey and E. Ash (eds), *Child Abuse and Neglect: Facing the challenge*, London: Batsford in association with The Open University, pp. 119–26. [X]
Cannan, C., Berry, L. and Lyons, K. (1992), *Social Work & Europe*, Houndmills, Basingstoke: Macmillan. [X]
CCETSW (1991a), *DipSW: Rules and Requirements for the Diploma in Social Work*, London: Central Council for Education and Training in Social Work. [18]
CCETSW (1991b), *Teaching, Learning and Assessing Social Work Law*, Report of the Law Improvements Project Group, London: Central Council for Education and Training in Social Work. [18]
CCETSW (1991c), *One Small Step Towards Racial Justice*, London: Central Council for Education and Training in Social Work. [16]
CCETSW, (1995), *Review of the Diploma in Social Work*, London: Central Council for Education and Training in Social Work. [18]
Challis, D., Davies, B. and Traske, K. (eds) (1994), *Community Care: New Agendas and Challenges from the UK and Overseas*, Aldershot: Arena. [13]
Cheetham, J., Fuller, R., McIvor, G. and Petch, A. (1992), *Evaluating Social Work Effectiveness*, Buckingham: Open University Press. [19]
Chiu, S. (1989), 'Chinese people: no longer a treasure at home', *Social Work Today*, **20** (48) June. [16]
Clough, R. (ed.) (1996), *Abuse in Residential Institutions*, London: Whiting and Birch. [14]
Coady, M. and Bloch, S. (eds) (1996), *Codes of Ethics and the Professions*, Carlton South: Melbourne University Press. [3]
Colton, M., Hellinckx, W., Ghesquière, P. and Williams, M. (eds) (1995), *The Art and Science of Child Care: Research Policy and Practice in the European Union*, Aldershot: Arena. [X]
Constable, R. and Metha, V. (1993), *Education for Social Work in Eastern Europe*, Vienna: International Association of Schools of Social Work. [X]
Corby, B. (1996), 'Risk Assessment in Child Protection Work', in H. Kemshall and J. Pritchard (eds), *Good Practice in Risk Assessment and Risk Management*, London: Jessica Kingsley, pp. 13–30. [14]
Coulshed, V. (1991), *Social Work Practice*, (second edn), Houndmills, Basingstoke: Macmillan/BASW. [2,5]
Cross, T. et al. (1989), *Towards a Culturally Competent System of Care*, CASSP Technical Assistance Center, Washington, DC 20007, US. [16]
Curnock, K. and Hardiker, P. (1979), *Towards Practice Theory: Skills and Methods in Social Assessments*, London: Routledge & Kegan Paul. [19]
Dalrymple, J. and Burke, B. (1992), *Anti-Oppressive Practice: social care and the law*, Buckingham: Open University. [17]
Danbury, H. (1994), *Teaching Practical Social Work* (third edn), Aldershot: Arena. [1]
Davies, B. and Challis, D. (1986), *Matching Resources to Needs in Community Care: an evaluated demonstration of a long-term care model*, Aldershot: Gower. [13]

Davies, M. (1981), *The Essential Social Worker* (first edn), Aldershot: Gower. [2]
Davies, M. (1994), *The Essential Social Worker: a guide to positive practice*, (third edn), Aldershot: Arena. [P,1,X]
Davies, M. (1997), *The Blackwell Companion to Social Work*, Oxford: Blackwell. [2]
Deacon, B. *et al.* (eds) (1992), *The New Eastern Europe*, London: Sage. [X]
Dearling, A. (1993), *Social Welfare Word Book*, London: Longman. [10]
Department of Health (1989), *Caring for People: Community Care in the Next Decade and Beyond* (White Paper), London: HMSO (Cm 849). [13]
Department of Health (1993), *Guidance on permissible forms of control in children's residential care*, London: HMSO. [14]
Department of Health (1995), *Child Protection: Messages From Research*, London: HMSO. [11]
Devore, W. and Schlesinger, E. G. (1991), *Ethnic-Sensitive Social Work Practice*, (third edn), New York: Macmillan Publishing Company. [16]
DHSS (1978), *Social Service Teams: The Practitioner's View*, London: HMSO. [19]
Doel, M. (1988), 'A practice curriculum to promote accelerated learning', in J. Phillipson, M. Richards and D. Sawdon (eds), *Towards a Practice-Lead Curriculum*, London: National Institute for Social Work, pp. 45–60. [9]
Doel, M. and Lawson, B. (1986), 'Open Records: The Client's Right to Partnership', *British Journal of Social Work*, **16** (4), 407–30. [10]
Doel, M. and Marsh, P. (1992), *Task-Centred Social Work*, Aldershot: Ashgate. [5,8,17,19]
Doel, M. and Shardlow, S. M. (1993), *Social Work Practice: exercises and activities for training and developing social workers*, Aldershot: Arena. [P,5]
Doel, M and Shardlow, S. M. (1996), *Social Work in a Changing World: an International Perspective on Practice Learning*, Aldershot: Arena. [P]
Doel, M. and Shardlow, S. M. (1996a), 'The practice curriculum and practice teaching' in Doel and Shardlow (eds), *Social Work in a Changing World: an International Perspective on Practice Learning*, Aldershot: Arena. [P]
Doel, M. and Shardlow, S. M. (1996b), 'Simulated and live practice teaching: the practice teacher's craft', *Social Work Education*, **15** (4), 16–33. [P,7]
Doel, M., Shardlow, S. M., Sawdon, C. and Sawdon, D. (1996), *Teaching Social Work Practice*, Aldershot: Arena. [P,N,1,7,8,17]
Doueck, H. J., English, D. J., DePanfils, D. and Moote, G. T. (1993), 'Decision-Making in Child Protection Services: A Comparison of Selected Risk-Assessment Systems', *Child Welfare*, **LXXII**(5), 441–52. [14]
Douglas, R. and Payne, C. (1988), *Organizing for Learning: staff development strategies for residential and day services work: a theoretical and practical guide*, London: National Institute for Social Work. [P]
Douglas, R., Ettridge, D., Fearnhead, D., Payne, C., Pugh, D. and Sowter, D. (1988), *Helping People Work Together: a guide to participative working practices*, London: National Institute for Social Work, Paper no. 21. [12]

Douglas, T. (1976), *Groupwork Practice*, London: Tavistock. [4]
Eadie, T. and Ward, D. (1995), 'The "Scenario Approach" to teaching social work law,' *Social Work Education*, **14** (2), 64–84. [18]
Evans, D. (1987), 'Live supervision in the same room: a practice teaching method', *Social Work Education*, **6** (3), 13–17. [P]
Evans, D., Cava, H., Gill, O. and Wallis, A. (1988), 'Helping students evaluate their own practice', *Issues in Social Work Education*, 8 (2), 113–36. [8]
Everitt, A., Hardiker, P., Littlewood, J. and Mullender, A. (1992), *Applied Research for Better Practice*, Houndmills, Basingstoke: Macmillan. [19]
Fanon, F. (1970), *Black Skin White Masks*, London: Paladin. [4]
Findlay, Sheena B. (1995), 'Teaching the unteachable? The teaching of ethics in field education', in G. Rogers (ed.), *Social Work Field Education: Views and Visions*, Dubuque, Iowa: Kendall/Hunt, pp. 152–63. [4]
Fisher, R. and Ury, W. (1983), *Getting To Yes: Negotiating agreement without giving in*, Harmondsworth, Middlesex: Penguin. [7,12]
Flood, B. (1988), *Developing a Cultural Inventory*, Division of Continuing Education, Portland State University, OR 97207, US. [16]
Ford, K. and Jones, A. (1987), *Student Supervision*, Houndmills, Basingstoke: Macmillan. [N]
Fortune, A. E. and Abramson, J. S. (1993), 'Predictors of satisfaction with field practicum among social work students', *The Clinical Supervisor*, **11** (1), 95–110. [N]
Fortune, A. E., Miller, J., Rosenblum, A. F., Sanchez, B. M., Smith, C. and Reid, W. J. (1995), 'Further explorations of the liaison role: a view from the field', in G. Rogers (ed.), *Social Work Field Education: Views and Visions*, Dubuque, Iowa: Kendall/Hunt, pp. 273–93. [N]
Francis, J. (1992), 'Results without racism', 'Staff Supervision', *Community Care*, 30 July. [N]
Fuller, R. and Petch, A. (1995), *Practitioner Research: the reflexive social worker*, Buckingham: Open University Press. [19]
Furniss, J. (1988), 'The client speaks again', Pro-file, **3**, 2–3. [8]
Gardiner, D. (1989), *The Anatomy of Supervision*, Milton Keynes: SRHE and Open University Press. [N]
Garland, K. (1994), *Mr Beck's Underground Map*, Hemel Hempstead: Pineland Press. [P]
Goffman, E. (1968), *Stigma: notes on the management of spoiled identity*, London: Pelican. [4]
Gould, N. (1989), 'Reflective Learning in Social Work Practice', *Social Work Education*, **8** (2), 9–18. [19]
Griffiths, S. R. (1988), *Community Care: Agenda for Action. A report to the Secretary of State for Social Services*, London: HMSO. [13]
Grossman, B. and Perry, R. (1996), 'Re-engaging social work education with the public social services: The California experience and its relevance to Russia', in M. Doel and S. M. Shardlow (eds), *Social Work in a Changing World: an international perspective on practice learning*, Aldershot: Arena, pp. 43–56. [X]

Hämäläinen, J. (1989), 'Social pedagogy as a meta-theory of social work education', *International Social Work*, **32** (2), 117–28. [X]

Hanvey, C. and Philpot, T. (eds) (1994), *Practising Social Work*, London: Routledge. [2]

Hare, I. (1993), *New Developments in Hungarian Social Work*, Washington, DC: NASW. [X]

Harris, J. and Kelly, D. (1991), *Management Skills in Social Care*, Aldershot: Gower. [12]

Hawkins, P. and Shohet, R. (1989), *Supervision in the Helping Professions*, Buckingham: Open University. [N]

Heap, K. (1979), *Process and Action in Work with Groups*, Oxford: Pergamon. [2]

Heron, J. (1975), *Six Category Intervention Analysis*, University of Surrey. [6]

Heus, M. J. and Pincus, A. (1986), *The Creative Generalist: a guide to social work practice*, Barneveld, Wisconsin: Micamar. [20]

Hewitt, R. (1986), *White talk, black talk*, Cambridge: Cambridge University Press. [4]

Hill, M. (ed.) (1991), *Social Work and the European Community*, London: Jessica Kingsley. [X]

Hogg, B., Kent, P. and Ward, D. (1992), *The Teaching of Law in Practice Placements*, Nottingham: University of Nottingham, School of Social Studies. [18]

Hollis, E. V. and Taylor, A. L. (1951), *Social Work Education in the United States*, New York: Columbia University Press. [20]

Hollows, A. (1992), 'Resources for courses' 'Staff Supervision', *Community Care*, 30 July. [N]

Howe, D. (1993), *Introduction to Social Work Theory* (second edn), Aldershot: Ashgate. [2]

Huczynski, A. (1983), *Encyclopedia of Management Development Methods*, Aldershot: Gower. [P]

Hudson, B. L. and Macdonald, G. M. (1986), *Behavioural Social Work*, Houndmills, Basingstoke: Macmillan. [9]

Hugman, R. (1991), *Power in Caring Professions*, Houndmills, Basingstoke: Macmillan/BASW. [3]

IFSW (International Federation of Social Workers) (1994), *The Ethics of Social Work – Principles and Standards*, Oslo: International Federation of Social Workers. [3,14]

Ivey, A and Authier, J. (1978), *Microcounseling*, Springfield, Illinois: Charles C. Thomas. [6]

Jayaratne, S., Croxton, T. and Mattison, D. (1997), 'Social Work Professional Standards: an exploratory study', *Social Work*, **42** (2), 187–196. [3]

Kemshall H. and Pritchard, J. (eds) (1996), *Good Practice in Risk Assessment and Risk Management*, London: Jessica Kingsley, pp. 13–30. [14]

Kissman, K. and Van Tran, T. (1990), 'Perceived Quality of Field Placement Education Among Graduate Social Work Students', *Journal of Continuing Social Work Education*, **5** (2), 27–30. [P]

Knowles, M. (1972), 'Innovations in teaching styles and approaches based on adult learning', *Journal of Education in Social Work*, 8 (2), 32–9. [1]

Knowles, M. (1983), 'Androgogy: an emerging technology for adult learning', in M. Tight (ed.), *Adult Learning and Education*, Beckenham, Kent: Open University/Croom Helm. [P]

Laing, R. D. and Esterson, A. (1964), *Sanity, Madness and the Family*, London: Tavistock. [15]

Langan, M. and Day, L. (eds) (1992), *Women, Oppression and Social Work*, London: Routledge. [2]

Leonard, P. (1976), 'The function of social work in society', in N. Timms and D. Watson (eds), *Talking about Welfare*, London: Routledge & Kegan Paul, pp. 252–66. [2]

Leung, A. Y. L., Tam, T. S. K. with Chu, C. H. (1995), *A Study of the Roles and Tasks of a Field Instructor*, (Monograph Series No 24), Hong Kong: Department of Social Work and Social Administration, The University of Hong Kong. [P]

Lindow, V. and Morris, J. (1995), *Service User Involvement*, York: Joseph Rowntree Foundation. [2,11,13]

Lishman, J. (ed.) (1991), *Handbook of Theory for Practice Teachers in Social Work*, London: Jessica Kingsley. [2]

Lishman, J. (1994), *Communication in Social Work*, Houndmills, Basingstoke: Macmillan. [6]

Loewenberg, F. and Dolgoff, R. (1988), *Ethical Decisions for Social Work Practice* (third edn), Itasca, Illinois: Peacock. [14]

Lorenz, W. (1994), *Social Work in a Changing Europe*, London: Routledge. [X]

Marsh, P. and Crow, G. (1996), 'Family Group Conferences in Child Welfare Services in England and Wales' in J. Hudson, A. Morris, G. Maxwell and B. Galaway (eds), *Family Group Conferences*, Australia: The Federation Press, pp. 152–65. [15]

Marsh, P. and Fisher, M. (1992), *Good Intentions: developing partnerships in social services*, York: Joseph Rowntree Foundation/Community Care. [17,19]

Marsh, P. and Triseliotis, J. (1996), *Ready to Practise? Social Workers and Probation Officers: Their Training and First Year at Work*, Aldershot: Avebury. [P]

Martin, E. W. (1992), 'Themes in the history of the social work profession' in *International Social Work*, vol. 35, 327–45. [20]

Mayer, J. and Timms, N. (1970), *The Client Speaks*, London: Routledge & Kegan Paul. [2,11]

Means, R. and Smith, R. (1994), *Community Care: policy and practice*, Houndmills, Basingstoke: Macmillan. [13]

Meredith, B. (1995), *The Community Care Handbook* (second edn), London: Age Concern. [13]

Metcalf, J. and Curtis, C. (1992), 'Feeding on support', in 'Staff Supervision', *Community Care*, 30 July. [N]

Milner, P. (1986), *The Child Abuse Potential Inventory: Manual* (second edn), Webster, NC: Psytec. [14]

Moore, J. (1992), 'Staff supervision: are you satisfied?' in 'Staff Supervision', *Community Care*, 30 July. [N]
Morrison, T. (1992), 'A question of survival' in 'Staff Supervision', *Community Care*, 30 July. [N]
Moxley, D. P. (1989), *The Practice of Case Management*, Newbury Park, California: Sage. [13]
Munday, B. (1993), *European Social Services*, Canterbury: EISS University of Kent. [X]
NASW (National Association of Social Workers) (1996), *Code of Ethics*, Silver Spring, MD: National Association of Social Workers. [3,14]
Nixon, S., Shardlow, S. M., Doel, M., McGrath, S. and Gordon, R. (1995), 'An Empirical Approach to Defining Quality Components in Field Education' in G. Rogers (ed.) *Social Work Field Education: Views and Visions*, Dubuque, IA: Kendall Hunt, pp. 382–98. [P]
Norman, A. (1985), *Triple Jeopardy: Growing Old in a Second Homeland*, London: Centre for Policy on Ageing. [17]
Oliver, M. (1990), *The Politics of Disablement*, Houndmills, Basingstoke: Macmillan. [13]
Orme, J. and Glastonbury, B. (1993), *Care Management*, London: Macmillan. [13]
Øvretveit, J. (1986), *Improving Social Work Records and Practice*, Birmingham: BASW. [10]
Papell, C. P. (1996), 'Reflections on issues in social work education', in N. Gould and I. Taylor (eds), *Reflective Learning for Social Work*, Aldershot: Arena. [20]
Paré, A. and Allen, H. S. (1995), 'Social work writing: learning by doing', in G. Rogers (ed.), *Social Work Field Education: Views and Visions*, Dubuque, Iowa: Kendall/Hunt, pp. 164–73. [10]
Parsloe, P. (1981), *Social Services Area Teams*, London: George Allen & Unwin. [11]
Payne, C. (1992), 'A map for different models', in 'Staff Supervision', *Community Care*, 30 July. [N]
Payne, C. and Scott, T. (1982), *Developing Supervision of Teams in Field and Residential Settings*, London: National Institute for Social Work, Papers no. 12. [P]
Payne, M. (1993), 'Standards of Written and Spoken English in Social Work Education', *Issues in Social Work Education*, 13 (2), 37–52. [10]
Payne, M. (1995), *Social Work and Community Care*, Houndmills, Basingstoke: Macmillan. [N,8,13]
Payne, M. (1996), *What is Professional Social Work?* Birmingham: Venture Press. [20]
Payne, M. (1997), *Modern Social Work Theory*, (second edn), London: Macmillan. [2]
Pease, A. (1984), *Body Language*, London: Sheldon Press. [4,7]
Phillipson, J. (1992), *Practising Equality: Women, Men and Social Work*, London: CCETSW, Improving Social Work Education and Training, 10. [P]

Pinchot, G. (1985), *Intrapreneuring*, New York: Harper & Row. [12]
Pincus, A. and Minahan, A. (1973), *Social Work Practice: Model and Method*, Itasca, Illinois: Peacock. [20]
Pinker, R. A. (1982), 'An Alternative View', Appendix B in P. M. Barclay, *Social Workers: Their Role and Tasks* (The Barclay Report), London: Bedford Square Press. [2]
Preston-Shoot, M. (1993), 'Whither Social Work Law? Future Questions on the Teaching and Assessment of Law to Social Workers', *Social Work Education*, 8 (1), 65–77. [18]
Priestley, P., McGuire, J., Flegg, D., Hemsley, V. and Welham, D. (1978), *Social Skills and Personal Problem Solving: a handbook of methods*, London: Tavistock. [6]
Pritchard, J. (1995), 'Supervision or practice teaching for students?' in J. Pritchard (ed.), *Good Practice in Supervision*, London: Jessica Kingsley, pp. 193–201. [N]
Reamer, F. G. (1993), *Ethical Dilemmas in Social Service: A Guide for Social Workers*, New York: Columbia University Press. [4]
Reid, W. J. and Epstein, L. (1972), *Task-Centred Casework*, New York: Columbia University Press. [6]
Reid, W. J. and Smith, A. D. (1989), *Research in Social Work* (second edn), New York: Columbia University Press. [19]
Rhodes, M. L. (1986), *Ethical Dilemmas in Social Work Practice*, London: Routledge & Kegan Paul. [4]
Richards, M. (1988), 'Developing the Content of Practice Teaching (Parts I and II)', in J. Phillipson, M. Richards and D. Sawdon (eds), *Towards a Practice-Led Curriculum*, London: NISW, pp. 9–16 and 69–74. [3]
Richards, M. et al. (1991), *Staff Supervision in Child Protection Work*, London: NISW. [N]
Roberts, H., Smith, S. J. and Bryce, C. (1995), *Children at Risk*, Buckingham: Open University Press. [14]
Rodrigues, F. and Monteiro, A. (1998) in S. M. Shardlow and M. Payne (eds), *Contemporary Issues in Social Work: Western Europe*, Aldershot: Arena, pp. 93–115. (X)
Rojek, C., Peacock, G. and Collins, S. (1988), chapter 3 in *Social Work and Received Ideas*, London: Routledge. [2]
Sacco, T. (1996), 'Towards an inclusive paradigm for social work', in M. Doel and S. M. Shardlow (eds), *Social Work in a Changing World: an international perspective on practice learning*, Aldershot: Arena, pp. 31–41. [X]
Sainsbury, E., Nixon, S. and Phillips, D. (1982), *Social Work in Focus*, London: Routledge. [8]
Sawdon, C. and Sawdon, D. (1995), 'The supervision partnership', in J. Pritchard (ed.), *Good Practice in Supervision*, London: Jessica Kingsley. [N]
Sawdon, D. (1986), *Making Connections in Practice Teaching*, London: National Institute for Social Work. [P]
Schneck, D., Grossman, B. and Glassman, U. (eds) (1991), *Field Education in Social Work: Contemporary Issues and Trends*, Dubuque, Iowa: Kendall Hunt. [N]

Schön, D. A. (1987), *Educating the Reflective Practitioner*, San Francisco: Jossey-Bass. [N,1,19]
Schön, D. A. (1995), *The Reflective Practitioner*, Aldershot: Arena. [P,19]
Secker, J. (1993), *From Theory to Practice in Social Work*, Aldershot: Avebury. [P]
Senge, P. M. (1990), *The Fifth Discipline: The Art & Practice of The Learning Organization*, New York: Doubleday. [P,N,6,7]
Shardlow, S. M. (ed.) (1989), *The Values of Change in Social Work*, London: Routledge. [3]
Shardlow, S. M. and Doel, M. (1996), *Practice Learning and Teaching*, Houndmills, Basingstoke: Macmillan. [N,1]
Shardlow, S. M. and Payne, M. (eds) (1998), *Contemporary Issues in Social Work: Western Europe*, Aldershot: Arena. [X]
Sheafor, B. W. and Jenkins, L. E. (1982), *Quality Field Instruction in Social Work*, New York: Longman. [N]
Shemmings, D. (1991), *Client Access to Records: participation in social work*, Aldershot: Avebury. [10]
Shulman, L. (1982), *Skills of Supervision and Staff Management*, Itasca, Illinois: Peacock. [N]
Shulman, L. (1983), *Skills of Helping Individuals and Groups* (second edn), Itasca, Illinois: Peacock. [5]
Simpkin, M. (1983), *Trapped Within Welfare* (second edn), Houndmills, Basingstoke, Macmillan. [2]
Singleton, W. T. and Holden, J. (eds) (1994), *Risk and Decisions*, London: John Wiley and Sons. [14]
Smale, G. (1993), *Empowerment, Assessment, Care Management and the Skilled Worker*, London: National Institute for Social Work, Practice Development Exchange, HMSO. [5]
Smale, G., Tuson, G., Ahmad, B., Davill, G., Domoney, L. and Sainsbury, E. (1994), *Negotiating Care in the Community: The Implications of Research Findings on Community-Based Practice for the Implementation of Community Care and Children Acts*, London: HMSO. [13]
Smith, M. and Campbell, J. (1996), 'Social Work, Sectarianism and Anti-sectarian Practice in Northern Ireland', *British Journal of Social Work*, **26** (1), 77–92. [X]
Social Services Inspectorate (1991), *Care Management and Assessment: Manager's Guide*, London: HMSO. [13]
Stevenson, O. (1988), 'Law and social work education: a commentary on The Law Report', *Issues in Social Work Education*, **8** (1), 37–45. [18]
Stevenson, O. and Parsloe, P. (1993), *Community Care and Empowerment*, York: Rowntree Foundation with Community Care. [14,17]
Taylor, P. (1994), 'The linguistic and cultural barriers to cross-national groupwork', *Groupwork*, **7** (1), 7–22. [16]
Thomas, M. and Pierson, J. (1995), *Dictionary of Social Work*, London Macmillan. [10]
Thomlison, B. (1995), 'Student perceptions of reflective team supervision'

in G. Rogers (ed.), *Social Work Field Education: Views and Visions*, Dubuque, Iowa: Kendall/Hunt, pp. 234–44. [N]

Thomlison, B. and Collins, D. (1995), 'Use of structured consultation for learning issues in field education', in G. Rogers (ed.), *Social Work Field Education: Views and Visions*, Dubuque, Iowa: Kendall/Hunt, pp. 223–8. [N]

Thompson, N. (1997), *Anti-Discriminatory Practice*, (second edn), Houndmills, Basingstoke: Macmillan. [17]

Thompson, N., Osada, M. and Anderson, B. (1994), *Practice Teaching in Social Work* (second edn), Birmingham: Pepar. [N]

Titmus, R. (1968), *Commitment to Welfare*, London: Allen and Unwin. [13]

Tolson, E. R., Reid, W. J. and Garvin, C. D. (1994), *Generalist Practice: a Task Centred Approach*, New York: Columbia University Press. [20]

Tropman, J. E. (1980), *Effective Meetings: improving group decision-making*, Beverly Hills and London: Sage Human Services Guide no. 17. [12]

Video Arts, *Meetings, Bloody Meetings* (video), London: Video Arts. [12]

Walker, J., McCarthy, P., Morgan W. and Timms, N. (1995), In Pursuit of Quality: Improving Practice Teaching in Social Work, Newcastle upon Tyne: Relate Centre for Family Studies, The University of Newcastle. [P]

Watson, D. (ed.) (1985), *A Code of Ethics for Social Work*, London: Routledge & Kegan Paul. [3]

Welsh, T. M., Johnson, S. P., Miller, L. K., Merrill, M. H. and Altus, D. E. (1989), 'A practical procedure for training meeting chairpersons', *Journal of Organizational Behavior Management*, **10** (1), 151–66. [12]

Whitaker, D. and Archer, J. L. (1989), *Research by Social Workers; Capitalizing on Experience*, London: Central Council for Education and Training in Social Work, Study 9. [19]

Wilcox, R., Smith, D., Moore, J., Hewitt, A., Allan, G., Walker, H., Ropata, M., Monu, L. and Featherstone, T. (1991), *Family Decision Making, Family Group Conferences*, available from Practitioners' Publishing, PO Box 30–430, Lower Hutt, New Zealand. [15,16]

Woodcock, M. (1989), *Team Development Manual* (second edn), Aldershot: Gower. [12]

Younghusband, E. (1981), *The Newest Profession: A Short History of Social Work*, Sutton, Surrey: Community Care/IPC Business Press. [X]

Index

accelerated learning 26
   see also learning
access as a factor in choice 134
accountability 4, 100, 138
   lines of 9
actions (of social workers) 43–52
administration (as a function of
     supervision) 4
advocacy 52, 69–77, 161
age as a factor in legal matters 197–9
agency expectations 101
agendas for meetings 126
agreement 58, 73, 75, 86, 129, 183
ambiguity 193
appeals 58–9
appointments *see* diaries
appraisal (in supervision) 4
approval-disapproval continuum in legal
     knowledge 196–7
assertiveness 72
assessment
   in care management 136, 141
   in supervision 4, 57
   of risk 152–3
attitudes 21, 47
authenticity 63
authority 72
   see also power
autonomy of social workers 9
availability as a factor in choice 134

backward mapping (technique) 85
beginnings of processes 79–85
behaviour 4, 35–6, 39, 40, 47, 66, 110, 154–5,
   169, 174
beliefs 13, 14, 23, 26, 28, 40, 46, 97, 107, 211
Believe it or not (training technique) 23–5,
   28
bipolar thinking 221
blame (as a weapon) 169
Block contracts 142
body language *see* non-verbal
   communication
Boundaries (training technique) 33–5
boundary behaviours 37
breaks (from work) 120
budget as a factor in choice 135

care and control 147, 155, 192
care in the community 136–41
   management 140–51
care planning 141–2
case paths 28
cast-iron diaries (concept) 119
chairing meetings 123, 126–8
challenge 127
change 29, 82, 129, 187, 207
choices 98, 131, 134–6, 142, 183
clarifying (in supervvision) 6, 7
climate as a factor in choice 135
closing of services 186

see also endings of processes
coaching supervision 5
communication skills 51–2, 73, 138
   see also non-verbal communication;
      verbal communication
comparative social work 231–8
competencies 4, 6, 20, 27, 57, 193, 228, 229
complaints 58–9
concept leakage 4–5
concerns 83, 84, 91–2
conflict 54, 69, 193
conflicts of interest 184
confrontive responses 67
consent 183
consumerist approach to services 186
contact with clients 60–2
contacts 19, 88, 121
   with other professions 121, 236
context (in supervision) 7–8
continuity record keeping 108
contracts in social work 142
control approach to services 186
convenience as a factor in choice 135
cost and volume contracts 142
creative generalists 227
creativity 57, 227
criteria in social work 75, 96, 97, 98, 101, 102
   ranking of 100
cultural inventories 170–1
culturally competent practice 165–176
culture as a factor in social work 138, 165–7
curiosity 63
cynicism 60

data 118
   see also information
decision making 9, 19, 102, 127, 131, 157,
      181, 182, 185
   in families 158, 159, 161–2, 163
deficits model of families 160
definite diary entries 119
delays in taking action 100
Dial 'D' for Danger (training activity)
   147–51
diaries 115–6, 119
   see also time management
diet as a factor in choice 135
dignity 142
dilemmas in social work 33, 39, 108, 193–4
direct observation 62, 73–4
disadvantage
   degrees of 101
disagreement 54
   in meetings 126
discretion 58
discrimination 47, 170, 177, 194

disgust 205
disinterest 63
double jeopardy 181, 206
dual purpose times in diary entries 119
dual relationships 36
duty 194
dysfunctional families 160

eclecticism 52, 224, 227
education (supervision aspects) 4
effectiveness of social work 103, 209
elastic-diaries (concept) 119
emotional risk (as a reason for intervention)
   151
emotions 14, 84
empathy 19
   empathic responses 67
empowerment 151, 177–87
   barriers 184–5
enabling (in supervision) 4
ending meetings 127
endings of processes 87–90
ends and means in processes 89
entertainment as a factor in choice 135
errors 7
Essence (training activity) 217
ethics 46, 103, 205
   ethical principles 82
Ethnic realities (training activity) 165–7
ethnicity 19, 165–176
   see also race
exchange model in assessment 58
expectations 36, 40, 56, 63, 119
   of an agency 40, 101
experiential learning 47, 207
expertise 58, 222, 227
   see also skills
explicit methods of practice 82

facilitating (in supervision) 4
facilities as a factor in choice 135
facts (differentiated from opinions) 109–10
fairness 58
Families as Allies Project (USA) 161
family centred practice 157–63
feedback 40, 61, 73–4, 110
feelings 13, 14, 43–52, 76, 84, 222
finding out *see* inquiry skills
first impressions 21
flexibility of diary entries 119
friendships 14, 33, 158
fulfilment 142

gender 25, 28, 85, 180, 181, 213–15
generalist practice 217–29
   defined 224–5

generalizations 110, 160, 165, 167, 175–6
  in research 204, 215
generic practice 222–5, 228
  defined 224–5
goals 85, 86, 91, 92–4, 179
Griffiths Report 140
group supervision 8
groupwork 224
guilt 169
Gulliver's travels (training activity) 231–4

helping (in supervision) 4
hidden agendas 69, 70, 129
humour 176

ideas 72, 123
identifying with a group 180
impressions (of situations) 21
imprint effect (concept) 119
improvisation 207
In My View (training technique) 69
in-person introduction to clients 61, 62
independence 142
inequality 181
  see also power
informal contacts 121
information 18, 19–20, 72, 118, 123, 134–5, 136, 138, 183, 211
  gathering 81, 209, 215
  giving 6
informative data 118
informative responses 67
initial contact with clients 60
inner thoughts 76
inquiry skills 63–8, 73
  barriers to 68
insecurity 193
insiders (concept) 180
inspection of services 142
integrity 63
intensive model of liaison 10
interests (as a determinant of position) 75
interpersonal skills 52, 68, 82
intervention 86, 147, 151–5, 179, 183, 221
  intervention technology 208
intimate relationships 36
intrapreneur's ten commandments 130
introduction to clients 60–2
investigative record keeping 108

jargon 109
jeopardy 181, 206
Johari window (technique) 49, 50
judgements 20, 58, 201

knowledge 4, 10, 14, 83, 97, 107, 194, 196, 205, 207, 221, 223, 224, 225, 226, 227, 228
  legal knowledge 193, 195
  previous knowledge 101
  receptiveness to knowledge 211
  theoretical knowledge 206–7

labelling of people 109
  see also generalizations
language 26, 62, 104–5, 109, 110, 138, 139
learning 4, 6, 7, 9–10, 19, 46, 62, 70, 73, 146, 194, 207, 234–5
  context of 7–8
  see also accelerated learning
left-hand column technique 76–7
legal considerations in social work 101, 189–99
letter introduction to clients 60–1, 62
liaison between college and agency 9–10
lifestyle as a factor in choice 135
live supervision 5
location as a factor in choice 135

managerial accountability 4
Matter of fact (training resource) 105–7
meals (cultural factors) 173–4
mediation (in supervision) 4
meetings 96
  agendas 126
  chairing 123, 126–8
  defined 124
  minutes 126
  organizing 123–30
mentors 171–2
middles of processes 85–7
minimalist supervision 7
minutes of meetings 126
mistrust 161, 205
mixed modality relationships 36–7
moods 14, 84
motivation 86, 89
mutual discovery 26
mutual gain 75
mutual understanding 60

needs 135, 137, 194
  degrees of 101
  of ethnic groups 168
needs-led assessment 57
negotiating skills 75, 129, 182
neighbourhood work 224
netting-diaries (concept) 119
networking 56–7
non-specific concerns 92
non-verbal communication 14, 46, 66, 72

objective criteria 75
observation in research 204, 210
Open ends (training technique) 63–5
open records 110, 111
opening of services 186
opinions 6, 7
   differentiated from facts 109
oppression 28, 86–7, 165, 177, 181–2, 184
optimism 60
organizational culture 40
orientation (within placements) 13, 15–22
outcomes 39, 79–94, 101, 184
outsiders (concept) 180

pacing of diary entries 119
partnerships 81, 96, 177–87, 227
   in family work 157
past experiences 7–8, 204
Perfect timing (training resource) 115–17
personal appearance 35, 38, 40
personal philosophy 26
Personal Social Services Research Unit (USA) 140
physical risk (as a reason for intervention) 151
placements 5–6, 8, 9–10, 15–22
planning skills 51–2
Playing field (training activity) 53–5
positional bargaining 75
power 19, 72, 86–7, 101, 127, 165, 177, 180–2, 184, 185, 194
   redistribution 187
   in families 158
practice methods 4–7, 52, 79, 80, 81–2
   see also processes of work
practice teaching 4, 5
   introduction of teacher 61–2
preferences 101
prejudices 181
   see also discrimination
preparation for meetings 126
prescriptive data 118
prescriptive responses 67
previous knowledge 101
price as a factor in choice 135
primary processes in social work 79–94
principled negotiation 75
priority of diary entries 119
priority setting 84, 96, 97–103
privacy 21, 142
problem defining 83–4, 91, 179
problem sensitization 101
problem solving 75, 92, 108, 169, 208
procedural model in assessment 57, 58
procedural record keeping 108
process records 110

processes of work 39, 79–94
   in care management 136–8
professional development 120
professional relationships *see* working relationships
professionalism 14
providing services 131–43
purchasing services 131–43

quality management 9, 142
quality of service as a factor in choice 135
questioning model in assessment 58
questions 6, 15, 16

race 44, 45, 46, 68, 87, 167–8, 182, 194, 211–13
reactive practice 90
reasoning 72
receptiveness to knowledge 211
record keeping 64, 96, 105–13
referrals 56–7, 99, 102
   source of 101
Reflections on supervision (training technique) 1
reflective learning 207
reflective practice 1–11, 206, 224
reflective responses 67
reflective students 10
relationships 5, 14, 18, 36, 49, 75, 84, 86, 88, 142
   with other professions 121, 236
   see also working relationships
reluctant clients 56, 86, 183
report writing 109
reported supervision 5
   see also record keeping
representativeness 185
research in social work 201–215
   findings 83
   purposes 209
resources 194
   availability 101, 136
resources-led assessment 57
responses (variations in) 67
responsibilities 28
   of social workers 9, 59, 101, 136–7
responsive practice 90
rights 59, 142, 194
risks 14, 100, 148–50, 151–3, 169, 194
   assessment 152–3
role conflict 193

scenario approach to legal training 194–5
selected observation (research technique) 204
self-awareness 67, 100
   cultural considerations 174

Index 255

self-disclosure 49
self-presentation 14
   see also personal appearance
sensitization of problems 101
service provision 131–43
service purchasing 131–43
shared records 110
Signposts (training technique) 201–3
skills 4, 8, 14, 58, 101, 137, 182–3, 195, 205–6, 207, 211, 221, 224, 225, 226
social pedagogy 237
social pressures 101, 181
social risk (as a reason for intervention) 151
social skills 66
social work 231–8
   autonomy of social workers 9
   comparative social work 231–8
   contracts 142
   criteria 75, 96, 98, 99, 100, 102, 103
   cultural factors 138, 165–8
   defined 221–2
   dilemmas 33, 39, 108, 193–4
   family centred practice 157–63
   forms of 236
   generalist practice 217–29
   generic practice 222–3, 228
   legal considerations 101, 189–99
   neighbourhood work 224
   primary processes 79–94
   research in social work 83, 201–15
   specialist practice 217–29
   training 1–11
   variations of practice in other countries 235
specialist practice 217–29
   by method 224
   by territory 223
   'specialist' defined 222
specific concerns 92
speculative record keeping 108
Spirit and letter (training activity) 189–93, 196
spot contracts 142
statements of concern 91
status of diary entries 119
Steps (training activity) 177–9, 182
stereotypes *see* generalizations
Sticky moments (training technique) 97–8, 100
strengths model of families 160
style of work 40, 62
style of working 38, 40, 60–61
success 103
   likelihood of 101
summarizing skills 6, 7
supermarket approach to services 186

supervision 1–11, 59, 209
   content 6
   purposes and functions 2–5
   techniques 6
   theory (use of) 6
   types of 5
support (in supervision) 4, 9
supportive responses 67
systematic methods of practice 82, 225–6
systemic sources of problems 169
systems theory 227

Taboo (training activity) 43–8, 49
telephone introduction to clients 61, 62
tentative diary entries 119
terminology *see* language
theory and theories 7, 26, 28, 82, 207, 210
   see also research in social work
time management 115–22
   cultural considerations 121–2
time of year as a factor in choice 135
timing for meetings 126
timing of appointments 119
Topical islands (training activity) 123–6
training of social workers 1–11
Travel agent (training activity) 131–4
Tree (training technique) 79–80
triage (prioritization in decision making) 103
triple jeopardy 181–2
trouble-shooting model of liaison 10

UN Declaration of Rights for Disabled People 135–6
uncertainty 53, 193
   in meetings 126
understanding 100, 195, 211
unexpected work 90, 119
unlearning 7
unspoken agendas 129
unstructured time 121
urgency 100, 119

values 13, 14, 26, 40, 46, 47, 97, 107, 205, 221, 224, 225, 226
variations of practice in other countries 235
venues for meetings 126
verbal communication 14, 66, 73
viewpoints 72, 84
voice intonation *see* non-verbal communication

walking the game (concept) 73
Whanau (training activity) 157–60, 161–2
Who takes the sugar? (training technique) 15, 17, 19

work patterns 19, 120
working relationships 33, 35, 38, 39
workload 96, 115–22
worldview (concept) 23–31